SALEM COLLEGE
LIBRARY

The Archie K. Davis
Collection of
Southern History & Literature

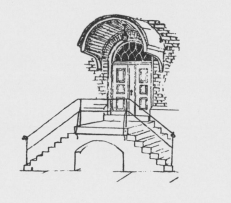

SOUTHERN LITERARY STUDIES

Fred Hobson, Editor

More Lights Than One

On the Fiction *of* Fred Chappell

EDITED BY Patrick Bizzaro

WITH A FOREWORD BY
Robert Morgan

LOUISIANA STATE UNIVERSITY PRESS · BATON ROUGE

Designer: Andrew Shurtz

Typeface: Adobe Caslon

Typesetter: Coghill Composition Co., Inc.

Printer and binder: Thomson-Shore, Inc.

LIBRARY OF CONGRESS CATALOGING-IN-PUBLICATION DATA

More lights than one : on the fiction of Fred Chappell / edited by Patrick Bizzaro ;

with a foreword by Robert Morgan.

p.   cm.

Includes index.

ISBN 0-8071-2939-9 (alk. paper)

1. Chappell, Fred, 1936——Criticism and interpretation.

2. North Carolina—In literature.

I. Bizzaro, Patrick.

PS3553.H298Z77   2004

813'.54—dc22

2003022752

for my wife,

RESA CRANE BIZZARO

❦ CONTENTS ❧

The Birth of Music from the Spirit of Comedy

ROBERT MORGAN

THE BOOK OF linked stories is one of the special genres of American literature. Beginning with Sarah Orne Jewett's *The Country of the Pointed Firs* and continuing with Anderson's *Winesburg, Ohio,* Faulkner's *Go Down, Moses,* and Katherine Anne Porter's *The Old Order,* the form has shown a renewed vitality in recent years with Louise Erdrich's *Love Medicine* and Tim O'Brien's *The Things They Carried.* The genre has included some of the finest American fiction. Combining the compression, implicitness, and completeness of the short story with the cumulative complications of the novel, the book of linked stories seems to be a particularly American genre. It is, in effect, two genres at once. Each story stands on its own, has the rondure and wholeness of a short story. At the same time, the stories connect to build the larger intimacy, the sustained complexity, of a novel.

Reading a book of linked stories such as *Winesburg, Ohio* or *The Things They Carried* is not unlike listening to an oratorio. Some sections are intense and brief, some are longer and more reflective. Some are choral, and others suggest solo recitation. Motifs and images recur and vary, are amplified and embellished, echoed and extended. The sense of repetition and return is as strong as the sense of progression.

There is no finer example of this genre than Fred Chappell's *I Am One of You Forever.* Like most of the other examples I have mentioned, Chappell's book is written with a powerful sense of place and time, and the stories have a vivid intimacy of voice. They are narrated by Jess Kirkman, who is looking back on his childhood and youth during World War II and shortly after. It is a voice of remarkable exactness, sophisticated but perfectly natural. It is also a voice of the southern Appalachians, and both the narration and dialogue are rich in the idiom of the place and time. The linked story genre enables Chappell to combine the liveliness of the oral tradition of storytelling with the allusiveness and subtlety of modern fiction. This book also links up with the three novels that follow it to create the range and scope of a much larger family narrative.

The work of Fred Chappell fits another special category in modern American writing as well. Chappell belongs to a small company of writers known equally for their poetry and their prose fiction. In English literature we have Thomas Hardy, D. H. Lawrence, Robert Graves, and perhaps Philip Larkin. In American literature there are only Poe and Robert Penn Warren. The list shows just how rare such a dual talent is. Chappell has done outstanding work in both fiction and poetry, and he is widely known as one of the leading critics of poetry. In this age of specialization, and overspecialization, his range is rare—a marvel and a treasure.

My first encounter with Fred Chappell's writing was with his fiction. I read his novel *The Inkling* soon after it was published in 1965 and was dazzled by the vivid, lyrical prose, the sinister atmosphere, the special combination of familiarity and mystery that have always been earmarks of his work. But in his early fiction Chappell had not yet discovered the comic talent that would make his later novels and stories even more distinctive.

As a young writer, I was most deeply influenced by Chappell's poetry. While enrolled in the graduate writing program at UNC-Greensboro in 1967, I held two part-time jobs. The faculty generously excused me from attending most of my classes and let me do much of my course work as tutorials. I met with Fred Chappell once every two weeks in his office or at a little café called the Pickwick, about a mile from campus.

Chappell was the best teacher of writing and of poetry I had ever met. His comments on my poems were always surprising, often provocative. As he read through the poems line by line, commenting on texture and diction and implicit metaphors, I remember thinking that this man knew exactly how these poems were made. I had never encountered that kind of practical critical intelligence before. The experience was inspiring. In the summer of 1967 I wrote more and more poetry, less and less fiction. Because I had met someone who understood what I was trying to do, I worked harder and better and more ambitiously than ever. I saw possibilities that had been unimaginable before.

I believe young writers are looking for the true reader, the authentic reader, of their work. They look for the reader who understands not only what they are doing but what they are capable of. When they go to graduate programs, to writers' conferences, to San Francisco or Paris, that is what they are searching for—the true reader. I believe this is why the best writers and poets have often come in pairs. Coleridge enables Wordsworth, Goethe enables Schiller, Sherwood Anderson discovers Faulkner, Marianne Moore discovers Elizabeth Bishop. But most young writers never find their true reader. They may go on searching all their lives. In the spring and summer of 1967 in Greensboro, North Carolina, I was lucky. I found Fred Chappell to read what I had been scribbling.

Many other young writers had similar experiences at UNC-Greensboro. Building on the work that Randall Jarrell had begun, and that Peter Taylor and Robert Watson had continued, Fred Chappell and his colleagues at UNC-G created one of the finest writing programs in the South. Because of their work, Greensboro has become a literary center of the contemporary South. I believe that teachers of writing teach more by what they do than what they say. The quality and range of his writing, as well as his learning and critical insight, have made Chappell an outstanding teacher and model for the young.

When I left graduate school I asked Chappell for a reading list. On a sheet of notebook paper he jotted down thirty or forty titles. They included theoretical and critical texts such as Lessing's *Laokoon* and Berkeley's *Siris,* as well as science-fiction classics such as Olaf Stapledon's *Last and First Man* and *Star Maker.* It took me five years to work my way through the complete list. But that reading was a happy and helpful part of my continuing education.

Looking back at Fred Chappell's stories and novels, what is most distinctive—besides the exactness, richness, and liveliness of the language—are the humor and humanity of the stories. There is such a warm presence in the narration, and in the characters of father, mother, and grandmother, and such a savoring of words. In the Jess Kirkman tetralogy we come to know a whole family and community, its roots and offshoots, its losses and secrets, its failures and affections.

And what a memorable portrait of a time and place it is: western North Carolina from the late 1930s to the present. Chappell's descriptive powers are matched only by his gift for living speech. And there is a special dimension to his fiction, what used to be called Magic Realism. There is a wonderful expressive and imaginative freedom in the stories as they range from precise realism to dreamlike fantasy, from documentary detail to tall tales. This element is as much a part of Chappell's work as the father Joe Robert's dry wit and pranks, or Virgil Campbell's drinking, or the earthy sternness of Grandmother Sorrells. The exaggerations have perfect emotional and psychological shape and accuracy. In "The Beard," Uncle Gurton's whiskers, freed from the bib of his overalls, crawl out, fill the bedroom, and flood down the stairs, threatening to entangle and bury Joe Robert and Jess. In "The Overspill," the single tear on the mother's cheek swells until it contains the young narrator and his whole world. In "The Telegram," the sad sheet announcing Johnson Gibbs's death in the army reappears no matter how often it is destroyed or how far away it is carried and left.

This magic element gives many of Chappell's stories the air of fables. Building on the tradition of the tall tale, the stretchers and windies and rusties of southern writing, these narratives have wonder; they have allegorical and psychological depth beneath the facts and the fun. The tall tale is one of the watersheds of American fiction, and in the hands of Fred Chappell a story like "The Beard" seems as old as Rip Van Winkle and as fresh as the breeze at the window.

Perhaps Chappell's finest single story is "The Maker of One Coffin," in which almost everything he does best is brought together in one narrative. We have the awe of the young Jess who tells the story, the farfetched character of Uncle Runkin who sleeps only in the coffin he carries wherever he goes and to whose construction and perfection he has devoted his life. It is his ship of death. The story is precise and realistic in its details yet surrealistic in atmosphere. And it is superbly comic. Like so many of Chappell's stories, the plot is about a joke that rebounds, a prank that backfires on the perpetrator. The story is also a satire on the sadness and mournfulness of Appalachian culture.

Another special feature of Chappell's fiction is the way he uses storytelling as a metaphor for music or square dancing, and the way he uses music and square dancing as narrative forms. No one writes better about music than Chappell does. In one way or another, almost all his fiction is a celebration of mountain music and mountain dance. He writes best of all about the mountain music associated with a character based on Aunt Samantha Bumgarner of Jackson County; in the stories, she is called Aunt Sam Barefoot. She first appears in the story "Bright Star of a Summer Evening," and she is a haunting presence in *Look Back All the Green Valley*, which takes its title from a line in one of her songs. In the earlier story Jess describes her singing "Come All You Fair and Tender Ladies."

Her singing transfigured the music entirely. She had a dark contralto that sounded like it had mellowed in an oak barrel for slow decades, a voice as rich as damask soaked in burgundy wine. The song began to take on strength and shape. (178)

The portrait of The New Briar Rose Ramblers in *Look Back All the Green Valley* is among Chappell's most delightful writing. The repartee among the members of the quartet, named in honor of Aunt Samantha's band, and the description of their playing on the porch in Hardison County, are unforgettable.

"Money!" exclaimed Junior. "You mean actual cash dollars?"

"Hush, Junior," Harley instructed. "The man said money, but he didn't go as high as a dollar."

"I was thinking two hundred for the four of you," I said. "How you split it is up to you. That's if you take the offer, of course."

"We took that offer as soon as you showed up in your yellow car," Harley said. "You didn't even need to say. Last few times we've been paid with the promise of a chicken."

"And ain't seen even a feather yet," Junior assented. (150)

The comedy and the music go together. They are both at the heart of Fred Chappell's fictional world. It is a world of both wit and sentiment, memory and magic. The past that is evoked is timeless. The pleasure of the music suggests possibility and hope, and the firmness of the opening future.

But it was John, John, that fiddling man, who most thoroughly stole my heart away. After one clear statement of the tune, he set out to embroider it with flourishes surprising but inevitable, to decorate it from above and from below, always teasing and never punishing it, and the long lines he played kept looping and coiling, uncoiling and relooping in my mind like threads of silver. (258)

When Jess describes The New Briar Rose Ramblers playing "Look Back All the Green Valley" and quotes the haunting lyrics, he says he expected to feel sad, even close to tears. But that turns out not to be the effect at all:

> . . . for all its full-hearted mournfulness, for all its lonesome elegiac keening, there was a dignity in it that held it steady to its starry truth. Aunt Sam's song brought the story to its close. If it remedied no sorrows of the world, if it could not console the time-abused heart or assuage all the distresses of the weary spirit, it brought them into the light and offered them an understanding to be found in nothing else but music, in the music that echoes beyond its own proper sound into that place where no sound is ever to be heard. (267)

Perhaps the finest description of the power of music and memory in all of Chappell's fiction is the narrative about the visiting scholar Dr. Barcroft in *Farewell, I'm Bound to Leave You.* While he is studying and collecting the music of the mountains, Dr. Barcroft attends a square dance. As recounted by Jess Kirkman's grandmother, Dr. Barcroft knows the history and meaning of the music and dance he witnesses. As he observes the dancers he understands the significance of the event.

> Dr. Barcroft had the impression—and not for the first time that evening—that he was involved with a place and a people, with a time and circumstance, that was not only human in all its affections and interests but linked also with nonhuman nature, with sky and stream and mountain, in its reverences. He felt that he was standing near the origins of a strength that helped to animate the world, a power that joined all things together in a pattern that lay just barely beyond the edge of comprehension. (215)

That is a good description of Fred Chappell's fiction. The stories are musical, and they also dance. They are ritualistic and realistic. They are about a particular place and time, and they are about all people and all times. And the effect of the stories is to make us feel part of the pattern, part of the current, part of the larger music that sounds just beyond our comprehension.

{ ACKNOWLEDGMENTS }

VARIOUS PEOPLE in various capacities have made it possible for me to give this proper critical appraisal to the fiction of Fred Chappell. I would be remiss not to mention John Easterly who, along with Fred Hobson, encouraged this project while serving as executive editor of Louisiana State University Press. Sylvia Frank Rodrigue has been patient as all this material came together and has advised me wisely as these essays became a book. And, of course, Fred Chappell's kindness has made this book much easier to compile. I cannot thank him enough for the essay that appears at the end of this book and for his continued good humor as I blunder my way through his astounding array of poems, stories, and essays.

I also want to thank Dean Keats Sparrow and my chair in English, Dr. Bruce Southard, at East Carolina University for a semester research leave during which time I managed to get a good start in compiling these essays. I also want to thank Mr. Phil Adams, Mr. Michael McClanahan, Mr. Josh Hasty, Ms. Shelley Leach, and Ms. Brandi Gooch for assistance in producing a readable copy of this book. And, of course, I want to thank my wife, Resa Crane Bizzaro, with and because of whom everything begins.

More Lights Than One

Chappell's Community of Commentators
An Introduction

PATRICK BIZZARO

THIS COLLECTION of essays on the fiction of Fred Chappell will right-fully draw some comparisons with *Dream Garden: The Poetic Vision of Fred Chappell,* published in 1997. Perhaps the most important question one might ask about this collection of essays is why Chappell's work merits the sort of attention these essays bring to it. First, Chappell is unique among writers of his generation, one of a select few who have influenced our thinking by what he has written in poetic, fictive, and essay form. Chappell is at once a poet, novelist, critic, and essayist, and his work is held in the highest regard by his contemporaries. In this collection, critics and writers of the stature of Robert Morgan, R. H. W. Dillard, Peter Makuck, and John Lang, among others, argue—in essays written specifically for this book—Chappell's stature as one of the foremost figures in contemporary southern, Appalachian, and American literature.

But the fact that their argument is no longer limited to *whether* Chappell's work merits this attention but engages, instead, in discussions of *how we might read and interpret* Chappell's writing offers a second reason for this book's existence. There is much more criticism of Chappell's works to read, digest, cite, and dispute now than at the time *Dream Garden* was published. In 1997, it seemed enough to give voice to those who had some-thing to say about Chappell's *oeuvre,* who wanted simply to argue that Chappell, among his contemporaries, is a writer who deserves critical ap-praisal. Now so much has been said about not only the worth of Chappell's writings but about how his writing portrays the culture he writes about, how it advances notions of narrative and point of view, how it has evolved from his earliest works of fiction, that it seems unavoidable that critics will voice dissenting views on particular issues, including Chappell's use of autobiographical, metafictional, and rhetorical strategies in his writings. We now have not so much a "community of readers" paying close attention to Chappell's progress as "a community of commentators" arguing, oftentimes, for the correctness and ingenuity of their own readings of his work. Much of that debate goes on in the pages of this book. From the conversation that has taken place since 1997, it is clear that Chappell has risen beyond being merely notable and into the top echelon of his generation of American writers, his work being representative of the best by members of his generation.

This collection of essays is especially timely, then, since it comes on the heels of the completion of Chappell's most significant work to date: a quartet of novels about the Kirkman family that parallels the quartet of volumes of poetry that make up *Midquest*. Many of the essays here do the hard but necessary work of placing these works side by side in an effort to understand Chappell's accomplishments, to learn from them as writers and critics, to make them more teachable for our colleagues, and to begin the hard work of critical appraisal for generations of Chappell scholars to come. Needless to say, future scholars, teachers, and students will want to understand how Chappell's contemporaries read his work, how they quarreled with one another over matters essential to an understanding of his accomplishment, and inevitably to argue with many of the assertions made in these essays.

Of the essays in this collection, all are new except a portion of R. H. W. Dillard's "Letters from a Distant Lover: The Novels of Fred Chappell," in which Dillard assesses the view he took of Chappell's early novels in an essay originally published in a 1973 issue of the *Hollins Critic*. That review/essay, which focuses on Chappell's fiction up to and including *The Gaudy Place*, which was published earlier that same year, ends with "a postscript, written in 2000, one that looks back upon the essay, makes an additional confession or two, and goes on to make a couple of observations about Chappell's second set of four novels and their poetic mirror image, the four-volume poem *Midquest* (1981), as well."

This collection of essays is arranged chronologically. It moves forward from Kelly Cherry's poem, "On Reading *The Inkling* by Fred Chappell in a Building on the UNC-G Campus," and Shelby Stephenson's "Chappell's

Women: Models from the Early Novels," which argues that, even in Chappell's earliest works, including *It Is Time, Lord; The Inkling; Dagon;* and *The Gaudy Place,* women "are the initiators and protectors of the men, the stabilizers of generations, and the managers of the homes," much as they are in the Kirkman tetralogy. George Hovis, in his essay "Darker Vices and Nearly Incomprehensible Sins: The Fate of Poe in Fred Chappell's Early Novels," argues that "[t]hough it is not surprising to hear a writer distance himself from his early work, in Chappell's case this dismissal is regrettable, since the early fiction shows such marks of genius, and three of the four novels—*It Is Time, Lord; Dagon;* and *The Gaudy Place*—are, in their own ways, as accomplished as his later work." Hovis makes it clear, however, that these early novels come from a different sensibility and atti-tude toward the subject of Chappell's Appalachian past than the Kirkman novels do.

My contribution to this collection, "'Growth of a Poet's Mind' and the Problem of Autobiography: Distance and Point of View in the Writings of Fred Chappell," turns from theme and subject matter in the early novels to a treatment of technique, specifically Chappell's intricate use of point of view. In this essay I employ Wayne C. Booth's notions of how, by use of an implied author as well as a narrator, Chappell is able to distance himself in terms of time, place, and moral value from the events he tells about. He does this consistently in his writing, in his essays, in poems from *Midquest,* and in the Kirkman tetralogy. Using the insights this approach permits, I argue that, though Chappell has written about the growth of a poet's mind in the tetralogy, he is wrongly accused of having written autobiographically. What I address from this Boothean perspective, J. Spencer Edmunds ap-proaches from the perspective that Chappell has written metafiction, elabo-rating the position voiced briefly in the earlier essay by Dillard. Edmunds writes: "Written between 1985 and 1999, the [Kirkman] novels share a com-mon strategy of metanarrative that marks them as uncommon, a strategy that might be overlooked."

Though much space is allotted to Chappell's novels, he is well known for his short fiction as well. Thus his two major books of short stories are addressed in this collection. Rebecca Smith writes about "The Search for Moral Order in *Moments of Light,*" arguing that this, Chappell's first short-story collection, presents "a chronological history of human moral development, from the beginning to modern times." Traci Lazenby in "Myth and Mundane in *More Shapes Than One*" and Rosemary Cox in "The Shape of Truth: Men and Women in Fred Chappell's *More Shapes Than One*" take aim at Chappell's second collection of stories. Lazenby argues for Chappell's insistence, in these stories and in other works, that people must necessarily attend in their lives to both the spiritual world and the material, and she argues that Chappell demonstrates that commitment in the characters and events of his stories. Cox's essay deepens and extends Stephenson's treatment of women in Chappell's first four novels, arguing that "virtually all of the relationships between men and women in *More Shapes Than One* are flawed in some way, yet women seem invariably to hold the key to enlightenment, even if that enlightenment is still an enigma."

The remaining essays, in one way or another, address the Kirkman tetralogy. Peter Makuck connects these novels with *It Is Time, Lord,* which he believes is "a false start for what was to come. . . . What links Chappell's first novel to the Kirkman books is, among other things, its first-person point of view, James Christopher's religious formation and interest in science fiction, James's uneasy relationship with his father, the character of Virgil Campbell, strongly religious grandparents, a house fire, a significant brother-sister relationship, and the importance of dreams." In "The Flashing Phantasmagoria of Rational Life," Warren Rochelle applies the dialectic of the exaggerated and the mundane, first introduced in this volume in Lazenby's essay but a trademark of Chappell's fiction, to the Kirkman quartet. According to Rochelle, "the rational and the irrational are not separate. There is a 'blurring of boundaries' between the fantastic and the realistic; they occupy a mutual borderland between two worlds that often seem not to touch." Rochelle comments on this borderland as it exists in the Kirkman novels.

The final three essays address Chappell as storyteller. In "Windies and Rusties: Fred Chappell As Humorist," John Lang argues that "Chappell has established himself as one of the premier humorous writers of late twentieth-century America." He continues: "What has become increasingly clear with the publication of each new volume in the Kirkman tetralogy is Chappell's stature as the rightful heir, perhaps the fullest twentieth-century embodiment, of the tradition of Old Southwest humor and of Twain's and Faulkner's transformation of that tradition." In making this argument,

Lang sets up the final two critical essays. In the first, Karen Janet McKinney's "Tracing the Hawk's Shadow: Fred Chappell As Storyteller," the case is made by reference to an essay by Walter Benjamin that storytelling in Chappell, specifically in *I Am One of You Forever* and *Farewell, I'm Bound to Leave You*, "binds the web of community together." James W. Kirkland writes, in "Tales Tall and True: Fred Chappell's *Look Back All the Green Valley* and the Continuity of Narrative Tradition," that "[s]tories are, in fact, the essence of [*Look Back*], appearing early and late in varied forms and contexts, ranging from isolated, single-motif anecdotes to extended storytelling events." Kirkland, thus, brings the insights of the folklorist to bear on Chappell's most recently published novel.

The last and perhaps least traditional component of this book is an essay by Chappell himself, "Too Many Freds," in which he responds to issues raised in this collection of critical pieces. Chappell responds specifically to accusations of having written autobiographically, to the suggestion that he has written metafiction, and to questions of "rhetorical manipulation" of his readers raised by giving Jess Kirkman in *Look Back* the pseudonym Fred Chappell. More than an interview, this piece gives Chappell the opportunity to respond to essays in this collection and gives him the last word on many of the issues raised here. In the end, Chappell notes that "[b]y means of reflection, inversion, translation, rotation, and that mathematical process known as screwing, we can produce as few as seventeen Freds and as many as two hundred and thirty—all in the literary, metaphorical sense, of course." In any event, I feel certain the author of that essay is none other than Fred Chappell, the guy whose picture can be found on the backs of his novels and collections of short stories.

ONE

Letters from a Distant Lover
The Novels of Fred Chappell

R. H. W. DILLARD

THIS ESSAY was written for and published by the *Hollins Critic* in 1973. It was the first critical essay to consider Fred Chappell's first four novels as a whole, as a body of work by a new, relatively unknown American writer of substance and promise. It was intended to be an introduction to those novels, for readers who might not know them, rather than a definitive reading of them. Looking over it twenty-seven years later, I realized that any attempt to revise it and its tentative conclusions for this volume would be a disservice to its young, relatively unknown author, a person with whom I feel a close kinship but with whom I identify in only the least substantial ways. Therefore, I offer it here with only a few housekeeping changes—a bit of dust flicked away here, a bibelot moved slightly there.

I have added a postscript, written in 2000, one that looks back upon the essay, makes an additional confession or two, and goes on to make a couple of observations about Chappell's second set of four novels and their poetic mirror image, the four-volume poem *Midquest* (1981), as well.

{ I. 1973 }

Consider Fred Chappell.

(As he considers the world.)

In the last decade, Fred Chappell has written four novels, a book of poems, and a number of uncollected short stories. In France, like his predecessors Poe and Faulkner, he is a critical and popular success, a best seller. In this country, his novels have been praised by such varied readers as Wright Morris, Granville Hicks, and the Prescotts (Orville and Peter).

William Blackburn, when asked who was the best writer among the students he had taught at Duke University (they included Mac Hyman, William Styron, Reynolds Price, and Anne Tyler) answered without qualification, "Fred Chappell. He's the best of them all."

The best of them all, and possibly the one we know the least.

The reasons for his audience in this country's not being larger are not hard to find. In the first place, he is a southerner, and his novels are set in the mountains of North Carolina. The phrase "Southern Gothic" has all too easily been attached to his work, and that phrase has automatically excluded him from much of the audience he deserves—readers who savor the wonders and complexities of Barth, Coover, or Hawkes. Even the dust jacket of his new novel *The Gaudy Place* will only allow that his works "have earned him the reputation of being one of the most gifted of the younger North Carolina writers."

And not only is he southern, but he is Gothic. The landscape of his fiction is often frighteningly ugly, and it is peopled with grotesques—with grotesques and with ordinary people awash in the flesh, drowning in its pains, suffocating in an absence of spirit. It is a world which, at least at first acquaintance, is as barren and deadly as Lovecraft's Arkham or Kafka's castled K-land. Or, if it is not barren, its very fecundity can be deadly. When Peter Leland, in *Dagon,* first visits the Morgans' house tucked away like a hidden sin on the land of his inheritance, he comes face to face with this nightmarishly living world:

> He entered. At first he couldn't breathe. The air was hot and viscous; it seemed to cling to his hair and his skin. The black wood range was fired and three or four kettles and pans sat on it, steaming away industriously. The ceiling was low, spotted with grease, and all the heat lay like a blanket about his head. The floor was bare, laid with cracked boards, and through the spaces between them he could see the ground beneath the house. There was a small uncertain-looking table before the window on his right, and from the oilcloth which covered it large patches of the red-and-white pattern were rubbed away, showing a dull clay color. From the ceiling hung two streamers of brown flypaper which seemed to be perfectly useless; the snot-sized creatures crawled about everywhere; in an instant his hands and arms were covered with them. And

through the steamy smell of whatever unimaginable sort of meal was cooking, the real odor of the house came: not sharp but heavy, a heated odor, oily, distinctly bearing in it something fishlike, sweetly bad-smelling; he had the quick impression of dark vegetation of immense luxuriance blooming and momentarily rotting away; it was the smell of rank incredibly rich semen.

No wonder a reader might hesitate before willingly entering such a place.

But, of course, his being southern and Gothic are not the whole answer. Styron, Price, and Dickey—not to mention O'Connor, McCullers, and Capote, have made the southern grotesque quite acceptable and even profitable. The difference between the work of these familiar Southern Gothic writers and that of Fred Chappell is that, despite the clarity and ease of his prose, Chappell is a difficult writer—a consciously, uncompromisingly, and originally difficult writer. He is what used to be known as an "experimental" writer, a writer deeply and intensely involved with the complexity of his vision who writes fiction that demands of its reader an imaginative commitment of an equivalent depth and intensity. Like Alain Robbe-Grillet or John Hawkes or Borges or Nabokov, Chappell demands of his reader that he "read the page, every page, as hard as if it were a letter from a distant, and reticent, lover. Which is, in a way, exactly what a page from a novel is."

The difficulty of Chappell's fiction is further compounded by the nature of his perception. The sources of his understanding are not psychological or social like those of Thomas Wolfe or Styron. They are, rather, philosophical. In the early 1920s, Wolfe complained to his notebook that North Carolina seemed incapable of producing any genuine thought. "Can there be," he asked, "any advanced intellectual life where a condition exists, where people look furtively about before even arguing the existence of truths which have been known and accepted for over half a century?" And so Wolfe, logically enough, set out to devour the whole of the vast world of impenetrable fact that his upbringing seemed to deny him. Fred Chappell's is a new generation, however, one raised on science fiction, to whom the galaxy seems and feels as real and immediate as the stonecutter's lot down the street or the whores at the foot of the hill. His is a generation ready for and at ease with ideas and no longer able to write a fiction which is unaware of the vast curve of space or the lawless variety of subatomic matter, even though it may be focused on the conversation in the room or the mysterious events next door. (How many of Chappell's generation, I wonder, came to Kafka not as adult readers or as students in a classroom but in the pages of Ray Bradbury's *Timeless Stories for Today and Tomorrow*?)

"I've written two novels which are philosophical novels," Chappell told John Graham in a 1970 interview. "They're not easy to read. None of my books are easy to read. But what I try to do . . . is let the philosophical structure stand behind the novel, and the drama that the philosophical notions generate just takes place in it. And if you follow the story perhaps the system would be intimated to you. But if you don't ever get the system, the story may just appear to be nonsense."

Consider, then, Fred Chappell.

(Southern, Gothic, difficult, philosophical.)

Edgar Allan Poe, who was also southern and Gothic and difficult and philosophical, whose work has often seemed "to be nonsense," felt the need to assure his readers in the preface to the 1840 edition of *Tales of the Grotesque and Arabesque* that his work was not of the school of German "pseudo-horror" that was popular at the time. Instead, he wrote, "If in many of my productions terror has been the thesis, I maintain that terror is not of Germany, but of the soul,—that I have deduced this terror only from its legitimate sources, and urged it only to its legitimate results." Like Poe, Fred Chappell has deduced his terrors from their legitimate sources; they are not of the South but of the soul, the mind, and the heart. If his pages are, as he says, letters from a distant and reticent lover, then I should like this essay to be read as a hesitant, uncertain but enthusiastic and excited reply.

I

Herr: est ist Zeit. Der Sommer war sehr gross.

—RAINER MARIA RILKE

James Christopher, the narrator of Fred Chappell's first novel *It Is Time, Lord* (1963), is a familiar figure in modern (and romantic) literature. He has just entered his thirtieth year, and he has come to a halt. He has resigned his job with the local university press, and he has settled into a life of surrender. He drinks; he rereads the books of his youth; he examines the universe for signs and portents; he gives in to sin and despair. Like Melville's Bartleby, he has reached a point of preferring not to do anything active or positive. The sole code of behavior that he attempts to live by and to understand is the army Code of Conduct, which does not seem to apply to him, since it states that "I will never surrender of my own free will." He is sporadically writing his story ("I was born May 23, 1931, in the house of my grandmother"), while at the same time recognizing that "There is no story to tell, there is only a story to look for." James Christopher is a prisoner of life, like Bellow's dangling man or Mailer's nameless watcher on the Barbary shore, "obliged to live waiting for the signs which tell me I must move on again."

It Is Time, Lord is not, however, just another existential tale of entropic decline, for James Christopher is a great deal more than he seems to be. For one thing, he is a liar, to himself, to those around him, and to the reader. His life story moves along for three chapters with few surprises, handsomely composed, meditative, intelligent; the third chapter is a sermon concluding, "Do not love your neighbor as yourself; love him as your brother. One loves oneself too dangerously." But, then, in the fourth chapter, James Christopher's sister finds the manuscript of those chapters and asks him, "The story of your life?"

"No," he tells her, "The way that thing turns out, I'm a Methodist preacher."

"It's not your life then?" she says, and he replies, "I don't think so." And what are we to think? We are forced to think, to unravel fact and fancy, and to see with great clarity the inextricable complicity of truth with the lie, and of the lie with truth. "What is paramount here," Christopher the preacher tells us, "is that I am by nature blind to a greater part of the world about; I am sealed away from the most of my life. This is an invaginate existence: much too dull to think about for its own value." The liar tells the truth; Christopher has become blind to most of his life. But the truth-teller cannot see the truth of his telling; at least not yet.

Christopher's clouded perception sees his thirtieth summer as the beginning of a draining autumn (even as a child in the dead cold of winter, he dreamed not of summer but of the fall). The last stanza of Rilke's "Herbsttag" defines the tone of Christopher's stalled thought and life (the translation is Annie Dillard's):

Who now has no house, never will build one.
Who now is alone, alone will remain,
and will wake, read, write long letters,
and wander the roadsides, up and down,
restless, while all the leaves rain.

James Christopher is homeless, having rejected his home even as he lives in it, and he is alone even when he is with his wife and children because of that same act of rejection: waking, reading, writing, wandering, and without rest. "It is time, Lord," he cries out in the foul rag-and-bone shop of his heart.

But James Christopher is more than one man. He was born under the sign of Gemini, the twins (as he carefully does not remind us, even as he discusses the sign), and the preacher James Christopher tells us in his sermon that "I do not trust my friendly Doppelgänger who ranges my dreams and daydreams." Just as the liar and the truth-teller live together in the same phrase, so James Christopher the false preacher and prisoner of life shares the same identity with James Christopher the true Christ-bearer and free man. It is this inner man who as a boy wrote the vast epic poem about the Ironbird, "a long, unrhymed, non-metrical poem about a bird whose wings were door hinges, whose brain was an abacus, whose tail was a poker hand of cards. This bird flew around the world twice daily. It could see into the far past and the far future, prophesying in unintelligible language. It preached against the horrible sin of cannibalism." It is the prisoner who later loses the poem. And it was the prisoner, even in the boy James, who decided to commit suicide at the age of twelve, his blood draining away like that of Petronius while he lay reading great literature, just as it was the living James who did not commit suicide because he became so interested in *The Hunchback of Notre Dame* with which his double chose to die.

If Rilke's poem dominates the world of the prisoner, H. G. Wells's *When the Sleeper Wakes* stands as an emblem of the other James's nature, struggling to awake from the cannibalistic autumn dream of his double. The prisoner, in his guise as preacher, advises James that the past is not unchanging:

It grows up soon with weeds and underbrush like a dangerous trail. It sours and rots like old meat in the mind. It is a huge sea with titanic currents—like any sea. And he who fishes it must use a golden hook, he must plunge himself as bait into its depths, and if his past does not destroy and devour him wholly, his luck is insuperable. The self is the golden hook which is too valuable to cast into former days; no line is strong enough to hold it to the present and to the hope of futurity once the cast is made.

But James Christopher makes the cast into that mutable past, and instead of losing himself, he awakens the sleeper in his heart. By descending into the sea of sin and betrayal and the darkness of himself, by losing hope and gaining vision, James Christopher learns the lessons of the day and finds the summer of his life. By accepting the blame for burning down his grandfather's house (and we never really know if he did it, or whether the mysterious and devilish red-haired man whom he had previously blamed really did), he learns the lesson of forgiveness, the healing and regenerative lie, the truth beyond all lies. He regains his home and his loving wife by betraying them and redeeming his own betrayal. He learns to love his neighbor only after he is able to forgive (and love) himself. His no-good drinking buddy (who is named Preacher, appropriately and ironically) is killed for James's sins, and he gains from that death and his own betrayals and recoveries a set of three recurring dreams (not nightmares) in which he is able to enact his fall and redemption again and again. In the last of them he finds the sleeping giant of himself, and he struggles to awaken him even as he knows "that when this cold figure wakes I myself, a figure in his dreaming, will be forever obliterated."

"I dream my dream," he says, "and swim slowly awake." And awake, he finds himself to be not a giant but a man, living again in time, not alone, not wandering, rested and waiting for his family to awake and rise. "The roof is dripping with the morning dew, a patient zodiac sprawls the sky." He has ceased to demand of himself and of life the purity of absolute truth, and he is now able, by his refusal to surrender himself or "his men" for good and all, to see the day for what it is and to live in it, summer moving into fall, fall into winter, secure in the present and the hope of futurity.

2

Mon âme éternelle,
Observe ton voeu
Malgré la nuit seule
Et le jour en feu.
—ARTHUR RIMBAUD

It Is Time, Lord is a rich and complex novel, difficult and rewarding far beyond the outline I have suggested, but its duplicitous narrative and textual complexity seem nevertheless clear and uninvolved beside the difficulties of Chappell's second novel *The Inkling* (1965).

Like the first novel, *The Inkling* is at first glance simple enough, even familiar—the story of a small and fatherless family, a mother who is fading away in her loneliness; her brother who is the type of ordinary fallen man ("as long as Uncle Hake was around you knew the universe was still identical with the one you had always known: it had not suddenly been cleansed overnight"); her son who is nearing madness in his attempt to master his life and the world around him by the exercise of his will; and her daughter who is a mentally retarded visionary. After the introduction of an outsider—Lora, Uncle Hake's young, sexy wife—into the family, the mother dies, the boy commits adultery with his uncle's wife, the sister finds them, and the boy shoots his uncle in the heart.

Simple and familiar, that is, in the light of countless southern tales of distorted families and mad children which have followed in the strong wake of *The Sound and the Fury*. And *The Inkling* is that story, the story of a group of people who allow themselves to be cut off from the normal flow of life around them. But it is much more, for it is also the story of the awful and essential struggle within the human consciousness between will and desire, between mind's desperate need to subsume the material unto itself and flesh's equally desperate need to assert its own reality by joining that materiality utterly and without cease.

The Inkling begins and ends at one moment in time. In it, the small boy Jan and his sister Timmie are warned by a terrible yellow-haired man, are given an inkling of what is to come. But all the man says is, "Hanh, you goddam kids! . . . What if you was to die? What if you was to die one day?" They cannot see what stands before them, and their lives move into tragedy because neither of them can see the terrible and awesome fact of mortality as something integral to their own needs and desires. When the scene occurs again at the end of the book, the reader discovers what the children did not, that the yellow-haired man is Jan, that he has burst back through time propelled by the fury of his thwarted will like one of Feynman's positrons, unable "to warn them . . . to admonish this Jan, to preach to him," able only to stagger away, laughing at the joke he has discovered at the heart of his own being, the very earth ebbing and swaying beneath "his confused feet . . . as it might ebb and sway beneath the feet of a man who had been hanged."

The events of that day on fire—when the yellow-haired man of sixteen stands in the field, existing "so weightily . . . that he might have created it," the sun reflected in the plain glass of his spectacles "a tiny yellow dot, the size of the pupils of his eyes," and cries out his terrible question to his silver-haired six-year-old self—cannot be explained by the terms of the familiar tale of the southern decaying family. Nor can it really be explained by the terms of science fiction, from which it borrows the time warp that enables the confrontation to occur. A science-fiction reader might explain that the older Jan, moving in negative time, is now composed of contraterrene (or anti-) matter and that, had he touched his younger self, they would have merged in an act of collision and would have vanished completely leaving only a new ray of free energy, a day even more brightly on fire. But that would not explain the nature of the two Jans' meeting nor its terrible significance.

The Inkling is not a rerun of either *The Sound and the Fury* or of Jack Williamson's *Seetee Shock*. It uses the familiar ground of the Southern Gothic just as it uses the metaphorical freedom of science fiction to give imaginative substance and aesthetic value to a philosophical examination of the awful and awesome tension in the human mind and flesh between will and desire and of the terrible consequences for us all if that tension is not resolved in understanding.

Jan Anderson is a boy who looks hard at the world and attempts to master it with the force of his stare. He stares down the family cat Buddha and then kills it with a stone. Having mastered the animate and sentient, he turns to that inanimate and insentient weapon itself:

The stone he took up and carried back from the field to the house and put down near the back door. It was smeared on one awkward side with blood and there were other, whitish, stains here and there upon it. It was to be a new obstacle for him to vanquish; and in time he came to know every mark, the contour of every stain, each minuscule protuberance, the vague course of every vein, each tiny pit in the texture of the surface. He squatted before it, gazing hotly, and it looked as if he might be worshiping a god in the stone. This time he managed the exercise without gathering rancor and he and the stone in the end became brothers, and Jan was satisfied that he had overcome the will of the stone without having to displace it.

Jan's sister Timmie is a creature of "unwillingly sentient desire," possessed of visions of bleeding hands and feet, the extremities of Christ's sacrifice without the central significance. Jan attempts to protect her from reality by telling her that all evil is just "joking," not understanding that what she desires is a world of tangible reality, of bleeding good and evil available to the senses. And she, in turn, sees Jan's coming to terms with the stone as an act of worship and his acts of will as a "willing himself out of being" and therefore attempts to protect him by blunting his will, by covering his eyes with the plain glass spectacles to prevent "him from seeing clearly, or even guessing clearly, what he was to bring upon himself." Jan strives to control everything; Timmie yearns "to allow everything, to let it come down."

These two characters are enriched by a subtle web of allusions to the relationship of Rimbaud and Verlaine. Jan has Rimbaud's features, his stare, his powerful will; Timmie has Verlaine's sensuous and sensual imagination, his desperate need for physical love, his commingling of ecstasy and painful despair. As Verlaine shot Rimbaud finally, so Timmie stabs Jan in the hand. She makes him bow to her gods, phallic and obscene, and she sacrifices him to her need for an evil that cannot be explained away. Caught "under the paw of that one big tiger, his will," blinded by that will, by his sister's desire, and by the physical presence of his uncle's wife whose breasts are "sealed but observant eyes" and whose sex is "a coy sticky sidewise wink," Jan misses the admonitory signs around him, does not see (as his sister does) "how the clean path he had laid was curling back upon itself under his feet." He is caught up in the fate of his blind making, kills his uncle, and enters literally the sun-blazing world of Rimbaud's day on fire.

In the field under the sun, he waits for "things to make sense." Instead a baseball lands at his feet, contesting "his supremacy of existence" by its very fact, its simple being apart from Jan's will. He wishes to crush it, but he merely throws it away. It bounces against a tree, and Jan sees at last the joke of his life. The world simply is, like the ball and the tree. He simply is, alive in a world that one need not master but in which one is free to live, filled perhaps with will and desire but above all simply and amazingly alive.

Jan laughs and walks away; he turns "a big invisible corner of the airy light," out of negative time and into time, the world ebbing and swaying beneath his feet as beneath those of a hanged man, confused, lost perhaps in time but also possibly found at last, a burnt-out case moving in the heat of the day. "As soon as he had begun to walk he felt cooler," we were told in the first chapter of the book, and perhaps we can believe that, freed now of will and desire, alert to the cosmic joke, Jan may say, as Rimbaud did before him, "All that is past. Today I know how to greet beauty."

3

What but design of darkness to appall?

—ROBERT FROST

Fred Chappell's third novel, *Dagon* (1968), picks up strands of idea and metaphor from the first two novels and weaves them into an utterly different substance. Peter Leland, its central character, is a preacher as James Christopher dreamed of being, and like Jan he is appalled by the power of materiality, "the invalidity of his desires, how they could be so easily canceled, simply marked out, by the impersonal presence of something, a place, an object, anything vehemently and uncaringly itself." The novel is the story of a man who comes into his inheritance in his thirty-third year, a puritan inheritance of revulsion toward the living world, of surrender to the evil that he finds in the very urgings of his blood. Peter Leland is Young Goodman Brown in the modern world. Aware of sin, of the "fast deep iciness, pure recalcitrant cold" at the center of the earth, of "the fault in mankind to act without reflecting, to *do* without knowing why, to go, without knowing where," he loses his faith (and his wife, whom he kills) as fully as did Hawthorne's young puritan. He becomes increasingly passive, losing everything that he was and had, becoming finally a helpless and happy sacrifice on the idol of the mutilated god *Dagon,* the embodiment to Leland of "naked will uncontrollable."

Dagon is an elaborate texture of allusions to and parodies of the puritanical works of many of our literary forebears—Hawthorne, Melville, and especially H. P. Lovecraft, from whom the book takes its title and its central metaphor. Lovecraft was really the final and fullest expression of the dark vision of American Puritanism in our literature, a Puritanism in which God is finally not only silent but actually nonexistent. Lovecraft saw himself as a materialist, a believer in a mechanistic and meaningless universe, so vast in time and space that it reduces all human significance to nothing. But his Puritan needs asserted themselves in the creation of a "mythos" with ancient gods (among them Dagon) and future ones, dark and horrible gods who once ruled and may again rule an earth on which humans are mere passing shadows, less permanent than mayflies, smaller than motes of dust. He gave himself over in his dreams and his fiction to these dark gods, sure in his surrender that, no matter how man may strive to endure or prevail, endless time and his own unending decay will finally destroy him and leave him forgotten in the "paleogian gulfs of time."

Chappell's Peter Leland, whose name should have warned him that he was of the earth, earthy, stone and soil, a weak man whose wife pins him easily when they wrestle playfully, is a preacher who is more interested in the horror of the world (sex, money, needless productivity) than in the love of God and the promises of life. He inherits his grandfather's house and with it apparently the Morgan family, whose daughter Mina, noseless and rank as a beached fish, priestess of the cult of Dagon in the back hills of North Carolina, is an emblem of Leland's own "self-minatory" nature. Once he has seen her, he cannot "unthink her image," and he sinks into the darkness that she represents for him. He sinks into materiality because he is unable to see that he was of it from the first. He creates out of the stuff of himself a new theology of the snake; unable to bear the weight of Adam's sin, of his own progenitors' worship of Dagon, he abandons his humanity and its strength, choosing the dark source of sinful temptation itself as his totem:

> We live as serpents, sucking in the dust, sucking it up. The stuff we
> were formed of, and we ought to inhabit it. We ought to struggle to

make ourselves secret and detestable, we should cultivate our sickness and bruise our own heads with our own heels. What's the profit in claiming to walk upright? There's no poisonous animal that walks upright, a desecration. It's better to show your true shape, always.

As he debases himself, he preserves himself. He does not reconstruct and free himself like James Christopher, nor does he see through his blindness like Jan; he merely maintains his static identity: "He had faced the incomprehensible manifestation and he still maintained himself, he was still Peter Leland." It is this sort of self-maintenance that Chappell has referred to in another context as "existential desperation." Leland dies at the hands of Mina, still himself, nothing more, nothing less (for to his own eyes, there could be nothing less).

Dagon is not, however, just a reworking of Kafka's *The Trial* in an American Puritan context. It is much closer to that sad novel's cheerful Doppelgänger, Nabokov's *Invitation to a Beheading*. Peter Leland may not find beings akin to him at the end of the novel in the way that Nabokov's Cincinnatus C. does, but he does come through death to a new mode of existence. In the concluding chapter, which alludes to and parodies Chaucer's *Troilus and Criseyde*, Leland looks back at his life and laughs "without rancor and without regret." He swims in a realm of metaphors, contemplating "with joy the unity of himself and what surrounded him," deliberating "what form his self should take now." He does not choose the serpent, but rather the fish, Leviathan: "Peter took the form of the great fish, a glowing shape some scores of light-years in length. He was filled with calm; and joyfully bellowing, he wallowed and sported upon the rich darkness that flows between the stars."

Peter Leland was his own executioner just as Nabokov's Cincinnatus C. almost was in his novel, and *Dagon*, for all its overwhelming physicality, is an interior adventure, again like that of Nabokov's novel. Peter, a self-mutilated man, dives into the depths of his consciousness; the line does not hold for him as it did for James Christopher, and he destroys his life as surely as he murdered his wife *within himself*. He chooses his own evil but finally finds the only unity available to him beyond that evil. The novel may be the account of a descent into madness, but to limit its realities to hallucinations is to deny its metaphysical implications. The human mind believes what it sees, but it also sees what it believes and shapes its world to the needs of its belief. Peter Leland's Puritan consciousness gives him literally the fallen and nightmarish world of Puritan belief. The joke is on him, and he is the unwitting joker as well.

Perhaps Peter Leland's Nabokovian namesake, "the melancholy, extravagant, wise, witty, magical, and altogether delightful Pierre Delalande," states the moral (for what Puritan book would be without a moral) of *Dagon* best in the epigraph to *Invitation to a Beheading:* "Comme un fou se croit Dieu, nous nous croyons mortels."

4

If design govern in a thing so small.

—ROBERT FROST

Of course, *Dagon* may also be read as a criticism of American society, of the dark puritanical sources of its commitment to blind productivity, but it is in Fred Chappell's new novel *The Gaudy Place* (1973) that we find the fullest rendering of society, of the social and economic levels of a small town from bottom to top, from A(rkie) to Z(ebulon Johns Mackie). The novel is a tracing of the events leading up to an act of violence, an act comic and trivial in itself but which reveals with a startling clarity the terrible patterns of human striving and knowing.

The novel is comic; its tone is far lighter than anything Chappell has written before, the prose lively and witty. Its characters are the familiar victims of vice and folly that we have come to know from centuries of comic art—Arkie, the fourteen-year-old boy who ranges tawdry Gimlet Street and his fourteen-block world looking for a good con; Clemmie, the nineteen-year-old whore tied to her life because the rest of the world seems to her "as flossy and unbelievable as a Technicolor movie"; Oxie her pimp who is rising above Gimlet Street toward politics and respectability; Linn Harper, an idealistic and intelligent seventeen-year-old boy who learns the limits of ideas and ideals by discovering for himself "whether a code of behavior crudely extrapolated from the printed page can find an arena of action in quotidian reality"; Andrew Harper, Linn's historian father, whose "muddied perceptions and not particularly admirable life" have led him to believe in a "humanity helpless because choice is absent"; and Zebulon Johns Mackie, Andrew's uncle by marriage, a corrupt small-town political boss and businessman, an expert at urban charading, a gangster who looks like our sentimentalized image of Benjamin Franklin. Assorted characters mixed ready to begin the morning right, and their lives do mix and mingle, all of them ready, for one reason or another, to turn their backs "on this feverish gaudy place for good," all of them knowing that Gimlet Street "could take you anywhere in the world, it was joined to all the other streets there were," but none of them able to leave that gaudy place behind.

Chappell's first three novels, dark in texture, filled with physical and spiritual suffering, all have at center a faith in life, in something inexpressibly larger than the bare self in the barren world. But *The Gaudy Place*, the brightest and lightest of them all, has at its heart the deepest darkness of them all, for at the center of this exercise in cause and effect is an absence of meaning, of first cause. It is as if, in these lives, design does not govern at all.

The book takes its epigraph from Yeats: "What's right and wrong? / My grand-dad got the girl and the money." The lines are from *Purgatory*, the play that, as John Rees Moore reminds us, "goes further than any other Yeats play in the direction of unredeemed and apparently unredeemable blackness." The characters in *The Gaudy Place* all feel themselves to be at a turning place, but when the turn comes it is unexpected, and the road leads into a new and strange country quite different from anything they might have dreamed. "I don't know whether a novelist believes finally and philosophically in cause and effect," Fred Chappell admitted to John Graham. "I don't frankly philosophically believe in it. I've studied too much Erwin Schrödinger to go with that. But, in human terms, I think there is a cause and effect. In sub-atomic physics, I'm sure there isn't." In *The Gaudy Place*, this purgatory without apparent exit, the chaos of the subatomic world seems to be the metaphorical figure at the moral center of the novel.

"Anything can happen," Clemmie says when discussing a science-fiction book with a barfly named Teacher, "but I don't believe in it." But anything can and does happen, believe it or not. Arkie gets up his courage and tells his dream to Clemmie. When it begins to come true, partly because he told it, she invents a lie to tell back to Arkie. Arkie, who has come to love Clemmie, acts upon her lie, leading Clemmie to believe that she is "on the verge of a strange and important revelation. She was going to know things that she had never known before. . . . Something big was going to take place and she was going to have a piece of it." And it does, but with consequences neither of them could imagine. Dreams feed fact; new fact gives rise to new dreams which feed new fact; the whole process careening along, a giddy nightmare of cause and effect, unpredictable and formless, the mad world of "anything can happen."

Even Linn Harper, the boy whose world is the largest in the book, whose imagination (fed by science fiction) can expand to galaxies and even to the farthest reaches of the universe, lands in jail, lured there by the very mental integrity that enables him to see so far. Science fiction has led him to physics and to the writing of Conrad, and from Conrad the path has led dangerously on to Kafka, to Sartre, and to Camus's *The Stranger*. Linn's faith in the course he has followed makes him willing to risk himself for what he believes, which happens to be a dim understanding of Meursault's gratuitous act. So he lands in jail, a place far worse than anything he had ever imagined. He begins there to see for himself a free and exhilarating future life of crime, apart from all morals, but he ends up in the grip of a dream in which his old faith in the right and the good reasserts itself, but now (and forever) mixed with "other images, unrelated, discordant and dismaying."

We consider them all, and we consider ourselves.

But there is more to the gaudy place than this random mix of blind cause and effect. We do live "upon this lonely blue planet Earth, burning like a sunny atom of dust on the farthest rim of its galaxy," and "The universe is, after all, a gaudy place in which to live." Andrew Harper, speaking of the shooting at the end of the novel, does manage to find a way of coming to terms with events:

> What happened next was at first almost incomprehensible to me—and, in fact, I do not yet understand it. That is, I cannot know the causes and mechanics of the event. But it does take a shape in my mind, it does make itself at least credible. Even at the time it occurred it must have appealed to me as a pattern, for by the time it was over I was laughing uncontrollably.

Laughing out of control, but laughing; unaware of causes and mechanics, but taking pleasure in the shape of things. Andrew Harper's laughter rings with Jan's and Peter Leland's. Oh, we learn the hard way, the hardest ways, but we learn. And we forgive. And we love. We care for these poor fools in Gimlet Street, and by that caring, we love life itself a bit more. Like Camus's Meursault, we at least come to appreciate the wonder of the gaudy place.

"The act of literature is a moral act," Fred Chappell told John Carr and John Sopko in a 1969 interview, and certainly the care and caring at the heart of *The Gaudy Place* make it a moral act. "What's right and wrong?" That we cannot ever know, because the right and the wrong are as fluid as the chaotic moment itself. But we can know the good. "I think the human spirit can surmount its materialism," Fred Chappell continued. "After all, materialism is really just an invention of the spirit. Anything we can invent we can get over. I hope." And that hope is at the source of *The Gaudy Place* as well as the earlier novels. The universe is, after all, such a grand and gaudy place in which to live.

5

A confession and one last anecdote:

I have, despite all my efforts, failed to do the novels of Fred Chappell justice, but I hope that I have managed to convey some of their values and something of their value. But perhaps this personal anecdote will at least say simply what I have been struggling to express. One of the best of our graduate students asked me not long ago which novelist of my generation (and by generation, she meant my age) did I really think she ought to read. Really read, grapple with, learn from, experience.

I could have named a great number. I did name a handful to myself; all, writers whose work I value. The list came easily, and it was an honest list. But I knew from the start that the exercise was futile, because I knew the answer all along.

"Fred Chappell," I said. "He's the best of them all."

{ II. 2000 }

To that concluding confession, I should like to add three others:

1. In the section of the essay dealing with *The Gaudy Place*, I called Zebulon John Mackie "an expert at urban charading." Since the phrase makes sense in its context (or at least I think it does), its oddness may have

slipped by its readers unnoticed, but I now feel the need to confess that it is actually a reference to an even more odd mistake in one of Fred Chappell's interviews (which I alluded to obliquely a bit further down the page). The transcriber of the taped interview, not entirely familiar with Chappell's western North Carolina accent, made Fred into a student of "urban charading" rather than of the physicist Erwin Schröder-inger. I confess that I could not resist the joke. Mea culpa.

2. Although I could not have been expected to know how important the number 4 with all of its Pythagorean solidity would become in Chappell's later work, I confess that I should nevertheless in my discussion of *It Is Time, Lord* have made mention of James Christopher's wife's lying by him in bed at the end of the novel, "her slender legs crossed with her right ankle on her left knee, making the number 4." I remember developing a tentative theory about it, one actually based on post-Pythagorean numerology (in which that most primitive of numbers stands for steadiness and endurance—certainly appropriate to Sylvia in the novel), but I must have lost my nerve. That it may also refer to the four elements (earth, air, fire, and water), I had not a clue. Mea culpa.

3. I will also confess that I was immensely pleased to discover, in a most startling and pleasant way, that Fred Chappell approved of at least one part of my essay. In his poem, "Burning the Frankenstein Monster: An Elegiac Letter to Richard Dillard," he says, "You were right, Richard, / What I mostly ripped off from Rimbaud was the notion of fire / As symbolic of tortured, transcendent-striving will." I was perhaps even more pleased by being in *Bloodfire* (1978, the second volume of *Mid-quest*) at all and, thus, like James Dickey, attaining immortality the easy way. For being so pleased and even worse for bragging about it here, I can only say, "Mea culpa."

I should also like to make three comments or observations having to do with Chappell's second group of four novels, the Kirkman tetralogy:

1. Once, when writing a notice of the first volume of the tetralogy, I attempted to locate or "place" the novel's unique nature by a process of what might be called literary rectangulation, i.e., a process using three fixed points rather than the usual two used in trigonometric triangulation. Since I now believe that the discovery I made using this process

applies equally well to the entire tetralogy, I shall repeat it here. If one wishes to define the special flavor of these books, one would do well to draw a line stretching from Gabriel García Márquez's *One Hundred Years of Solitude* (1967) to Erskine Caldwell's *Georgia Boy* (1943) to Ray Bradbury's *Dandelion Wine* (1957), closing the rectangle with Chappell's tetralogy. By examining closely the literary context formed by these books, each unique and radically different from the others, I predict that one will find at least a clue as to just what gives Chappell's novels their satisfying and unique taste. Of course, there are references and echoes and allusions to the work of many other writers in Chappell's novels, ranging from Robert A. Heinlein (in chapter 9, "Into the Unknown!" of *Look Back All the Green Valley*) to Dante, Virgil, Shakespeare, et al., but I still believe that those particular three novels I've hitched to the Kirkman tetralogy's star will give an interested reader at least a good start toward a richer understanding of Chappell's achievement.

2. I do have one bone to pick with Fred Chappell. In *The Finish Line*, the Leidig lecture that Chappell gave at Emory and Henry College on April 10, 2000, and which was published by the college the following fall, he delivers himself of an unusually tart attack on "postmodernist metafiction":

> For my money, metafiction is a nasty adolescent habit one strives to outgrow—like smoking. . . . When I depart this world and a just Deity hands out my allotted punishment, he shall set me to writing metafiction. That is a sign of his mercy, of course, for he could condemn me to an eternity of reading the stuff.

As a fully accredited (and aggrieved) writer of "postmodern metafiction," I guess that it is up to me to take on the onerous task of pointing out to Fred Chappell that the Kirkman tetralogy is, whether he likes it or not, and whether he admits it or not, a metafiction. How could it not be, with its shifting narrative strategies, cross-genre devices and references, multilayered allusions, and, of course, its playing of the significant game that "Fred Chappell" is the pseudonym used by Jess Kirkman to write his tetralogy of poems (*Midquest*)? Why else would I have put Chappell in the company of "a Barth or a Coover or a Hawkes" in my 1973 essay had it not been that his first four novels struck me as being metafictional, too? I don't know exactly why he is denying the metafictional nature of his fiction so much these days, but I have to admit that, while doing so, he sounds to me an awful lot like an adolescent farm boy caught smoking behind the barn, who protests his innocence loudly while one of his horny heels is busily grinding the still smoldering butt out in the red clay.

3. In *The Finish Line*, Fred Chappell also speaks tellingly of the Kirkman tetralogy and the four volumes of *Midquest* as a "double quartet, or octave, of books: about 1,000 pages of fiction, about 200 pages of poetry." There is no need for me here to explore the connections between the parts of that octave, a task begun so well by Richard Abowitz in Patrick Bizzaro's *Dream Garden: The Poetic Vision of Fred Chappell*. That work is now safely, I am sure, in better hands than mine. I would like, rather, to make the possibly heretical suggestion that the first four novels, the four *Midquest* volumes, and the four Kirkman novels form an even larger, twelve-volume work, a *Divina Commedia Nuova*, if you will. The connections between the first four novels and the octave are, at least to my mind, clear enough—the autobiographical echoes and parallels, for example, or the parallels among Fred Chappell, Jess Kirkman (as Abowitz pointed out, *chapel* and *churchman*), and, say, James Christopher (*Christ bearer*) in *It Is Time, Lord*, or, for that matter, Preacher in that novel and the preacher Peter Leland in *Dagon*. The connection of Chappell's work with Dante's great *Commedia* is quite explicit in both the situation and design of *Midquest* and is brought full circle in *Look Back All the Green Valley*, in which not only is Jess Kirkman translating the *Commedia*, but his quest for his father's secrets comically and significantly replicates Dante's revelatory journey. The first four novels are also to my mind sufficiently hellish to form an *Inferno;* Chappell admits in his autobiographical essay in the *Contemporary Authors Autobiography Series* that his design in the early novels "was as much to harrow the reader as to entertain him." *Midquest*, I think, could also interestingly be read as a *Purgatorio*, and the Kirkman tetralogy as a *Paradiso*. I offer this observation not as a fact, but as a speculation. I doubt that Chappell had this *Commedia Nuova* in mind all along, but then, since he is such a complicated and thoughtful and quite duplicitous artist, I also wouldn't be surprised if he did. It may just be that I see this larger pat-

tern in Chappell's work because I am concerned that Chappell's first four novels not be overlooked in the midst of all the quite legitimate interest in the last four; for I still believe, as I did in 1973, that they are major novels, certainly worthy of thorough and serious critical examination. To further that cause, I'll even make another and final confession: like many readers of Dante, for all my admiration of the books that make up what I've called Chappell's *Purgatorio* and *Paradiso,* I nevertheless still like his *Inferno* best.

TWO

On Reading *The Inkling* by Fred Chappell in a Building on the UNC-G Campus

KELLY CHERRY

THE BUILDING that had been allocated to
the writing students: one main room in which
we wrote, hoping our words were right, and true
to life, that we had snagged the *Ding an sich.*
I settled in a corner of the couch
to read, and read until the light grew dim.
Lamps now. Outside, snow had begun to slouch
across the sky in search of Bethlehem,
or like a poet, hands in pockets,
très Rimbaud and existentialist,
a mind electric as the lamps' sockets.
I read as in a dream of night, snowmist
spiraling, brilliant as poetic insight,
beyond the window, in lovely starlight.

THREE

Darker Vices and Nearly Incomprehensible Sins
The Fate of Poe in Fred Chappell's Early Novels

GEORGE HOVIS

THE AMAZING DIVERSITY of Fred Chappell's literary productivity was perhaps already apparent during his years as an undergraduate and graduate student at Duke (1954–64). Chappell studied under the legendary William Blackburn—who also taught such notable writers as William Styron, Anne Tyler, and Reynolds Price—and in these workshops Chappell demonstrated a sort of raw genius that later prompted Blackburn to call him "the most gifted writer and the best of the bunch," even while admitting his doubts that Chappell would "ever 'succeed' as a writer" the way the others had (Garrett xiii). Chappell's "success" in the form of widespread recognition was slower in coming than it was for the other writers mentioned, which may be due to his penchant for experimentation. Looking back on his days at Duke and the presence of Reynolds Price, who had already published several mature stories in *The Archive*, Chappell admits surprise that the upperclassman's style did not much influence his own: "But maybe it was already clear to me that Reynolds and I were headed in different directions. There seemed to be a tacit agreement that I was to be intense and wild and experimental, while he was to be traditional, Olympian, and successful" (*Plow* 24). When Chappell's popular success as a fiction writer finally did arrive, it was due to the 1985 publication of a novel that, like Price's early success *A Long and Happy Life*, depicted rural folk in a sublime state of innocence. Although Price's novel and *I Am One of You Forever* differ in many respects, they have in common their depictions of agrarian communities in which the members exist in harmony with each other and with the natural world—an image of the South that has always appealed to readers. Chappell had actually begun working in this pastoral mode during the

1970s with the composition of the four volumes of the Bollingen Prize–winning poem *Midquest,* and he continued this approach with each of the novels in the Kirkman Quartet (1985–99).[1] All based on Chappell's Appalachian boyhood, these eight works compose an octave for which Chappell is best known by critics and general readers of fiction and poetry. Despite an impressive variety of literary forms, the octave sustains a pastoral vision characterized by a reverence for nature and family, a preoccupation with social order out of which meaning and value are derived, and an imagining of the past as an innocent Golden Age whose disappearance the adult narrator elegizes. Chappell's earlier novels present such a radically different worldview from that presented in his later octave that they hardly seem the work of the same pen. In contrast to Jess Kirkman's idyllic boyhood in the bosom of a supportive family, Chappell's first four novels are dominated by a fascination with alienation, social disintegration, and degenerating states of the self (including alcoholism, deviant sexuality, prostitution, paranoid schizophrenia, and nihilism). All four of the early novels—*It Is Time, Lord* (1963), *The Inkling* (1965), *Dagon* (1968), and *The Gaudy Place* (1973)—were out of print until *Dagon* was reprinted in *The Fred Chappell Reader* (1987) and the others were recently reissued in Louisiana State University Press's *Voices of the South* series. Given their publishing history, these works have received considerably less critical attention than Chappell's later work. This essay explores *It Is Time, Lord* and *Dagon* as studies in alienation and goes on to examine *The Gaudy Place* as a transitional work that anticipates Chappell's later pastorals.

Though Chappell claims that Jess Kirkman is by far a more autobiographical figure than the protagonists of his earlier novels, he admits that Jess has been "highly romanticized and cleaned up a great deal" (Hovis 71). For a sense of just how much Jess has been "cleaned up," we need only look at Chappell's memoir-essays "First Attempts" and "Welcome to High Culture," collected in *Plow Naked,* and "A Pact with Faustus"—all three classics of their genre. In contrast to Jess's basically harmonious childhood, these essays portray a young artist alienated from his family and community, and, despite the mature writer's comic deflation of his own youthful angst, these accounts of romantic aspiration help explain the mood of the early novels. It comes as no surprise that Chappell, a boy with an intense interest in books and writing, seemed something of an oddball in his community and was less than perfectly content with life on the farm. Like Thomas Wolfe in Asheville, twenty miles to the east, Chappell grew up seeing the hills around his native Canton as a prison holding him back from the cosmopolitan experience—and the writing career—of which he dreamed.

By the age of fifteen he was determined to become a writer and was already publishing stories in science-fiction and fantasy magazines, whose editors gave him what little encouragement and instruction he received. "My experience with [these] editors," he writes, "was that they were sinister spectral entities who occasionally scribbled crabbed notes on little blue rejections slips: 'Your exposition is silly'; 'This is not how Martians talk to each other' " (*Plow* 20). Aside from the thanks he gives certain high school teachers who at least did not discourage him from writing, the picture Chappell gives us of his adolescence is the one we might expect from an aspiring writer growing up on an isolated mountain farm: the dreamy autodidact, who began teaching himself to write through "an eon of trial . . . followed by an infinitude of error" (*Plow* 14). Although he believes that his schoolteacher parents had themselves once entertained literary aspirations, they strongly discouraged his own as impractical (10).

In "A Pact with Faustus," Chappell recalls his adolescent friendship with Harry "Fuzz" Fincher, another Canton boy, who aspired to be a composer. Chappell recalls their mutual "conspiracy against the placid town and against [their] perfectly nice parents": "We felt—God forgive us!—superior in some way that we could not articulate, and much put upon, despised for our interests and aspirations" (480). The boys felt cut off from any meaningful discussion of the arts beyond their own company of two, and, in typical adolescent fashion, they luxuriated in their alienation and eventually joined in a spree of vandalism through the nighttime streets of Canton, "breaking random store windows and wreaking other damage," a night which for Fred resulted in "severe" and "unforgettable" punishments involving "physical ordeals" and an "interminable" ban on reading, an activity his parents associated with his waywardness (481). If he was taught that reading was a guilty pleasure, writing seemed to have been doubly so. In a community of farmers and mill workers, a pursuit of the arts was seen as self-indulgent. Parents, teachers, and "everyone else" constantly lectured Fred about the lack of value in his pursuits (481). In "First Attempts,"

Chappell recalls his parents' feelings about the long evenings he spent secluded upstairs, writing:

> My bedroom was too small to accommodate a desk and typewriter, but I had found a niche in the upstairs hall. When I set the Royal clattering the sound could be heard all over the house. Visitors who asked about the racket were informed that Oh, that's only Fred working on his typing. Their embarrassment was just that acute; I was not trying to write, I was learning to type. Typing was a useful skill that might come in handy someday. Writing was impractical and impracticality was worse than heresy, thievery, or some kinds of homicide. These were the tag-end years of the Depression; it was imperative to be practical. (*Plow* 12)

He had discovered that to be a writer was to be at odds with his culture, and he clung to this new-found identity of the outsider.

Chappell makes comically clear in "First Attempts" that what fascinated him as a young person was the glamour of "being a writer" rather than the daily task of writing. The problem he faced was a lack of models:

> The only other writer [besides Hemingway] of whose personal life one ever heard anything was Poe—and he was regarded as both scandalous and tragic. Whenever my parents, teachers, and ministers tried to dissuade me from a life of writing—as they did regularly and assiduously—it was the fate of Poe they threatened me with. They pictured him as a wild-eyed genius who was an alcoholic and drug addict, and they hinted too at darker vices and nearly incomprehensible sins.
>
> Well, I could see that being Edgar Allan Poe had it all over being Ernest Hemingway. . . . To all of us [writing] seemed such an exotic occupation, such a dangerous ambition, that when we tried to imagine the way of life a writer might trace we could come up with only the most lurid and improbable scenarios, visions that horrified and repulsed my elders while they attracted me with all the force a two-ton electromagnet exerts on a single crumb of iron filing. (*Plow* 9)

Poe would serve as an appropriate icon to represent the alienation felt by the adolescent Chappell. Along with the French symbolists, Poe would fix very firmly in the boy's mind the image of the young genius at odds with his world, composing obscure lyrical gems that would some day (most likely after his early death) bring him the fame he had deserved. In the poem "Rimbaud Fire Letter to Jim Applewhite," Chappell recalls the decade of his apprenticeship at Duke and parodically describes the long nights of drinking and the "artificial fevers" necessary to become a poet (58–61) with the word his mother uses to describe farm labor, "hard."[2] Throughout "Fire Letter," as in his memoir-essays, Chappell looks back in amusement at his own self-indulgence and pokes fun at the pose of the romantic genius.

He takes a similarly dismissive attitude toward the vision behind his early fiction. When asked about the earlier novels, Chappell unequivocally distances himself from them: "There was a kind of claustrophobic feeling about those first three novels that derived from a kind of determinism that I could not get out of my fiction. It didn't bother me in poetry, but as soon as I started writing fiction, I could feel the prison walls closing in. So, the philosophical ideas stated in the first four novels are surely not my own" (Hovis 71). Though it is not surprising to hear a writer distance himself from his early work, in Chappell's case this dismissal is regrettable, since the early fiction shows such marks of genius, and three of the four novels—*It Is Time, Lord; Dagon;* and *The Gaudy Place*—are, in their own ways, as accomplished as his later work. But they do obviously derive from a different sensibility, a different attitude toward the subject matter of his Appalachian past. In each of these first four novels, there is an intense ambivalence toward home and society that results in alienation and in some cases psychological collapse. One easily recognizes in this earlier fiction the influences of Faulkner and Camus[3] and even more so of Poe, whom Chappell names as his "first and most lasting influence" (Hovis 75).

The protagonists in the first four novels are Appalachian Quentin Compsons, trapped and determined by their environments and by their personal and familial pasts. James Christopher, the first-person narrator of *It Is Time, Lord,* describes the past as "an eternally current danger, in effect, a suicide. We desire the past, we call to it just as men who have fallen overboard an ocean liner call. . . . [I]t sours and rots like old meat in the mind" (34–5). In *Dagon,* Peter Leland returns with his wife to his family's Appalachian home place, which he has just inherited and which he finds to be haunted by a familial past that, like Poe's Roderick Usher, he cannot escape. Upon first exploring the downstairs parlors, Leland remarks that "the pastiness which these two rooms . . . enclosed was not simply the impersonal weight of dead personality but a willful belligerence, active hostility. Standing still in the center of the first room, he felt the floor stirring faintly beneath his feet, and he was convinced that the house was gathering its muscles to do him harm" (53). Over the following weeks, the house does in fact do him serious harm, exerting an influence over his moods and his frame of mind, leading him to morbid thoughts and ultimately to the brutal and seemingly motiveless murder of his wife. One is reminded of Monsieur Meursault in Camus's *The Stranger* and, perhaps more obviously, of Poe's many demented criminals who seem compelled by a force beyond their understanding.

Of Chappell's novels, Poe's influence is, indeed, most intensely felt in *Dagon,* a horror tale that anticipates Cormac McCarthy's *Child of God* (1973), just as Chappell's depiction of Asheville's red-light district in *The Gaudy Place* (1973) anticipates McCarthy's tale of 1950s Knoxville derelicts in *Suttree* (1979). I mention this similarity to McCarthy in part to call attention to their common inheritance of that southern gothic tradition extending back through O'Connor, Erskine Caldwell, Truman Capote, Faulkner, and finally to Poe—and to the darker earthy elements in the work of the frontier humorists. But rather than comparing the gothic elements of *Dagon* to any one of these previous literary sources, it might be more profitable to trace the germ of its horror—the sociopathic behavior of the protagonist—to similar behaviors found in so many folk ballads of the Appalachian frontier.

These folk songs often examine the darker side of yeoman independence, which in its most extreme cases ends in an antipathy and indifference to the claims of society. Steve Harvey notes that "According to their songs, mountain folk have an assortment of ways . . . to kill each other. Silver daggers and the hangman's rope are two. Drowning is common" (63). Harvey finds in these songs an uncanny fascination with violence and criminality for its own sake and sees, for example, the ballad "Little Sadie"—which begins "Went out last night to take a little round / I met little Sadie and I blowed her down"—as "one of the most compact murder stories ever composed." Harvey notes the nearly comic swiftness with which the ballad shifts from romance to murder, as well as the crime's apparent randomness and lack of motive (63–4).

The same seemingly motiveless killing appears in the traditional ballad "Knoxville Girl":

I met a little girl in Knoxville, a town we all know well,
and every Sunday evening, out in her home I'd dwell.
We went out to take an evening walk about a mile from town.
I picked a stick up off the ground and knocked that fair girl down.[4]

The song continues with a graphic description of the murder told by the killer in a dispassionate, detached, almost curious voice. Like Lee from "Little Sadie," the nameless murderer of "Knoxville Girl" returns home and pretends innocence, in this case to his mother who notices blood all over his clothes, which he almost comically attributes to a bloody nose. He ends up in prison, haunted by his crime and yet not fully capable of comprehending his motives for killing or the reasons for his punishment. In his retelling of the event, he focuses on the details of the murder itself and thereby demonstrates a psyche alienated from any social context that would give his tale meaning. The juxtaposition of romance and murder in these Appalachian ballads emphasizes the young mountaineers' problems with intimacy, a major issue for Chappell's early protagonists and still very evident in his later pastorals.

In *Dagon*, Peter Leland is guilty of the same motiveless, nearly unconscious killing that we find in "Little Sadie" and "Knoxville Girl," and, like the protagonists of these ballads, he is never capable of or much interested in understanding the social ramifications of his act. Immediately after bludgeoning his sleeping wife to death with a fire poker, Leland flees to the home of a sharecropping family named Morgan, who for generations have sustained themselves on the sale of moonshine. Leland, by profession a Methodist minister, and normally of puritanical disposition, gives himself over to the Morgans' moonshine and spends the rest of the summer drunk in the bed of the daughter Mina, who serves as his dominatrix, subjugating him to her every whim, delighting in his increasing degradation. At the end of the summer, Mina uses Leland's automobile to drive eastward with Leland and another young man to a Piedmont town where they settle into an abandoned house. Mina employs two other women as prostitutes and begins a campaign of ritually desecrating Leland's body through torture and tattooing. The story ends with Leland emaciated and covered in tattoos, reduced to a state of bestiality and total withdrawal. His level of communication has been degraded to grunts and mooing, and a metal bar that he identifies as his "man-thing" has become his only source of consolation. When Mina finally takes his life in ritual sacrifice, Leland welcomes the knife.

In an ironic and detached epilogue that chronicles the life of Leland's spirit after the death of his body, we find that he achieves a state of sublimity, for which it seems his debasement was necessary. One is again reminded of Poe's fascination with annihilation; in *Eureka,* his long treatise devoted to cosmology and metaphysics, Poe puts forth a deterministic theory that necessitates not only personal annihilation, but the ultimate annihilation of all matter in the universe, as a fulfillment of the Divine plan for spiritual renewal. A similar idea underlies the apparently fated action of *Dagon;* early in the novel we learn that Leland has left his parish for a summer sabbatical at his family's home place in order to complete a book to be entitled *Remnant Pagan Forces in American Puritanism,* in which he traces through history the worship of an evil god called Dagon, who represents the mindless pursuit of instant personal gratification, especially through sexual and material means. Leland identifies this god as having dominated the course of American history, which he believes to be controlled by consumer culture:

> And wasn't the power of money finally dependent upon the continued proliferation of product after product, dead objects produced without any thought given to their uses? Weren't these mostly objects without any truly justifiable need? Didn't the whole of American commercial culture exhibit this endless irrational productivity, clear analogue to sexual orgy? And yet productivity without regard to eventual need was, Peter maintained, actual unproductivity, it was really a kind of impotence. This was the paradox which the figure of Dagon contained. . . . Dagon was symbol both of fertility and infertility; he represented the fault in mankind to act without reflecting, to *do* without knowing why, to go without knowing where. (70–1)

One hears in Leland's treatise the unmistakable echo of the Agrarians' manifesto, which similarly indicts modern industrial/consumer America as doomed by an irresponsible, unthinking impulse toward consumption that leads to a destructive and nonsustainable lifestyle.

Unlike *I'll Take My Stand*, however, Leland does not spare agrarian society from his criticism. And unlike Chappell's later pastorals, which are careful to draw a distinction between a corrupted urban present and an innocent rural past, in *Dagon* all of humanity is infected with destructive and self-indulgent urges—arising from something akin to Original Sin. Leland traces these same impulses from biblical times through the Puritans at Merry Mount down to his own age. Nowhere in his research of the past does he come upon an unpolluted Golden Age. The "disease" to which Leland falls prey similarly doomed his father and is active in the lives of the sharecropping Morgan family and the other nearby farmers who visit the Morgan home. With the exception of Leland's wife—who is murdered a third of the way into the narrative—the novel does not offer a single healthy character. In particular, the poor farmers are shown to be ignorant, brutal men and women who delight in violence for its own sake. This is a world where might makes right, where in any situation a pecking order obtains and one's identity is constituted as a result of one's position in that order, instilling in the protagonist—and the reader—a claustrophobic desperation for liberation, a desire for detachment and independence. One feels, at least throughout the first part of *Dagon*, that if Leland could only escape the home place of his ancestors, he could avoid the malaise that has overtaken him.

Similarly, in each of the other first four novels, family and community are shown to be a trap from which one must find a way to extricate oneself. The claustrophobia felt by each of these protagonists recalls Chappell's account in "A Pact with Faustus" of his own adolescent desperation to escape the parochialism of his hometown, a desperation that led to a spree of vandalism and afterward guilt for the rebellion, followed by an intensification of alienation. We note that a similar destructive cycle provides the basic tension for his first novel; in *It Is Time, Lord*, James Christopher at age thirty-one is still wrestling with the guilt of having, as a nine-year-old, burned down his family's ancestral home place. The first-person narrative begins with James Christopher's rehearsing two memories, upon which he is fixated and which he spends the rest of the novel revising. The first memory is of seven-year-old James returning from the barn with his younger sister Julia on a bitterly cold winter evening and being reprimanded harshly by his father for exposing his sister to such dangerous cold. The father's words seem overly harsh, and much later in the novel, when we learn that the sister is whimpering not because of the cold but because she has just witnessed her brother being raped or molested by strange men out at the barn (148), the father's reprimand takes on a horrific resonance. The second memory is of the home place's being set on fire; the culprit is at first identified as a red-headed stranger who has been regularly parking out behind the barn with women he takes there for sexual purposes. Through a series of vignettes, each of which revises these two memories—the children's return from the barn, and two years later the night of the home place burning down—the rapist is associated with the red-headed stranger who supposedly set the fire, and then we discover that nine-year-old James has falsely blamed the red-headed man and that he set the fire himself, in an unthinking and seemingly unmotivated act—much like Peter Leland's murder of his wife.

Like Faulkner's *Absalom, Absalom!* Chappell's first novel *It Is Time, Lord* is a detective story in which past event and motive are filtered through fragmented memories, many of them proven to be false. Of all his novels, his first is easily his most demanding; rather than employing a linear plot, *It Is Time, Lord* relies upon repetition of images and fragments of dialogue to suggest in a very modernist, and often postmodernist, fashion the constructedness of meaning. The protagonist, James Christopher, is obsessed with his past: his office is cluttered with pieces of broken souvenirs from boyhood; he is writing a largely autobiographical novel (which begins with the same first lines as *It Is Time, Lord,* a metafiction designed to suggest further the constructedness of meaning—and the claustrophobia of personal memory). Despite James's obsession, however, he feels intensely dislocated from his childhood, declaring, "As far as event is concerned, the mind is an isolated citadel standing in a desert. Miles of sand surround it. A starry sky stretches overhead. The face of God never leans toward it, and in the desert nothing moves. The citadel itself is peopled only with thin ghosts" (35). This first novel was written shortly after Chappell's time at Duke, when he claims to have labored upon a "longish, heavily Eliotic" poem through as many as forty drafts (*Plow* 23), and *It Is Time, Lord* clearly shows the influence of Eliot and other modernists whose epistemological anxieties resulted in the fragmentation of meaning into multiple subjectivities, here within the same person.

Among the unstated questions inevitably raised in *It Is Time, Lord* are these two: first, what happened in James Christopher's childhood that could have led to his inexplicable burning of his family's home place at the age of nine? And a related question, what exactly has caused his current crisis of purpose at the age of thirty-one, leading him to give up his job at a local university press, drink himself to sickness daily, and pursue a sexual relationship with a "redneck" woman named Judy who disgusts him—an involvement that, predictably, threatens to destroy his marriage and family? James comes to realize that his present life and his past are inextricably linked, but not in any easily decipherable fashion. Not only do repressed childhood traumas motivate him toward self-destructive behaviors, but his present relationships insinuate themselves into and pollute his already unreliable memories of the past. After reaching a crisis point in his present life, he tells his wife of his plan to straighten things out by visiting his parents in the mountains, whom he has not seen or corresponded with in five years. "Isn't it true," he says, "that if I could get my past settled in the right groove my present life would trundle along the way it's supposed to? It's like getting a nut cross-threaded on a bolt: you have to twist it back and try until it fits correctly" (160).

His attempts to "settle" his past depend largely on making peace with his father, a plan that fails abruptly; when James first enters the front yard, his father begins a withering speech, monotonously pointing out all of his son's failures, past and present. In effect, he verbally divests James of his manhood, just as he had done throughout James's boyhood, constantly criticizing his bookishness and his disinclination for farm labor and reminding him of his guilt for burning down the home place. Like James, his father is a man threatened by any degree of intimacy, and his rebuff of his son appears to be a spontaneous response to that threat. Shortly thereafter, James's mother comes to his bedroom and explains that she is supposed to let him know that his father is still his "good buddy." "Your father's got in his head," she says, "that the only way a real masculine man ought to talk is in grunts and profanity. But the trouble is, he likes to talk too much for that to satisfy him. So he runs on. I've lived with him long enough to know he doesn't mean anything he says for an hour at a time." She further remarks that he "almost jumps out of his skin" when he hears the word "love" (161). In *Look Back All the Green Valley* Jess Kirkman observes that "to be well spoken is not in the tradition of the Appalachian mountaineer, whose sometimes inscrutable taciturnity is locally regarded as a virtue having something to do with valor and manliness" (183). If to show oneself a "well spoken man" in Appalachia is to invite suspicions of one's masculinity, to show oneself as "bookish" confirms those suspicions. In both cases, not only emotional warmth, but communication through language, is degraded in contrast to "action." James's father has obviously internalized these cultural values and, since, as his wife observes, he is a compulsive talker, he compromises by divorcing any emotional warmth from his speeches to his son. These speeches are characterized by the abstraction, nihilism, and self-absorption of Faulkner's Jason Compson III (Quentin's father), with the addition of an icy hostility born of long hours laboring on the farm for diminishing returns.

Except for demeanor, James Christopher's father very closely resembles the heroic father, Joe Robert Kirkman, of the Jess Kirkman novels. Both fathers are farmer-teachers who lose a job teaching science at a nearby high school because of their unwillingness to refrain from teaching evolution. Both men are rugged individualists who cultivate a friendship with a local grocery store owner named Virgil Campbell, the hard-drinking epitome of Appalachian independence. In these respects, both fathers closely resemble Chappell's own father. What changes, obviously, is Chappell's attitude toward his father. One finds in the early novels a painful ambivalence for the father that is absent, or at least muted, in the four Jess Kirkman novels. In these later four novels, the father is a benign, harmless, fun-loving trickster figure, whom the boy idolizes and emulates. For all his adolescent pranks, one nevertheless notices in Joe Robert Kirkman an emotional distance from his son, Jess. Chappell himself has remarked of Joe Robert, "It's noticeable in my work that the father actually says very little, except when he is showing off and teasing" (Hovis 71). Chappell acknowledges "the taciturn farmer father" as a staple of American realism, finding examples in Hamlin Garland, Sarah Orne Jewett, Mary Wilkins Freeman, and "all the regionalists" (Hovis 71). This taciturnity and emotional paralysis appear in all of Chappell's fiction as the downside of yeoman independence. The emotional distance of the father lends the Jess Kirkman novels a pathos that enhances the longing of the adult narrator for unity with his family, and especially with the father; in the earlier novels, by contrast, the father's distance engenders only bitterness.

It Is Time, Lord launches a steady critique against Appalachian ideals of manhood, viewing the figure of the yeoman farmer as insensitive, alienated, and completely incapable of nurturing. In attempting to teach their male children strength, they only turn them into bullies, as indicated by James's redirecting the aggression he feels for his father to his crippled, sympathetic grandfather, habitually calling him an "old hopping Jesus." Similarly, little nurturing takes place in the relationship of the father and son tenant farmers, with whom James spends much time. Though Uncle George, the tenant father, is consistently abusive to his son Hurl, he serves James as a surrogate father, joking with him and teaching him many traditional rural skills, from bee-keeping to animal husbandry, while James's father always resorts to belittling him in order to force him to perform his chores. The failure of the son to mirror the father in the case of James leads to an unstable sense of selfhood, one that is subject thereafter to threats of insinuation by other strong male figures. It is even possible that the memory of the rape is actually a false memory, a projection of James's vulnerability evoked in response to certain recollections of his father.

This inability of the father to form a healthy bond with his son results in a cycle of male emotional paralysis, which in James's case becomes so severe that he exhibits symptoms of paranoia and schizophrenia, believing that he has been overtaken by a Doppelgänger: "For a long time now, someone else has been living my life. Or living in my life, inside. It's clear to me that I have been completely usurped" (50). The opening paragraph from H. G. Wells's *War of the Worlds* is also invoked to communicate his paranoia: "No one would have believed in the last years of the nineteenth century that this world was being watched keenly and closely by intelligences greater than man's . . ." (*Time, Lord* 14). At night he dreams that he is the victim of a plot designed to "bar [him] from conscious awakening, to seal [him] forever in this circular dream" (179). Despite his abortive attempt at a more hopeful resolution, James discovers that the mind takes whatever means necessary to hold the past at bay. Returning home from his failed meeting with his parents, James lies in bed paralyzed and muttering to himself like Eliot's Prufrock, or like Hamlet, repeating, "What shall I do?"

(182). Instead of more firmly securing his relation to the past, or rethreading the "cross-threaded" nut on its bolt, he resorts to another metaphor, one that views repression in the most positive light: "Bad, naked event will cover itself over again with my mind like an old man pulling the blankets about himself in a winter night" (182). James Christopher resigns himself to the loss of the past, to the fact that his memories are not conduits but rather barriers to past experience, thereby allowing him to function in the present. The novel ends tentatively but hopefully with James turning in bed to his sleeping wife and seeing in her the path to his future.

Like Poe's stories of dementia, which Chappell so admired as he was growing up, the energy driving Chappell's first three novels[5] derives from within the self rather than from the social milieu in which the self finds itself. For all their intensity and frequent lyricism, the first three novels lack the breadth and social scope typically associated with long fiction. Admittedly, each novel is less than two hundred pages long; considering the economy and intensity of the narratives, these novels have the advantage—which Poe attributes to the short story—of possibly being read in a single sitting. Nevertheless, one might make of them the same criticism that W. H. Auden makes of Poe's stories: "There is no place in any of them for the human individual as he actually exists in space and time, that is, as simultaneously a natural creature subject in his feelings to the influences and limitations of the natural order, and an historical person, creating novelty and relations by his free choice and modified in unforeseen ways by the choices of others" (vi). As with Poe's stories, each of Chappell's first three novels demonstrates an unease with society. The characters' self-destructive behaviors result not from interactions with others so much as from internal compulsions they cannot escape. Chappell has acknowledged this problem in his early fiction, noting a "claustrophobic feeling . . . derived from a kind of determinism that [he] could not get out" (Hovis 71).

In my estimation, the "claustrophobia" of Chappell's earlier work is not necessarily a problem; as with Poe's stories, Chappell's early novels are so engaging precisely because of the characters' withdrawal into dementia. Alienation is not only a very real part of the modern experience, but, as we have seen, of the traditional yeoman experience in Appalachia. One might, in fact, describe James Christopher or Peter Leland in the very words Joe Robert Kirkman uses to describe one of his shy rural students who is more comfortable alone in the woods than in a high school classroom: "It was the mountaineer strain in his blood as pure . . . as it might have been a century ago" (*Brighten* 57). Nevertheless, having acknowledged the insight of Poe and of Chappell's early work into the alienated psyche, one is forced to agree with Auden and declare that not all the world looks so dark and determined. Even in the loneliest valleys of Appalachia, people form communities, however small, in which they creatively engage and in which they define themselves. *The Gaudy Place*, Chappell's fourth novel, marks his first attempt in long fiction to escape the prison of the self and to describe a social world.

As satire, *The Gaudy Place* takes the first step toward the pastoral vision of social order found in *Midquest* and the Kirkman novels. Frank Kermode argues that, like pastoral, satire is an urban genre, designed to contrast the "degeneracy" of the "metropolis" with some "better way of life—that is, some earlier way of life; the farther back you go the better" (15). One thinks, for example, of *The Adventures of Huckleberry Finn*'s juxtaposition of pastoral river life with the social quagmires the boy finds along the river's shores. *The Gaudy Place* offers no such easy demarcations, though one is confronted with moral differences among characters that do invite a comparison of possible innate benevolence with the corrupting influences of the city. Published two years before the first of the four *Midquest* volumes, *The Gaudy Place* (1973) departs from the earlier work in that it is Chappell's first and only urban novel. (Although parts of *It Is Time, Lord* take place in the suburbs, the setting is primarily confined to the suburban home.) *The Gaudy Place* takes in all of the bustle of the Gimlet Street red-light district of Braceboro, the fictional version of Lexington Avenue and Flint Street in Asheville, where Chappell spent numerous hours doing research.[6] One finds a strikingly different sensibility at work in this fourth novel; although the earlier fiction is replete with delicious irony, this is Chappell's first fully comic novel, a social satire reminiscent of Twain that pokes brutal fun at the American myth of the self-made man. *The Gaudy Place* turns away from the psychological introspection of the earlier Poe-inspired thrillers to take in a broad overview of society in this mountain town. With its Kafkaesque interest in the dissemination of power, this is easily Chappell's most explicitly sociopolitical novel, one in which not family so much as economics and politics determine social and personal realities. But then again, as Andrew

Harper discovers upon moving to Appalachia with his mountain-born wife, mountain politics *is* a family business.

Expanding beyond the limited perspectives in the earlier novels, *The Gaudy Place* contains five parts, each written from a different point of view: Arkie, the resourceful orphan who makes his living running cons along Gimlet Street; Clemmie, a nineteen-year-old prostitute; Oxie, a bondsman with political aspirations, who is also Clemmie's pimp; Linn Harper, a middle-class teenager who finds himself trapped by personal ideals into committing a meaningless misdemeanor that lands him in jail; and Linn's father Andrew Harper, a college history professor who, in attempting to extricate his son from the machinations of the law, finds himself trapped in a shady deal with his wife's elderly Uncle Zeb, a corrupt local politician with powerful connections throughout the city. The diversity of perspectives, motives, and voices represented in these five point-of-view characters, and in the novel's other various and colorful characters, create a very rich and convincingly real fictional milieu, one that seems at first to avoid Auden's criticism of Poe; these characters exist in such a busy and heterogeneous world that the creation of "novelty" through "free choice" seems inevitable and perpetual.

The sense of exuberant freedom is most apparent in the first section, which is devoted to the lovable young con man, Arkie, an urban Huck Finn, who has just turned fourteen, "according to his own cloudy reckoning" and is "little for his age" (8). Throughout this opening section, Arkie makes his rounds down Gimlet Street, conning slow-witted truck farmers who have just sold their produce, or unsuspecting "johns" waiting for their "girl friends." Arkie speaks a tough, comic street slang, full of both hyperbolic boasting and self-deprecation; he understands how his age and size give him both advantage and disadvantage in a place where no one but himself is concerned with his needs. His friend Teach, a teacher who hangs around the bars reading sci-fi novels and drinking too much, has informed Arkie that he does not exist, marshaling as proof the boy's lack of any official connections to the power structures that grant identity; the boy is in possession of neither driver's license, social security number, birth certificate, vaccination scars, doctor's or dentist's records, mailing address, and does not know his parents' names (3–4). Despite his uncertainty even about "what it mean[s], *to exist,*" Arkie belligerently affirms, "Yes I do, I do that" (3).

Like *The Sound and the Fury,* one of Chappell's favorites,[7] *The Gaudy Place* relies upon the modernist method of multiple subjectivities, a form that denies the possibility of omniscience and foregrounds the freedom of individuals to know their world, even if in a limited way. Their freedom, however, seems deliberately undermined by the periodic intrusions of an omniscient narrator. Immediately prior to Teach's challenge of Arkie's existence, an authorial voice condescendingly introduces the point-of-view character: "Consider Arkie. / (But it breaks your heart)" (3). This juxtaposition of the authorial voice and Arkie's self assertion creates a tension that continues throughout the novel between the desires of these fictional characters to define themselves and the intrusion of a limiting omniscience, which often occurs in dialogue with itself like a Greek chorus commenting on the action of a tragedy already written in the stars. Clemmie's section begins "Consider Clemmie. / (Poor speck of flotsam.) / . . . The rate she's going makes you want to bet that the machine will break down before she's twenty-one" (31). Here, as elsewhere, the intrusive voice is marked by a coldly sociological or scientific indifference, which further subverts the novel's basic structure.

Of all the novel's characters, Arkie, the youngest and least established (and least indoctrinated), is possibly the most optimistic about his agency. In this mountain city, where African Americans are virtually nonexistent, Arkie occupies the lowest socioeconomic rung, and is even known for a subservient song-and-dance routine that has all the characteristics of minstrelsy. Whenever a tense moment appears, he does his dance and sings out in his namesake couplet: "Fried cornbread and cold coleslaw, I'm traveling down to Arkansas" (26) or some variant thereof. The barkeeps allow him to hang around because he keeps the "johns" happy and laughing and not fighting each other (12). This repeated song expresses Arkie's essentially transient nature, like a hobo riding the rails ever farther westward to new opportunity and freedom from encroaching civilization and its restrictive responsibilities. The intrusive voice of the author undercuts the faith in freedom expressed in Arkie's song by cynically viewing the Old Southwest as merely myth: "Arkansas . . . / Man, was there really such a place as that?" (26).

In contrast to the boy's expansive vision of his prospects, the narrator informs us that "Arkie's universe was minuscule, actually comprising an area of about fourteen blocks" (14), but the boy is not daunted by this limitation and at the end of a day pursuing his various cons—especially the one designed to put him in close daily contact with the older girl, Clemmie—he feels euphoric:

> You couldn't keep him down now, he couldn't remember when he'd been so happy. He felt confident about his whole life. . . .
>
> . . . Suddenly it occurred to him that this street, Gimlet Street, could take you anywhere in the world, it was joined to all the other streets there were. He shook his head, grinning. Arkie couldn't go. This was his territory. He was chained to Gimlet and he was chained to Clemmie, that green-eyed girl he was so helplessly in love with.
>
> "River gonna rise, creek gonna thaw, I'm traveling down to Arkansas."(30)

This segment, which ends Arkie's section, emphasizes the tension between the determining influences of his environment and his ability as an individual to choose the manner in which he engages that environment; so far, Arkie seems a likely candidate for the sort of fictional character Auden is looking for. He demonstrates here an understanding of how his choice to stay on Gimlet Street pursuing the girl he loves will involve him in any number of unforeseen circumstances that will limit his freedom. The spontaneous utterance of his song in this context calls attention to his acceptance of his changing identity: the feeling of liberation associated with his song comes not in response to a romantic plan of escape but in a very real commitment to another person.

The following two chapters, told from the points of view of Clemmie and Oxie, respectively, diminish our hopes for Arkie's chances to determine himself. In Clemmie's chapter, she seems hardly aware of Arkie and instead is interested only in Oxie, her pimp, whom she identifies as her source of stability and protection. Similarly, in Oxie's chapter, he is hardly aware of Clemmie and is instead preoccupied with schemes to ingratiate himself with the "respectable" racket of local politics. In both chapters, these two characters express feelings of optimism about their futures in words very similar to those used by Arkie, and, in each chapter, we enter states of increasing self-absorption. In each case, their dreams of self-fulfillment echo and thereby undercut what at first seemed the innocence of Arkie's. Oxie, a first-generation immigrant, has discarded his ethnic name and is strug-gling to give up his street slang and rewrite his personal history in a move from Gimlet Street to the courthouse downtown. As aids to his project of self improvement, he reads Dale Carnegie and tapes to his shaving mirror the slogan, "appearance is important. You got to put your best foot forward" (137). When we discover that Oxie got his start running small-time cons on Gimlet Street at roughly the same age that Arkie is now, we become aware of other similarities between the two: Arkie's colorful vocabulary comprises the very words that Oxie is now coaching himself to avoid; the phonetic similarity of their names suggests a connection; and the condescension Oxie feels toward his prostitutes is mirrored by Arkie's attitude toward the truck farmers who are his source of income. Of Oxie's indifference to Clemmie, we learn: "For Oxie, of course, she held no attraction, no more than a razor or table or wallet he owned. Mechanism still in running order. Something doing what it was supposed to do with a minimum of attention" (114). Arkie similarly dehumanizes the truck farmers whom he cons for small change by calling them "mules." Even if the boy is in love with Clem-mie, the chances of this adolescent infatuation's becoming anything more significant are low—especially if his ambitious plan to become her pimp does, in fact, succeed.

Perhaps the novel's most devastating blow to self-determination and genuine human interdependence is the figure of Andrew Harper's uncle-in-law, Zebulon Johns Mackie, or Uncle Zeb, a local politician whom An-drew describes as a "dead ringer" for Benjamin Franklin. A member of both the city council and the board of directors for the local Green Ridge Con-struction Company, respectable Uncle Zeb has his own con in the works, which involves someone with Oxie's contacts on Gimlet Street. In a shady property deal worthy of Robert Penn Warren's Willie Stark, Zeb avoids charges of conflict of interest through a mixture of frequent casual briberies and good-ol'-boy charm. The official deal is supposed to result in a parking lot on Gimlet Street that would make the red-light district "more widely public" and more susceptible to surveillance and law enforcement (161), a plan eerily reminiscent of Foucault's Penopticon; the actual deal involves a more insidious distribution of power, with Uncle Zeb collecting profits, through a middle-man such as Oxie, from the properties housing gambling rackets and prostitution rings. Of course, the maintenance of power depends upon a careful distinction between private realities and public fictions; to augment his already high profile in local politics, Uncle Zeb has plans for his niece's husband, Andrew, to write the family's proud history, in which, of course, Uncle Zeb figures prominently. If Oxie hopes one day to fill Zeb's shoes, Zeb wishes to fill the shoes of his namesake and kinsman, Governor Zebulon Johns, whose bronze effigy stands in the town square. Like Ben Franklin, who took care not only to *be* industrious but to *appear* so, Uncle Zeb understands the importance of self-promotion to the acquisition and maintenance of power. In the world of this novel, the self-made man is made by insinuating himself into the available power structures and assuming the identity demanded by that structure; this holds true for Zeb, Oxie, Arkie, and even a high-minded idealist such as Andrew Harper, who is trapped into accepting the assistance of his powerful uncle-in-law in order to free his son from jail and avoid alienating his wife.

Of the novel's five sections, only the final chapter devoted to Andrew Harper is written in the first person, allowing him alone the artifice of objectivity. Andrew's voice is one of carefully studied judgments, both as a father and as a scholar of history. He begins his narrative in language that echoes but humanizes the omniscient voice that introduces the other four sections: "Is there anyone who *considers* himself a good parent?" [emphasis added] (139). His choice of a contemplative life stands out in relief when compared to the active lives of the other characters, including Uncle Zeb, who informs Andrew that he started out as a history major in college but gave it up because "there didn't seem much a feller could *do* with it" (155). Add to Andrew's profession the fact that, of all the characters, he alone is an outsider, from the middle-eastern part of the state, who intensely feels his difference and often wryly criticizes the ways of mountain folk. Nevertheless, he believes this difference allows his analysis to be more objective and accurate. To the degree that the reader makes this same assumption, the reader may participate in his critique and—considering his credentials—his generalization from this society to all societies. His unveiling of Uncle Zeb's corrupt plot makes Andrew an even more credible source, so that when he cynically concludes his analysis of cultural, socioeconomic, and political factors that determine the lives of mountain folk with the broad generalization that all "humanity [is] helpless because choice is absent" (166), one is inclined, at least for the purposes of the novel, to agree with him.

After swallowing three bourbon-and-waters in his kitchen and resigning himself to his fate, Andrew rides with his Uncle Zeb to the jail to meet the bondsman, Oxie, who will assist in extricating Andrew's son, Linn, from the machinery of the penal system. With two pages to go in the novel and a diminishing expectation for a satisfying ending, out of nowhere Arkie appears with a .25-caliber pistol (which Oxie had lent to Clemmie and she lent to Arkie). The boy has mistaken Uncle Zeb for the "creepy old pervert" who has been abusing Clemmie (177) (or perhaps it is not a mistake); he fires the gun's one round, which shears Uncle Zeb's collar bone and sends him to his knees cursing and covered in blood, but otherwise safe from serious harm. Oxie threatens Arkie with a call to the police, but the boy merely responds with his song: "Fuck them! . . . Fuck the law, I'm going down to ARKANSAS!" (177), with which he disappears, leaving Andrew Harper laughing hysterically at this unexpected turn of events.

This novel's considerable power derives from the vertigo of watching what at first seems to be a random sampling of society drawn into a web of power that robs each of them of agency. In *The Gaudy Place,* Chappell demonstrates at least the same mistrust of society that is apparent in his earlier novels of alienation. Furthermore, by deconstructing the American myth of the self-made man, he, in effect, attacks the notions of independence and personal autonomy that underlie the yeoman myth, which he celebrates in each of the four Jess Kirkman novels. The ending of *The Gaudy Place* may suggest a clue to this transition from social satire to yeoman idyll. Like so many of the unexpected endings to his novels, the final two pages of this one come as a delightful surprise and, like the final couplet of an Elizabethan sonnet, force us to reconsider everything that has come before. Arkie—the boy who according to all official statistics does not exist—is able to take action that at least symbolically challenges the power system for which Uncle Zeb stands, and he also challenges Andrew's nihilism; his spontaneous act at least provisionally restores our faith in the individual's freedom to choose. As in *Huck Finn,* however, Arkie's final statement that he plans to light out for the territory of the old Southwest suggests that, for Chappell as for Twain, freedom only exists for the individual who is removed from society.

Having discovered in *The Gaudy Place* that a city—even a young one with strong ties to the surrounding rural farmland—inevitably robs the individual of freedom and agency, Chappell limits the fictional milieu in his later novels to the family farm, the nearby high school, and the surrounding countryside. In the Jess Kirkman novels, we meet individuals who find their identities not exclusively in reaction *against* the social order but nurtured within it as well. Each of these four novels explores the extent to which personal autonomy and society are compatible. A broad overview of Chappell's eight novels suggests a prodigal's journey. In his earlier fiction, we find a withdrawal from society, motivated by personal ambivalence for what he then found to be a narrow and constraining Appalachian culture, combined with a romantic temperament and his artistic identification with Baudelaire's dictum that "the man of letters is the world's enemy." Sooner or later, however, even the most romantic temperaments tend to cool. It is not surprising that, when Chappell decided it was time to leave the prison of the self, his eyes turned westward toward home.

NOTES

1. *Midquest* (1981) is composed of the four previously published volumes: *River* (1975), *Bloodfire* (1978), *Wind Mountain* (1979), and *Earthsleep* (1980), all from Louisiana State University Press. The Kirkman Quartet includes: *I Am One of You Forever* (Louisiana State University Press, 1985), *Brighten the Corner Where You Are* (St. Martin's, 1989), *Farewell, I'm Bound to Leave You* (Picador, 1996), and *Look Back All the Green Valley* (Picador, 1999).

2. See "My Mother's Hard Row to Hoe," *Midquest* (Baton Rouge: Louisiana State University Press, 1981), 151–2.

3. Chappell acknowledges the important influence of Faulkner and Camus on his first novel in George Hovis, "An Interview with Fred Chappell," *Carolina Quarterly* 52, no. 1 (1999), 71. Also, in "A Pact with Faustus" he lists *The Sound and the Fury* among the five novels he has most often read, the others being *Doctor Faustus, Don Quixote, Adventures of Huckleberry Finn,* and *The Sun Also Rises.* "A Pact with Faustus," *Mississippi Quarterly* 37 (1984), reprinted in Dabney Stuart, ed., *The Fred Chappell Reader* (New York: St. Martin's Press, 1987), 479.

4. Louvin Brothers, "Knoxville Girl," 1956, rereleased on *When I Stop Dreaming: The Best of the Louvin Brothers* (New York: Razor & Tie Music, 1995), compact disc.

5. While I don't discuss *The Inkling* here, it very much fits the pattern found in both *It Is Time, Lord* and *Dagon*. The boy protagonist Jan and his sister Timmie both spiral into states of increasing dementia, which their dysfunctional home life only exacerbates. David Paul Ragan notes that the relationship between Jan and Timmie "almost seems an extension of the childhood relationship between James Christopher and his sister" in *It Is Time, Lord,* and that "the relationship between Laura and Jan at the end of *The Inkling* seems to prefigure the relationship between Peter Leland and Mina" in *Dagon.* David Paul Ragan, "Flying by Night: An Early Interview with Fred Chappell," *North Carolina Literary Review* no. 7 (1998), 111.

6. Fred Chappell, interview by George Hovis, Chapel Hill, N.C., 12 September 1999. (Note that the other citations of this interview are to the version published in *Carolina Quarterly* 52, no. 1).

7. "A Pact with Faustus," 479.

WORKS CITED

Auden, W. H. Introduction to *Edgar Allan Poe: Selected Prose, Poetry, and Eureka,* ed. W. H. Auden. New York: Holt, Rinehart, 1950.

Chappell, Fred. Interview by George Hovis. Chapel Hill, N.C., 12 September 1999.

Garrett, George. Foreword to *Dream Garden: The Poetic Vision of Fred Chappell,* ed. Patrick Bizzaro. Baton Rouge: Louisiana State University Press, 1997.

Harvey, Steven. "Bluing." *Five Points* 4, no. 1 (1999): 60–72.

Hobson, Fred. "Contemporary Southern Fiction and the Autochthonous Ideal." In *The Southern Writer in the Postmodern World.* Athens: University of Georgia Press, 1991.

Hovis, George. "An Interview with Fred Chappell." *Carolina Quarterly* 52, no. 1 (1999): 67–79.

Kermode, Frank. *English Pastoral Poetry: From the Beginnings to Marvell.* New York: Barnes & Noble, 1952.

Louvin Brothers. "Knoxville Girl," 1956. Rereleased on *When I Stop Dreaming: The Best of the Louvin Brothers.* New York: Razor & Tie Music, 1995, compact disc.

Ragan, David Paul. "Flying by Night: An Early Interview with Fred Chappell." *North Carolina Literary Review* no. 7 (1998): 105–19.

FOUR

Chappell's Women
Models from the Early Novels

SHELBY STEPHENSON

SOME OF Fred Chappell's most compelling writing has to do with women, exemplified best perhaps by his creation of the fugue of women's voices in *Farewell, I'm Bound to Leave You.* His women characters never actually speak for themselves or narrate their tales, except in a few poems from *Midquest.* More often they behave in direct response to the behavior of the men they care for, live with, and nurture. Often, however, Chappell's women come to dominate their men in a manner both controlling and, in some instances, destructive to the man. This essay will demonstrate the way many of the women Chappell creates protect and, by necessity, use their protectiveness to control the behavior of the creative men in their lives and how, in many instances, the controlled men are eventually consumed by their women. What's more, this essay will show that the women in Chappell's early novels seem to be rehearsals for the women in the later works, both short stories and novels.

MATERNAL PROTECTORS OF MEN

Since many of Chappell's lead male characters are writers, inventors, musicians, or, in any case, men who dedicate some portion of their lives to various creative acts, the women closest to them provide models for how to live with, protect, and control a creative man. In nearly all of these encounters between a woman and a creative man, the woman tends to be protective of the man, and she finds his creativity appealing, almost irresistible. As Norma Lang in "The Thousand Ways" says of writer Mark Vance, he "could arouse a motherly feeling in the carcass of a dead horse" *(Moments* 89).

Writer James Christopher is such a man. Though he narrates Chappell's first novel *It Is Time, Lord,* and, though it seems to be his story, he is profoundly influenced by the women around him. His wife Sylvia, for instance, is absolutely loyal to him. She never questions him. Rather, she is an accepting and protecting woman. But more than that, she seems to have insights unavailable to her husband, creative though he may be. And this is typical of one kind of woman—the protecting woman—who thrives in the various worlds of Chappell's making.

When James comes home from a bar drunk at four in the morning, Sylvia calmly tells him to "Come on to bed" (56), an attitude indicative of her sensibility throughout the novel. When they take a ride in their Alpine and James, on the verge of a breakdown, has a fender-bender with a Dodge driven by a young woman, Sylvia consoles him, even though he has ignored her plea to stop the car. What's more, she tells him she will go down to the police station the next day and report that *she* was driving the car. More central to James's desires, when he has finished writing *It Is Time, Lord,* he can sleep peacefully, knowing that Sylvia has straightened the papers and the pages of his novel and—for the time—his life. Like Deborah of "Mrs. Franklin Ascends," Sylvia allows her husband the space to try to be whatever he dreams or thinks he might be. If there is tension between them, it is negligible. Though James cannot do without Sylvia, he rarely "goes out" to her. His behavior highlights but does not enhance her status; she is simply one of Chappell's good women.

In *It Is Time, Lord,* James's mother Cory is presented as yet another insightful woman who uses the power of her understanding to comfort James. To emphasize this quality in Cory, Chappell contrasts her with David, her husband. David is a gruff father who thinks his son is lazy, wants him to get a job, and wants him to be responsible. David believes James should quit reading "all that literary stuff," the novels he describes as "hog wash. Bull shit" (158). Cory, on the other hand, is easygoing and seems able to look into the heart of another human being. She, like Annie Barbara Sorrells of the Kirkman novels, has a wonderful sense of humor and seems eager to understand her son. It is easy to see that Cory Christopher and James are early incarnations of Cora Kirkman and Jess. Cora, of course, is more developed, since Jess presents his mother's life from the time she is a young woman courting Joe Robert to her final days in the Graceful Days Retirement Community. Like Cora Kirkman, Cory Christopher consoles her writer-son, particularly when a family member dies. James acknowledges his mother during the death and funeral of his grandfather: "My mother's worn, thin hand rode my shoulder like a trained dove" (160–1). In an easy exchange of talk, he gets his mother's endorsement because she understands her husband: "Your father's got it in his head that the only way a real masculine man ought to talk is in grunts and profanity" (161). Cory understands differently from David and approves of the sensitivity required for a man to create.

Understanding the connections between an early novel such as *It Is Time, Lord* and Chappell's most recent work in the Kirkman quartet is essential to an understanding of Chappell's fiction, his continuing interest in the creative man, and the relationships of women with such men. Like James Christopher, author Jess Kirkman looks back on his life and his relationship with the women he has encountered, focusing particularly on his pre-teen years. In "The Overspill," a kind of prologue to *I Am One of You Forever*, Jess characterizes his mother as protector, creating her tear, which takes him into the world of the Kirkmans, the world he writes about. He also presents grandmother Annie Barbara Sorrells as a woman who understands and challenges men, as exemplified by a "rusty" played on her by Joe Robert and Johnson Gibbs. They eat her chocolate candy in the wrappers and wrap pullet eggs where the chocolates had been, waiting and gloating in their messy glee. The grandmother out-eggs them, so to speak, making for their meals a variation of egg recipes until Johnson Gibbs stops "dreaming about the underwear girls in the Sears catalog" (14), dreaming instead of pork chops. Chappell's women, sensitive though they may be, are not easily duped by the boyish, if creative, men who likewise populate the fiction. But the women of Chappell's novels do suffer from bias, gender and otherwise, that inhibits their creativity and requires that they protect men, often in order to control them.

Recounting the visit of Grand Ole Opry star Aunt Samantha Barefoot, cousin to Annie Barbara, Jess learns that his grandmother was forced by her pious father to quit music (she and Sam were a duo). The climax of the story comes when Sam and Grandmother Sorrells do the old number,

"Come All You Fair and Tender Ladies," with Sam singing lead and playing fiddle. Jess's recollection of the two women suggests that they challenge
and tease the men and clearly do not back down from them. Sam, for example, is characterized as a go-getter, a hustler, and funny as hell, although
she has suffered a life of trouble (for instance, her husband, a rube comic,
committed suicide), reminding Joe Robert when she needs to that he is
"mean and trifling" (168). Aunt Sam knows her public and private selves, as
Jess reports her response in an interview on WWNC in Asheville. The
radio announcer asks her to comment on the commercializing trend of old-
time music, to which she responds, "some people didn't know cow shit
from cake batter" (177). Jess's description of their singing and playing the
old out-of-tune piano is a poetic tribute in prose to Annie Barbara, showing the respect for her that Chappell displays for women throughout *Farewell, I'm Bound to Leave You*:

> Her singing transfigured the music entirely. She had a dark con-
> tralto that sounded like it had mellowed in an oak barrel for slow dec-
> ades, a voice as rich as damask soaked in burgundy wine. The song
> began to take on strength and shape. In the middle of a chorus Aunt
> Sam stopped singing and fiddling and all the music was my grandmoth-
> er's harmony chords with so many notes missing. She played on, hesi-
> tant but unfaltering, and those wistful broken shards sounded like the
> harmony that must lie beneath all the music ever heard or thought of—
> tremulous, melancholy, constant. It was a music you might hear down
> in the autumn grass on a cold hillside. (178)

In *Farewell, I'm Bound to Leave You*, Annie Barbara says she was a better
fiddler than Samantha, that she had a career, a life in music, but her father,
Ward Purgason, discouraged her: "The music was my other life, the one I
never had and never would have once my daddy said no. So I was always
bitter about it and held it against him, and that's a sin against me, and I
wish it was the worst one" (16).

Chappell is well aware of such inequities but these inequities make
Annie Barbara more reactive to the men around her. Jess remembers his
mother Cora saying that Joe Robert is "such pure mischief, you can see it
coming a mile" (18). She adds: "He's always trying to get her [Annie Barbara's] goat, but it usually works the other way" (19).

The grandmother's account of how she planned for her daughter Cora to win Joe Robert by letting him fly a kite made from her petticoat, is a wonderful example of how, by understanding the emotional and intellectual workings of a man, a woman is able to control and even manipulate him. Annie Barbara tells Cora to fib about the petticoat and say it was hers. When Joe Robert launches his soaring success in the manner of Ben Franklin, hoping to reenact Franklin's discovery of electricity, Cora shoots it down with her father's .12-gauge. She wins his heart, though, especially after he sees her shoulder bruised from all the practicing she had done to learn how to shoot the undergarment down. All this is to say that Grandmother Sorrells knows how men's minds work; she, like Sylvia, Cory, Deborah, and Cora, portrays the strength of character, insight, and human concern that characterize one type of woman that populates Chappell's fiction.

Grandmothers are also often maternal protectors in Chappell's fiction. James Christopher's grandmother, like Annie Barbara Sorrells, is an excellent example. She is a protector, nurturer, and healer, daubing alcohol on James's wound when he scrapes his body raw with a rope while climbing onto the barn roof. "Does it burn much?" she asks (33). "It hurts good," he says. Like Jess's grandmother Sorrells, James's grandmother talks to him constantly about the Bible, is glad that she lived long enough to see him as a preacher (all of chapter 3 is a sermon), and shelters him. But her influence does not keep her grandson from excessive drinking, just as Annie Barbara cannot do much with her son Luden, who shoots the dime-store dolls he lines up on the hog-lot fence, emptying his pistol, during one of his drunken escapades in *I Am One of You Forever*.

If James Christopher and Jess Kirkman remember and learn from the women in their lives, so does Mark Vance, another writer, the lover of the older and seasoned Norma Lang in "The Thousand Ways" (from *Moments*). When the young, aggressive, and totally spoiled Edwina Tumperling enters his life, however, and wants him to meet her mother right away, her shiny exuberance confuses him. The two women initiate Mark Vance in a way reminiscent of how sixteen-year-old Rosemary McKay introduces her fifteen-year-old playmate to sex in "The Weather." Like James Christopher, the boy seems uninterested; he wants to be a writer, as evidenced by the poetic flourishes of his prose. She "might have been my sister; it was a kiss companionable and a little defensive" (109), he muses in retrospect about his relationship with Rosemary, pointing out that she had already stuck her soiled cotton underpants under the hay.

"Mrs. Franklin Ascends" (from *Moments*) likewise enhances the notion that women have control adequate to the shaping of fictive worlds of their own in order to foster lives as creative as the lives of their men. Told in the third person, the story comes shaded by Deborah Franklin's consciousness: she loves her "Pappy" with an excessive love, accommodating him by arranging a dinner party on his first night back from England (he has been away for five years), exchanging witty repartee with him, and clearly looking forward to going to bed with him. In the dream that ends the story, she gets out of bed—this is after "they took pleasure of one another and fell asleep" (26)—and goes upstairs to a room that is neither in their house nor in heaven. She enters "this smallest ante-room to the Many Mansions" (27) in a state of being "neither truly awake nor truly asleep, but in a vague state between," and she sees her husband playing an "armonica" he first named *deboronica*—a musical instrument "of their after life" (28). In the dream, her husband, like Joe Robert, busies himself inventing, while she enjoys managing his life—when she can. She tells herself she will not move to England as he contemplates doing. There is no tension between them, just a gay acceptance of the terms of their marriage.

Many of Chappell's women, then, are protectors of men who are writers or, at the very least, men who are creative in some way, including inventors and musicians. Most of the women considered thus far have been wives. But in Chappell's various worlds, sisters also protect their brothers, often in order to control them, as does Julia in *It Is Time, Lord*. Thus the sister-brother relationship is worthy of consideration here.

Like Cory, Cora, and Annie Barbara, Julia helps James discover himself within the context of others. This theme emerges poignantly in *It Is Time, Lord*, when seven-year-old James introduces his three-year-old sister Julia, who follows him outside in the freezing cold. What Annie Dillard says of "January," a version of the James and Julia Christopher story, in her foreword to *Moments of Light*, makes clearer the brother-sister relationship. The boy, she says, "has learned the moral ambiguity at the heart of things, and the moral imperative" (xiii). But what of the sister? What does she learn? Perhaps she learns to go on the ambiguous way instinctively. In any case, the focus is on the boy's maturation. And so, as Julia grows up, she puts family first, sensing her role as her bother's counsel and foundation. Like Sylvia, she unconditionally supports James from childhood through his wayward indulgences into his virtually impending collapse.

Extra-sensitive to Julia's authoritativeness, seeing her at times as if she were a first lieutenant, James often thinks—and tells her—that she seems older than he. Gail M. Morrison's phrase to describe this sister-brother connection is "his sister's maternal protectionism" (52), a phrase that also might apply to Mitzi of *Look Back All the Green Valley*, though Mitzi seems independently proud to be an adviser to Jess; her manner is less grandly doughty and overbearing than Julia's. James begins this exchange with his sister:

> "Do you remember about my asking you how you got to be older than me? I want to know how you got to be bigger and stronger too."
>
> "I don't know what you're trying to say."
>
> "I'm not trying, goddammit, I *am* saying. I used to protect you. You were smaller than me, my little sister. And then somehow you got the notion you were protecting me, and some way you got me to believe it. That's what I mean."
>
> "Well," she says, "it's true. You've always had women—if it's the woman part of what you're saying that bothers you—to protect you. Sylvia—"
>
> "There," I say. "Right there. That sentence sounds just like Daddy."
>
> She hasn't even heard me. "Sylvia protects you, she doesn't let a thing get to you that you don't want her to. I'm doing my share too. You just resent it because I'm trying to get you to come out of it a little. Mother protected you when we were children; then, she was always standing by." (121–2)

In this world, the responsibility of caring in some maternal way for the creative man is passed from generation to generation, from Sylvia to Julia.

This gender requirement can be found in Chappell's second novel *The Inkling*, as well. The world is too much for Jenny Nolan Anderson and her daughter Timmie, the main female characters in the book. Jenny is a war widow: her husband, Robert Anderson, "burned to death, bathed in a splash of fired gasoline, at Pearl Harbor" (31). Her no-account brother,

Hezekiah (known as Hake), lives with her, having squandered money her husband sent home for investments. Jenny's role is to serve as Hake's protector while she grieves over her husband. Like James Christopher, Jan is Timmie's protector (he is a year older) until Timmie becomes a woman. But when Timmie has her first period, she imposes her will on him. Thereafter, like Julia, Timmie dominates her brother. Their changing roles suggest recurring patterns of sister-brother relationships in Chappell's fiction.

"Thank You," which appeared in the *Chattahoochee Review*, illustrates such form. Greta Morrison, a masculine outsider reminiscent of Mina in *Dagon*, befriends Sara Jane Bakes by suggesting new fashions in clothes, hairstyles, glasses, and so on. Prompted by Greta, Sara Jane agrees to try to change the dress habits of her jazz-pianist brother Mullison Bakes. Sister and creative brother, like Jenny Anderson and Hake in *The Inkling*, live together: for years Mullison depends on his sister to look after him—get his clothes ready, number them, line them up in precise order in his closet for his gigs at Hagan's Bar. His dominance quails, however, when she changes his wardrobe, leaving out one crisp scarlet bow tie. There is little evidence, however, that the inward man changes. And though Greta succeeds in bringing out Sara Jane's new exterior, the idea that the two women will go beyond lively companionship is merely suggested. Greta Morrison seems to entertain that thought with the passion of a person who has found in North Carolina a residue of happiness she did not know in Boston. She frees Sara Jane from being a slave to her brother.

We might find protectors of men elsewhere in Chappell, however. One reason the list of housekeepers in the Anderson home is so long is because of the demanding, volatile nature of Jenny's brother Hake. Those female housekeepers maintain a semblance of order until one, Lora Bowen, marries Hake; the marriage is doomed when Jan shoots Hake for trying to kill him after Hake finds Jan in bed with her. Mrs. Boggs, another housekeeper, supplies welcome comedy. Infuriated at Uncle Hake, who calls her a "goddam old bitch," she takes him "by the top of his greasy trousers and flung him across the room against the wall. He landed with a plop like a bag of wet laundry" (58). She leaves after her affray with Hake but feels compelled to give Jenny a set of pearl earrings, sensing her total powerlessness as a mother and as an individual. In this way Jenny Anderson differs from the other women in Chappell's first four novels and in the fiction here under consideration. It is possible to view her as an early turn on Little Mary (in *Farewell*), the woman whom only other women see and want to care for. "She [Mrs. Boggs] went from the house for the last time; the mother still held the earrings open in her hand" (61). *Things*, however, cannot help Jenny. She has lost her husband and the property he helped the family buy. Bereft and filled with a feeling that she might not be able to keep the family fed, she just seems to give out. Suffering loneliness and boredom, staring longingly at a photograph of her dead husband, then turning it over and closing it in a drawer, she looks at herself in the mirror, her eyes filling with tears that "flocked on her cheeks like condensed moisture on an icy glass" (36). As if to acknowledge that the world has passed her by, she gives up; the narrator describes her drab life in terms befitting a Charlotte Brontë heroine.

Unlike Cora Kirkman, Jenny Nolan Anderson cannot carry her burdens. It is as if she is a grown-up version of the "twelve-year-old girl" of "Children of Strikers," who keeps the nicely amputated doll baby's foot she finds in the dirty stream near Fiberville where she lives: "In the girl's dark face was something harsh and tired, as if she had foretold all her life and found it joyless" *(Moments* 134). Jenny's attempt to go on with the help of other women ends in knotted embroilments, fights, and tragedy. When Lora Bowen comes to work as a housekeeper, for example, Hake sets out to seduce her. But like most women in Chappell's fiction, Lora Bowen is the aggressor, wanting to ravish Jan. Hake and Lora, meanwhile, take the bus to Spartanburg, where they get married. Jenny endorses the marriage, giving her brother and his bride her own bedroom in the front of the house, as she takes her brother's room. This climate sets up the scene when Lora Bowen asks Jan for help with a zipper. Lora "was giggling; now she was laughing at him full out" (140). After the seduction, Lora has him for her very own, controlling him in a corrupt befuddlement of emotion, much as Mina controls Peter Leland in *Dagon*. The Anderson family disintegrates in failed hopes to a darkness where only the outcry that accompanies the first and last gestures in the world arrests in silence any possible future light for the family.

CHANGING ROLES: WOMEN WHO CONSUME THEIR MEN

Chappell's third novel, *Dagon,* tending toward symbol and allegory, probes the nature of humanity and why people do what they do. Mina, the daughter of trapper Ed Morgan, for example, lives in a place that smells like semen. Backward her name is Anim, as if to emphasize the brute force of her identity and to suggest the possibility of soul in the abstract. And Sheila, who is married to the central male character Peter Leland, is, like her name, all feminine aura, bright, always, like Mitzi, planning and hoping for the best. More pointedly than in *It Is Time, Lord* and *The Inkling,* *Dagon* may be read as a dramatization of what happens to Americans who play out their lust for obsessions. Peter Leland's marriage to Sheila ceases after a few years, when another woman, the beefy-bodied Mina, enters Peter's life. Mina Morgan exhausts her relationship with Peter Leland, turning it into a grotesque purification that allows him to appreciate for the first time a new and original humanity. Obviously the women of *Dagon* are wildly different from those of *Farewell, I'm Bound to Leave You,* yet there are parallels and correspondences that bring them all closer together. Unlike the lives of Annie Barbara Sorrells and Cora Kirkman, who fit within a conventional social order, Sheila's time in society does not last long. And Mina is another story completely, though her instinctive qualities represent the spunk and core of these women—and many of the others: Earlene Lewis, Jenny Summerell, and Alma, especially.

Introducing narrative alternatives, *Dagon* begins inside Peter Leland's head. He sees two pillows, one embroidered with the image of a girl "in pastoral splendor," who stands for placid and peaceful goodness. The other shows a scene of a girl whose "innocence is all torn away" (48), the representative contemporary ruination of perfect bliss. The two images link the pillows with *Dagon*'s women, Sheila prompting readers to note on the first its symbolic intent in the story. When she and her husband go picnicking, she is all light and singing. Leland ruminates often on his wife's face, watching it, "pink and oval but with the sharp chin, a face like a brightly buffed fingernail" (86), reminding the reader of the uninitiated Faith of "Young Goodman Brown." Morgan invites Sheila and Peter to his cabin in the woods, where he introduces them to his wife Ina and daughter Mina. The scene is set for a playing out of the story symbolized in the second pillow. Peter and Sheila Leland, like Andrew and Katherine Harper in *The Gaudy Place,* are knowledgeable and bored; Sheila, in her self-conscious way, imposes a suburban air, trying to manage Peter even as she ridicules everything. When Sheila's mind focuses on her husband's sermon on the subject of the crippled god Dagon, saying it is too "historical" and "distant" (73), Peter, a preacher and an intellect, asserts that the story is contemporary—which is to say that Americans indulge to ragged satiation in sex and money. Add Peter Leland's undue embarrassment about being childless after four years of marriage, and the forecast is plain: he and Sheila have a rough marriage ahead; the time, furthermore, is favorable for trying to have children.

Sheila wants "to find out firsthand all this crazy wild endless American sex you keep talking about" (73); she invites him to bed, a romp that promises to take them somewhere between the details embroidered on the two pillows. Peter, however, becomes obsessed with Mina, womankind exaggerated into monstrous proportions, an extreme parody of the woman embroidered on the second pillow. When he goes into the attic of their sixteen-room house and sees chains, together with a contraption of erotic and rusty cuffs, he clangs himself into the thing, acting in the manner of the hanged god, the dominant image of his religious work and of the western world.

Imagining that his father died in some way similar to his present predicament, all of a sudden Peter can't see. Sheila has put her blue coat on the electrical current's box, dropping the lever and putting the house in darkness, even as she cleans. Peter, in chains, thinks of Mina, seeing her shadowy perception as Sheila approaches, holding a lit kerosene lamp. True to her sprightly form, Sheila is unnerved, admonishing Peter for his propensity to self-destruction, reminding him that he would stick his hand in a fire to see what would happen. Neither protector nor nurturer, Sheila is more a contender for a domestic domain of bright hungers and sunshine—and, most of all, for a child—the kind of situation that Katherine relishes and at which Andrew Harper scoffs. Eventually Peter murders Sheila in a blurring fantasy, turning finally to Mina, who gives him coffee in the shack and liquor from her father's still.

Mina totally controls Peter, presenting an embellishment in disharmony of the theme of domination and role-shifts represented in the first two novels. Functioning as character and concept to satirize Peter Leland's lusts, Mina takes a photo of Sheila from Peter's wallet and sticks it to the jar. In his fuzzy perception, Peter sees his wife and then Mina as he waits for Mina sitting backward in a chair, engaged in a ritual of coupling instinct with a man, a farmer, muffing a serpent against his cheek in a climaxing frenzy. Mina knows that he is full to an emptiness with sex and stumphole whiskey and, to rub him sorely, she reminds him that he does not have enough energy to have intercourse with her. She gives him more whiskey, and he guzzles himself into a horrific state, moans of snakes, and conjures Sheila—"Sheila, whom he had murdered, lay out there somewhere, going to pulp in the southern weather" (126). In such a macabre parody of unfulfilled love, Peter "had become a queer experimental animal; Mina used him purposely to try to gauge through him the fiber of the whole species" (126). She supervises a ritual of etching art not on pillows but on Peter Leland's body; most of the tattooing is done by Enid and Bella, androgynous lovers. Bella, the manlier, continuously renders her "loving ministering to Enid" (146). As their names—read backward Alleb and Dine—suggest, they are anyone and all, born to be all things in all respects. They feed on one another. Jugs and mugs and pitchers come to mind. And bellows of rutting time. In this ludicrous and eccentric scene, the women terrorize Peter Leland, victimizing him until he dissolves into a miserable fleshy blob.

A different version of changing roles takes place in "Ladies of Lapland" from *More Shapes Than One*, as the Lapland sisters Ainu and Tslma, prompted by philosopher-scientist Maupertuis, alter their status as free and sensual women to disheveled ladies of the night when he removes them from their native land to Paris; their once unified identities are destroyed. From the same collection, "Alma" offers a lonely mountaineer compelled to tell his sorrowful story: "I feel different about women than a lot of men do and I'll tell you why. It's because I had me my own woman one time" (169). The woman, one of twelve "shoats" (women treated like young hogs), wrests free of bondage by "coming-on" to the storyteller, Fretlaw. She gains his consent to return to an island of women in the center of Weeping Lake only after they agree to have a baby; Alma says she will reappear to live with him after five years. A version of a grownup and wise Rosemary McKay, Alma seduces Fretlaw, and they capture the drover who keeps the women as slaves for trade. She becomes Fretlaw's soul, as her name sug-

CHAPPELL'S WOMEN · 63

gests, abandoning him for the peace and love of other women at Weeping Lake, telling him the guardians of the waters there will kill him if he tries to rescue her.

In the final scene of *Dagon*, by contrast, Peter Leland, like Fretlaw, gets his chance to be a better person, as Mina transfers her absolute animalism into her sacrifice, transforming Peter into transcendent pleasure. She takes "a handful of his hair in her left hand and Peter knelt forward on his knees and raised his head. Happily he bared his throat for the knife" (161). Mina's behavior turns Peter into a Leviathan, a "great fish, a glowing shape some scores of light-years in length" (163). Out of society, he understands ironically what it is to be a human being, for he learns suffering and fallibility. The reader, likewise, released from the heinous events, feels relieved. Poetic justice works in *Dagon* as it does in "Alma," as the abused women—Sheila and Alma—cannot get over their treatment by the men. Without their male partners, the women achieve stability and permanence on alternative spheres: Sheila in the new life-role of her husband who becomes "a kind of catalogue of physical existence and of the gods" (163); Alma on the island of women, a choice which punctuates the most memorable Chappell fiction affecting women.

Although it is a satire, Chappell's fourth novel *The Gaudy Place* achieves much of what *Dagon* gets done by holding up a mirror to the truths and contrarieties of the human predicament. If Mina's ritualistic violence transforms Peter Leland into a cataloguer-fish, an attempted theft and a violent crime prompt a mother to help her son in *The Gaudy Place*. As a consequence, her husband, Andrew Harper, sees for the first time the wreaking vanity of their lives, narrating the final section of the novel, a retrospective of his family-wife, Katherine, and son, Linn (the would-be burglar) and Katherine's corrupt uncle, Zeb Mackie, pimp of a Gimlet Street prostitute, Clemmie. Zeb, known as Uncle Zeb, is the person "with pull" touted to get Linn out of jail for trying to steal chicken feed, something he does not even want or need. Katherine, Zeb's niece, is the "contact" person. "Katherine lifted the white telephone into her lap and began to dial" (165), her husband says, arranging for her Uncle Zeb to meet her husband at the police station. Andrew reluctantly follows through on her plan, his reflections out of balance with the situation at hand: the son is in jail and they want to get him out. She tells him he is "pretty close to helpless, you know that?" (166).

She wonders how he can be of any help at all: "Mean and snotty and little. Thinking about your pride instead of Linn" (167). Although she is older, more domineering, unafraid, and more developed as a character, Katherine is like Sheila.

Katherine and Andrew's love life shows the flip side of Clemmie and Arkie's. Clemmie is a con artist, Arkie's true love. She knows how much to involve life—how much to drink, how far to go. When Oxie, her "john" and "boss," lets her go as one of his "girls," she celebrates by getting drunk. Like Jenny Summerell or Earlene Lewis, Clemmie affirms her attitude and social status, illustrated by her action when a guy tries to make her as she plays the jukebox, putting his hands on her waist. "Get your goddam hands off of me," she tells him, "I'm not one of your Gimlet Street whores. I'll blow the whistle so fast you won't know what hit you" (48). Andrew Harper's long first-person story of his and Katherine's social and academic lives contrasts with the low-lifes of Gimlet Street, suggesting that all the characters are edgy, vain individuals whose excessive pride glosses their social exteriors.

The world *is* a gaudy place in which Clemmie and Katherine hold to the order available to them; they do not equivocate. They know what they know and what they have to do and they do it with no regard for consequences. They seem to live mostly by instinct. Presented as satirical portraits, both function as controlling women who see their worlds plainly and strictly according to their relative social classes. "My wife, Katherine, comes from Family" (151), the intellectual Andrew Harper says. He pronounces it "a bare defiant tri-syllable: Family" (151). Harper recognizes that their seemingly successful lives languish in surfaces. Katherine does not share that knowledge, even if she cared to ponder it. Perhaps that is why his wildly derisive laugh surely must minimally be a cry, as he sees the ridiculousness of his life within the context of his job as assistant professor at William Watson College and husband to Katherine, the "professor's wife," who spends much of her time lounging and marking corrections in *The Joy of Cooking* and thumbing through "*Immaculate Homes* or whatever" (168). Her uncle Zeb Mackie, a wheeler and dealer—but, in any event, Fam-I-Ly— serves to reveal general corruption. As Charmaine Allmon Mosby points out, Andrew Harper is aware that his wife's Uncle "Zeb actually is a crook who has used his position on the city council to gain lucrative public-improvement contracts and to arrange the cheap purchase of extremely profitable Gimlet Street property" (61). In such a world, Clemmie is as "good" as Katherine; she lambasts Oxie in one of their last meetings, saying, "you might have lucked up into a fast con or two, but you ain't no better than me. You ain't no different" (134). Contemplating the first four novels, R. H. W. Dillard calls *The Gaudy Place* "the brightest and lightest of them all" and notes that it "has at its heart the deepest darkness of them all" (13).

A much gentler satire on the art of living and dying, *Look Back All the Green Valley* concludes the Kirkman tetralogy and foreshadows ongoing Chappell fiction. Jess Kirkman is a grown man, married (he does not marry Sarah Robinson), settled down. Like Andrew Harper, he is part of the respectable social class. Jess's wife, Susan, younger and not as flashy and social as Katherine, presents a similar attitude of the dutiful wife who forever waits for her husband to come home. Sylvia, Jenny, and Sheila linger in the mind, too. Further, if James Christopher listens for stories to write, so does Jess, although he keeps a more aesthetic distance from his subjects than James Christopher does. Jess understands his mother's slow time at the Graceful Days Retirement Community, her needling him, her always giving priority to his sister Mitzi in the light buzz of things routine, her talking about how ordered Mitzi is while reminding him that Susan runs his life, as if to salute Deborah Franklin and Sylvia in their attempts to manage their husbands' lives. "You're a dreamer. Head in the clouds. Nose in a book. Pointless schemes. If Susan didn't look after you, I shudder to picture the condition our affairs would be in. Making footnotes. Writing poetry nobody can understand" (12).

When he importunes his mother about being too hard on him, saying, "I manage to move about the world without continually falling on my face," she retorts: "Yes—because your wife props you up. Without her, you'd be facedown most hours of the day" (12). This sounds like something Julia might say to Christopher. To spare the family embarrassment, Jess announces that he writes under the pen name Fred Chappell, allowing his mother the deference and space she imposes, for when Jess writes about his sister, her clear prayer at the table, he considers it in the context of what he perceives as his muddled one, admiring her for standing up to Rollie Sikes, who called her a "baxter." She remembers her father's labeling a "bastard" the man he thinks responsible for opening the floodgates and flooding the valley, taking away the gift—that is, the bridge—he made for Cora. "As I watched her [Mitzi] sitting there, bathed in that mild celestial glow, I was ashamed of myself and began to make my usual private vows to improve the condition of my mind and spirit" (50). Compare this maturing person—his inclusive memory and consciousness—with James Christopher, who seeks counsel from his sister Julia while peppering his conversation with self-deprecating antagonisms. Jess allows Mitzi plenty of space to live her life and be as wise or foolish as she wishes. Working with her help, he takes on the assignment to fulfill one of his mother's requests—to put in order Joe Robert's workshop. Advising him not to get sidetracked, Mitzi understands her brother, knows that he is preoccupied with a map their father had marked with women's names. His mother weighs on his mind, too, while he imagines Joe Robert in his little retreat: "She had stood as symbol of adult business for Johnson Gibbs and my father in the old times and nowadays for me and even for Mitzi. Her own mother, my grandmother, had recognized this officiousness in her and would smile gravely" (68).

His mother, he emphasizes in *I Am One of You Forever*, protects Johnson Gibbs, the orphan who comes to live with the Kirkmans. "When my mother was introduced to him her hands went automatically to her hips, smoothing her skirt" (8). Cora holds on to this "officiousness" at Graceful Days; her quarrels with Jess gain emotion as she gets better, complaining about everything from the carpet trapping her walker to Jess's moving away from home to Greensboro where he invents an author's name for the books he writes: "*Fred Chappell*. Lord, what a silly name" (85), she says in *Look Back All the Green Valley*.

All the real, insoluble problems the practical-minded Mitzi turns over to Jess. She is good at helping the caterer, but finding a way to bring their parents together in death is not a thing she looks forward to. After Joe Robert's death and burial, through some mistake of planning, no plot was made available for Cora beside her husband's. Mitzi tells Jess, "You've been claiming that you want to do more to help me with managing our family affairs. If you can figure a way out of this dilemma, it will help immensely, believe me" (111). Wondering if his father could have had affairs with the women, the curious and impractical visionary continues to investigate the names on the list he found in his father's shop, appreciating alone the yield of his little side-quest, that the women he sought turned out to be flowers after all—roses! Translating the best possible future for his family, he imagines Annie Barbara Sorrells before St. Peter's bar, putting in a good word for her son-in-law: "*I wish you'd take notice when he comes along and maybe show a little mercy*" (130), and Jess sees her consenting to say good things on behalf of his father's friend Virgil Campbell. The women continue to lead him, his mother at Graceful Days and his wife at home.

SOME THOUGHTS ON WOMEN'S WAYS OF KNOWING IN CHAPPELL'S FICTION

Men in Chappell's fiction seem to learn a considerable amount from the women who care for them. As a result, an essay on the women in Chappell's stories and novels should end with some comment on what men learn. Though the majority of stories from which male characters learn come directly from *Farewell, I'm Bound to Leave You*, other Chappell works stress the theme of men learning from women. What exactly do they learn? They learn to listen patiently rather than to talk through people, to show respect for their elders, to accept and have insight into the world of the spirit, and to behave in accord with the blessedness of good intentions that lead to kind acts.

The Wind Woman in *Farewell* is a crucial voice for Jess's tutelage, as he accompanies his mother on visits to various women who also figure in his maturation as a person and as a writer. His mother cannot make the steep grade to the top of the mountain where the Wind Woman lives, so she stays behind, leaving her son to go on alone to hear a woman whose words are for the wind. "*Now I understand, I thought. This journey was for me to come here to this cabin and let these sounds come upon me. I can't figure them out by myself. The Wind Woman will teach me how to lay out these sounds in proper fashion. I will wait here for her to come and beg the favor of her aid. I will wait here as long as it takes*" (115).

The wind "takes," as Jess becomes a masterful listener and talebearer, speaking for women throughout *Farewell*.

But Jess has yet to learn respect for elders, as he recalls learning by being corrected in "The Shining Woman." If every person has a shining self, the parable of Little Mary figures tall. Talbot Lucas will not allow his wife

Mary to fulfill herself, reducing her to a short life of trouble. After her death, his second wife Sarah inherits the heavy marital carriage. At night Little Mary comes back as a "hant," dancing like a four-year-old over their beds. And when Jess—this is the way the tale is told—asks his grandmother Sorrells to tell about another of Aunt Sherlie's "figurings," "The Shining Woman" is the story she reports to him. She asks Jess if he can imagine his grandmother as a "tall blond Spirit Woman dancing in the air and showing her fanny" (153). When Jess says he can "see it in my head as plain as anything," she undercuts his vision, saying, "I think somebody ought to take a stick to you" (153), still protecting and mentoring her grandson. She can relax in Jess's company, though, have fun, articulate the parts of her memories which might have been, certain that he will understand and remember decorum proper to her life, giving shape and character to her zealous father who insisted she quit the music she loved for his imposed religion of restraints.

Little Mary's plight clearly relates to the disagreeable uncertainties in Annie Barbara's life and in Chappell's earlier fiction, particularly *Dagon*, for after Mina takes over Peter Leland's life, Sheila, like Little Mary, returns as a ghost in Leland's fantasies. Sylvia, likewise, projects her distressing situation. In the final scene of *It Is Time, Lord*, when she and James Christopher are in bed, she communicates with him in her sleep. Coming to terms with himself, though, requires James to momentarily hurl his perception into her night thoughts. One thinks of Miss Prue also, in the story of the same name. She thinks that "Men were so easily discouraged. It was a bad thing. To let oneself down like that, and something she never allowed herself" *(More Shapes,* 153–4). Miss Prue's imaginative fancies come after her suicide husband's ghost says he will not come to see her for conversation any more on Thursdays. He has been dead for twenty years, though she conjures him well and fully alive. A case, furthermore, may be presented for Jess as the extended and continuous shine of the troubled young writer James Christopher; or the writer-preacher Peter Leland; or Mark Vance; or Fretlaw, the teller of "The Weather"; or, for that matter, Andrew Harper, for whom Little Mary represents the missing significance of all or nothing, that pure, brightly innocent spirit in need of fulfillment. Annie Barbara tells Jess, "The truth was, she wore out. Just wore thin and then wore through, like a shirtsleeve at the elbow" (141). Sarah, Talbot's second wife, plus the other women in "The Shining Woman" (Annie Barbara Sorrells, Aunt Sherlie Howes, and Little Mary Talbot) understand this unrequited ache. To quote Jess, as his grandmother tells her story of what Sarah said to Aunt Shirlee Howes, who serves as counsel to Sarah and Talbot: "'It's the kind of thing a woman will know and a man might not, if you understand what I mean.' The sentence must have darted out of Sarah's mouth before she realized what she had said. Maybe she had contradicted her husband's word before on some dull winter day when they had been in the house too long together. But she'd never done it in public and never imagined that she ever would or could. She glanced at him quickly, but he appeared not to have noticed" (148).

Mysterious "hants" make no sense to a man who cannot but see himself. Her released spirit is the fulfilled person Sarah desperately wants to realize, even as she may be seen as an extension of Little Mary, recognizing that possibility by decorating Mary's grave with the help of Aunt Shirlee and Annie Barbara in the sensual surround of apple-blossom time.

If the grandmother and Aunt Shirlee resonate with bigger-than-life characteristics steeped in wisdom gathered from experience, so does Cora Kirkman create a sanctuary for the heart of good intentions. Her mythic essence lives on in Jess, solidified in his mother's distaste for dwelling on death, disclosing to her initiate boy a series of incidents involving Jenny Summerell, who had been brought up to stave off vile men who "big" girls for marriage for the purpose of keeping them as a kind of property, as slaves to their manliness. As a little girl, she refuses to put up with such violence, controlling Orlow Jackson by conking him on the head when he destroys her make-believe playhouse in the mountains. Growing up strong, she learns to shoot straight, hit the mark, and be independent. When he comes home from duty in the army, he is chosen by Jenny to be her husband; he gets cold feet because, as Jess's mother says, "Men like to feel they make the important decisions, you see, and the trick is to let them believe they actually do" (169). Too determined and capable for Orlow Jackson, Jenny challenges him to a duel to settle their differences. Wanting no part of her plan, he picks up a rock and knocks himself out, as Jenny falls across his body and passes out too, making an X in the grass where their bodies lie. Although they marry, when Jess wants to know how Orlow Jackson dies, his mother refuses to tell him, saying, "I'm not in the mood to recount sad stories" (176). His grandmother, however, "had not the slightest fear of death and would speak of it with warm familiarity" (195), as she does in remembering for Jess the story of Angela Newcome, who looks after Mr. McPheeter with such obsessive care that he feels relieved and rejuvenated when she becomes caregiver to a widow named Elsie Twilley who is ready to die.

The women lead the way, likewise, in Jess's appreciation of the old times, the dances, ballads, lyrics, ditties, and myths, helped out by the folklorist Dr. Holme Barcroft. Gaining the permanence of a series of stories, tales that people lived their lives by, these beliefs and legends of memory's texture reside now in Jess's imagination, as his grandmother introduces him to death. *Farewell, I'm Bound to Leave You* ends, suspended in time, as the grandson muses on past, present, and future, sitting with his father, waiting to go down the hallway to turn on the light. The father speaks first and then Jess. Finally, the two acknowledge that they need all the help they can get in a world they do not understand (they have just exchanged comments about the mysteries of death). His father acknowledges his son's emerging maturity by referring to his mother, not as "your mother" but as "Cora," as if to echo his lament at the beginning of the novel, when he says "Annie Barbara Sorrells," instead of "your grandmother," signaling that her death would mark the end and the beginning of the historical basis of a family and community the Kirkmans live to know and love so well. *"'Cora is trying to come down the hallway,' my father said. 'But it is dark and she can't find the switch and she is frightened. If you and I don't go to meet her halfway, she may not make it back to us. Are you ready to go with me into that dark hallway and bring your mother back here into the light?'"*

WORKS CITED

Chappell, Fred. *Dagon (The Fred Chappell Reader)*. New York: St. Martin's Press, 1987.

———. *Farewell, I'm Bound to Leave You*. New York: Picador, 1996.

———. *The Gaudy Place*. Baton Rouge: Louisiana State University Press, 1994.

———. *I Am One of You Forever*. Baton Rouge: Louisiana State University Press, 1985.

————. *The Inkling.* Baton Rouge: Louisiana State University Press, 1998.

————. *It Is Time, Lord.* Baton Rouge: Louisiana State University Press, 1991.

————. *Look Back All the Green Valley.* New York: Picador, 1999.

————. *Moments of Light.* Los Angeles: New South, 1980.

————. *More Shapes Than One.* New York: St. Martin's Press, 1991.

————. "Thank You." *Chattahoochee Review* 10, no. 4 (summer 1990).

Dillard, Annie. Foreword to *Moments of Light* by Fred Chappell. Los Angeles: New South, 1980.

Dillard, R. H. W. "Letter from a Distant Lover: The Novels of Fred Chappell." *Hollins Critic* 10 (April 1973).

Morrison, Gail M. "'The Sign of the Arms': Chappell's *It Is Time, Lord.*" *Mississippi Quarterly: The Journal of Southern Culture: Special Issue: The Work of Fred Chappell* 37, no. 1 (winter 1983–84).

Mosby, Charmaine Allmon. "*The Gaudy Place:* Six Characters in Search of an Illusion." *Mississippi Quarterly: The Journal of Southern Culture: Special Issue: The Work of Fred Chappell* 37, no. 1 (winter 1983–84).

FIVE

"Growth of a Poet's Mind" and the Problem of Autobiography

Distance and Point of View in the Writings of Fred Chappell

PATRICK BIZZARO

> Handling point of view is much more than a matter of picking a person or a narrative
> technique and sticking with it; rather, it involves carefully manipulating the distance
> between narrator and character, moving closer one minute, then farther away the next,
> so as to achieve the desired response from the reader.
> —DAVID JAUSS, "From Long Shots to X-Rays"

FRED CHAPPELL has been rightly praised for his ability to work in several genres effectively. Robert Morgan, for one, writes, "Among the poets of our time there are many with great ability for concentration of phrase and figure. . . . And there are many fine story writers and novelists among us. Since Frost, however, there has been virtually no one who can do both at once. . . . We should value all the more, therefore, a writer such as Fred Chappell, who can combine the two arts" (133). Morgan refers here to Chappell's use of narrative in both his poetry and fiction. For my purposes in this essay, I want to add to this praise of Chappell praise for his ability to write effectively in essay form, as both critic and creative essayist. So it should not surprise us that two of the matters brought to our attention in the Kirkman tetralogy—that the novels are concerned largely with Jess's education, with what Wordsworth calls the "growth of a poet's mind," and that, as a result, they invite us to pay particular attention to the relationship established between the narrator and the author—are perfectly comfortable in their relation to other of Chappell's works in other genres. No doubt one of Chappell's contributions to contemporary literature, indeed to postmodern thinking, is the way we view genre and voice since his central themes and his complex use of point of view are evident in his poems and essays as well as in his novels. This is particularly true of his major fictive accomplishment to date, the Kirkman tetralogy, novels structurally parallel to his four-volume poem *Midquest.*[1]

Both the Kirkman tetralogy and *Midquest* are in some ways concerned with the "growth of a poet's mind" and with the education of its narrators, Jess Kirkman and the "Ole Fred" or "I" of Chappell's poetry. In spite of his statements to the contrary, Chappell seems to self-consciously identify not only Jess and Ole Fred but his other narrators as well (including essayist Chappell and critic Chappell) with Fred Chappell the author. And he seems especially interested, in all three genres, in discussing the education of his narrators. That these narratives often overlap neither surprises the reader nor lessens the impact of the individual narratives. But the narratives do bring to mind other writers who, like Chappell, placed so much emphasis on themselves.

But Chappell seems to have already thought his way through this predicament. While readers still take quite seriously D. H. Lawrence's dictum to "never trust the teller, trust the tale," most will honor the author's denial that he has intentionally identified his narrators with himself. But in Chappell's case his various personae report similar narratives of the growth of the poet, if not narratives typically associated in all respects with *bildungsromane.*[2] No doubt the experiences given in these multi-genred, multi-volumed efforts are not identical with Chappell's life experiences any more than Wordsworth's "growth of a poet's mind," *The Prelude,* is an accurate depiction in every detail of Wordsworth's life. At most, these works are "partial autobiographies"—which, of course, in some ways erases them as autobiographies. We might look farther for comparisons. But more partial, and less autobiographical, indeed, are the other romantic works that come to mind, including Keats's *Endymion,* Byron's *Don Juan,* Pater's *Marius the Epicurean*—works in the subgenre "growth of a poet's mind" most often cited as prototypes of *bildungsromane* (see Buckley).

Still, in reading Chappell's writings, readers might rightly feel that their educations have betrayed them—or, if not betrayed them, been revealed as inadequate to the task. It is fairly standard these days to locate point of view in terms of "person." Though this is often a useful mechanism for discussing literature, since it enables us to determine "who" tells the story, it does not provide the tools necessary if our goal is to understand and appreciate narration, as we must in reading Chappell, in terms of what Wayne

Booth calls "distance." As Booth notes in *The Rhetoric of Fiction*, distance may mean "distance in time and space, differences of social class or [in] conventions of speech or dress" (156). These elements of narrative distance—to use Booth's language, the distance between narrator (the one who tells the story) and implied author (the author's presence in the story as a second self)—give us a way to discuss point of view in Chappell's writings. Though I am opposed to reading Chappell's essays, poems, and stories as rhetorical in any reductive way, if we hope to understand Chappell's method of narration we must accept the notion that Chappell as author has intended to manipulate his subject and his audience to achieve particular ends and thus works rhetorically himself.[3]

The term *distance,* then, is the one that best describes the rhetorical manipulation Chappell has in mind. As Booth writes: "The *narrator* may be more or less distant from the *implied author*" (156, my emphasis). This essay will read Chappell for the skill he employs in distancing his narrator from the implied author and test in Chappell's writings the viability of Booth's long-standing and widely accepted position on the use of the implied author—that is, that the narrator and the implied author may exist simultaneously in a text and that they may be (are apt to be) identified in that text by a single name. More specifically, in personal essays such as "First Attempts" and "Welcome to High Culture" from *Plow Naked,* Chappell, the implied author, speaks through a mature if judgmental voice and thus seems distant in time, place, and moral values from his youngish narrator, who describes the events that constitute growth as writer and poet. These events often bewilder the narrator, though they are understandable to the older, more experienced implied author. In poems from *Midquest,* Chappell uses a variety of strategies to manage point of view and manipulate his readers; "Rimbaud Fire Letter to Jim Applewhite" makes the most impressive use of distance through which Chappell the writer seems best able to demonstrate the point he wants to make about the poet's growth toward maturity. When read as we read *Midquest,* as a single work that comprises four parts, the novels likewise use a variety of means of distancing. And where Jess the narrator and the implied author agree, the implied author disappears entirely; the job of educating the poet is then complete. Since in all of Chappell's works the line separating Chappell as author from the narrators of his essays, poems, and stories (i.e., Chappell the critic, Ole Fred,

"I," and Jess Kirkman) is so thin—at times nearly invisible—that accusations of having written autobiographically have been and continue to be leveled against Chappell. This essay concludes with some observations about Chappell as an autobiographical writer.

THE IMPLIED AUTHOR IN ACTION:
HARPOONING THE "IRASCIBLE CRITIC"

Narrators of Chappell's essays work together, often to achieve comic effect. As a result, Chappell's implied author provides various reminders of his presence, usually by offering inside views about or interpretations of the narrator's experiences, much as the critic Chappell offers judgments and interpretations about the works he discusses. Bakhtin provides an interesting description of this literary event in his assertion that multiple voices exist simultaneously in a text (what he calls *dialogism* or *polyphony*). Readers are directed to these changing voices in Chappell's essays when changes occur in tone.

The existence of these voices (and the distances between them) is quite apparent in Chappell's criticism, where judgments made by Chappell the critic are juxtaposed with judgments made by Chappell the implied author. Both voices may be heard: the critic Chappell who discusses the literary works in question, and the implied author who discusses Chappell the critic and criticism in general. These judgments are sometimes at odds. The implied author often doubts or makes light of the wisdom of Chappell the critic and, in Chappell's collections of critical and personal essays, *Plow Naked* and *A Way of Happening*, this encounter—Chappell as implied author with Chappell as critic—gives the works their distinctive character. Through the conflict these two voices create, Chappell is best able to teach and delight. In fact, Chappell seems aware of the different voices that sometimes wrestle for dominance in his critical essays: the critic speaks while the implied author justifies, ameliorates, extends, or simply undermines the critic's efforts.

For purposes of demonstrating how these two voices work together, let's look at "Maiden Voyages and Their Pilots" from *A Way of Happening*. This essay addresses the first books of six young writers. The cantankerous critic Chappell reaches several logical conclusions that come from the single critical judgment: "One trait that generally betrays a book as being a first effort is the usage of the first-person pronoun" (79). Later Chappell the critic makes more specific use of this judgment (and might even be commenting on the use of first-person in his own poetry): "The I of a poem is one of its methods of control, and when the poet forgets that the speaking I is not and should not be the same figure as the live person writing the poem, the result can be shymaking" (81). And yet another: "In most contemporary poems the I is simply a reporter of feelings and observations about incidents enjoyed or endured; rarely is the I physically involved in any significant action the poem might record" (82). But the voice of the critic in these examples is balanced by the more urbane, almost self-effacing implied author who confides in a voice distant in time, place, and moral value from the above: "I am only trying to understand the dramatic function of the I in our contemporary lyric poems and finding it to be a more complex chore than I had reckoned on" (83). The most distinctive characteristic of Chappell's criticism—the juxtaposition of a judgment with the repudiation or harpooning of the judge—arises from Chappell's use of voices in his essays. These often conflicting voices render an interesting juxtaposition in terms of temporality: the critic, focused on the here and now, alongside the implied author, who seems outside the time constraints of the essay. By considering one of Chappell's personal essays, we are able to see how this technique of narration works when Chappell writes about the "growth of a poet's mind" where the time and place of the bewildered "I" of the events (the narrator) is by necessity distant from that of the judgment-making "I," who often by his comments reinforces moral distance as well (the implied author).

In "First Attempts," from *Plow Naked*, the implied author does not reveal his presence except through occasional intrusions. In this essay and the one that follows it ("Welcome to High Culture"), we assume the implied author/poet Chappell has already grown into maturity since he recalls his stages of development, creating a distance in time and place between the implied author and the young narrator. While the narrator of the essay has a story to tell, the implied author moralizes—often humorously—on that story and more often than not does so by speaking cordially and directly to the reader. The first sentence of "First Attempts" introduces the essay's warring voices: "The real beginning of a writer's compulsion to compose is difficult to discover and he must be a foolhardy author who will attempt to sound these strange, moiling storm-lit depths in search of an origin" (4). This is the voice of the implied author who recognizes in the narrator's willingness to tell the story of his origins as a writer a certain foolhardiness, separating himself, then, from the narrator, who seems not to know any better than to write such an essay. The narrator has a story to tell, as the implied author understands quite well: "He [the writer] has been forced to be objective about something, to try to see it in a light that permits description, however fumbling and inaccurate" (4). Because the implied author is a presence in the essay, a judge of the narrator's foolishness not only for writing on this particular subject but also for believing much that he believes, we tend to trust the voice of the implied author when we hear it, finding it, in Booth's term, "reliable," while we do not always trust or find reliable the voice of the one who narrates. That voice, after all, is often undermined and ridiculed in the essay by the implied author. A reader finds it difficult to trust them both.

Consistent with this view, the narrator goes on to portray the fantasies he held to as a beginning writer: "I knew what I would look like as a writer," he says, and "I knew too what I was supposed to look like while writing" (5). The author who is all along an implied presence soon intrudes, however, in the tone of the judgmental veteran: "I suspect that most writers are urged to their purpose by adolescent fantasies such as these, and that these daydreams do not entirely evaporate with adolescence" (6). And what's more, "The steely frost of publication soon lays this pastel hope a-withering but never kills it entirely." The distance between implied author and narrator here is great, a distance in time, place, and moral value.

In "First Attempts," the large pronouncements, the less cautious statements of value and thus the more eloquent generalizations, are offered by the implied author, which may be why we tend to find him more knowledgeable and reliable than the narrator: "For me it is in the work that the final perfection of a life is lodged; the work is the life." And, "I have known any number of writers who were drunks, buffoons, knaves, clods, blowhards, sycophants, trimmers, charlatans, and egomaniacs; indeed, I can find episodes of my own life in which I have matched each of these descriptions and sometimes all of them together" (8). And, "Not that writers as a group are scurvier than other groups. Maybe it is a holdover from my adolescent glamourizing that I expect them to be better . . . " (8). The narrator then returns us to the story he wants to tell, and he does so without making the judgments that seem reserved for the implied author: "When I was a teenager the only contemporary writer whose personal life I knew anything about was Hemingway." As in his critical essays, Chappell the author employs two voices, one telling a story we may justifiably call "growth of a poet's mind"—this the tale told by the narrator—and the other commenting on the person telling the story, what that person says, and how it is told—this told by the implied author.

POINT OF VIEW IN *MIDQUEST:* SOME OBSERVATIONS

The narrators of poems in *Midquest,* as Chappell notes in his preface, are most often either "Ole Fred" or "I," neither of whom, the author says, is identical to the author. They are simply representative characters, "to some extent a demographic sample" (x). As in essays such as "First Attempts," poems in *Midquest* that take up the subject of Ole Fred's education (and he seems to be an active learner in nearly all of the poems) use techniques of narration that are more typically used in fiction. Poems in *Midquest* that address the education of the poet are explorations. As such, they most often depend for success (and even in some poems, for development) upon the presence of an "other." Distance between implied author, narrator, and this other (characters) is a major consideration insofar as the inevitable expression of values is concerned. How are narrators of these poems and the characters themselves used to manipulate the reader?

Chappell's narrators in these poems employ a wide range of vantage points from which to see the world Chappell has created. Rare, indeed, are poems that employ narrators other than Ole Fred or "I," but they do exist (including the narrators of "Second Wind," "My Mother Shoots the Breeze," "Three Sheets in the Wind," "Susan's Morning Dream of Her Garden," and "My Grandmother's Dream of Plowing"). But these poems are dramatic monologues; as such, they imply the presence of a listener. The listener of these poems is the presence identified elsewhere as "I" or Ole Fred. The titles of these poems suggest the strategy used in *Farewell, I'm Bound to Leave You:* a poem titled "*My* Mother Shoots the Breeze" (emphasis mine) suggests that what follows in the poem is filtered and selected by someone other than the mother—the mother speaks through her child's recollection. In this particular poem, then, the implied author decides which details of the known experiences of "mother" will be given and how. The distance in this poem between implied author and narrator (the mother) is slim indeed. It is thus the implied author who decides to recall the "Old Times," for instance, as "cruelty and misery" or to recount the mother's post-secondary education and to make her "schoolbook proud." This strategy looks forward to *Farewell* and solves for Chappell some of the problems male authors confront when they narrate a story from a woman's point of view. By creating such close, almost shared, perspectives for the implied author and the narrator, the implied author's "mother," Chappell manipulates his reader into thinking that the stated values are those of the mother. In fact, the values are those of Ole Fred or "I" who speaks through the narrator and serves as the implied author.

Chappell employs a similar strategy in "Hollowind," in which the distance between implied author and the poem's characters is likewise manipulated. In his interview with Resa Crane and James Kirkland, Chappell says the conversation presented in "Hollowind" is a "[v]ery accurate reflection of a kind of continuing dialogue, or debate, that Reynolds [Price] and Jim Applewhite and I had in those days" (14). This is a trickier strategy for the reader to break through than the one used in "My Mother Shoots the Breeze" since one of the speakers here is identified as "Fred." But we cannot read this voice as that of the author Fred Chappell (or, in any case, if we do we cannot assume this person and the author of *Midquest* are one and the same). The Fred of this poem is a construction. If we assume he speaks for the author of *Midquest*, we are more apt to believe that Reynolds Price in the poem is, in fact, author Reynolds Price. But Reynolds of the poem is, likewise, a construction, perhaps sharing some qualities with the writer Reynolds Price; and the speaker who gives Reynolds his words and ideas is the implied author, so nearly identified with the multiple voices in this poem that a reader finds it difficult to tell them apart.

A third method of narration in the poems comprised in *Midquest* is the interview. This strategy seems to be a combination of the first two discussed, insofar as one speaker speaks to assumed listeners, as in "My Mother Shoots the Breeze," but often in response to questions asked by a curious listener, Ole Fred, who serves as an interviewer. This strategy helps

Chappell complete two tasks. For one, it gives the reader the sense that the "I" is distant from the speaker, called "father" in the poem, and at the same time it provides a mechanism in the poem for elaborating the events father wants to tell. The reader is thus given the sense that a distance exists between the implied author and the characters. But the implied author directs the exchange between the boy and his father; the boy serves as the doubting listener, pointing out inconsistencies and impossibilities in the father's story, and the father reacts to these intrusions with the refrain, "Don't interrupt me, boy. *I am coming to that*" (116). The values that insist that father adhere to reality, or at least argue logically, suggest the presence in the poem of yet another character entirely, the implied author.

"At the Grave of Virgil Campbell" provides a complex strategy for narration and looks forward to a similar strategy in the framework of *Look Back All the Green Valley*. This poem is spoken by the "I" who addresses a now-deceased Virgil who, even in his silence, is a curious interviewer. These two begin in agreement: "I visit you half-smashed, you'll understand . . . Let's you and me / . . . tell some lies / To the worms and minerals" (167). What choice does Virgil have here? But since Virgil is linked to the values of another, the poem's implied author, he soon disagrees and challenges even in his silence. The point of departure where the deceased Virgil disagrees with the poem's narrator is over "some epitaphs." The narrator credits Virgil with finding the first epitaph "A little naked maybe." After three more epitaphs are offered, the narrator sees that the deceased cannot object after all: "I've got no business scribbling epitaphs / For wiser sounder ones who can't hit back" (168). This, of course, is an ironic statement since it implies that the deceased do have some control—that, in fact, they do hit back. But this strategy serves the author well since, like the interview strategy, one result is that it enables the author, through his implied presence in the poem, to continue, this time with epitaphs he's written for himself. Virgil is able to "hit back" nonetheless: "Howzat, / Old Mole, you think it's junky—portentous" (168). The drunken narrator gives Virgil just enough animation to make possible certain judgments that, like the first-person narrator of Chappell's critical essays, echo in the voice of the implied author.

Since it focuses exclusively on the growth of the poet's mind, "Rimbaud Fire Letter to Jim Applewhite" offers an interesting comparison with the essays "First Attempts" and "Welcome to High Culture," which address the same subject. This poem not only addresses the topic "growth of a poet's mind" but also employs a strategy of narration similar to the strategy employed in those essays. Both the essays and this poem rely upon two voices to narrate. One, the poem's narrator, has a story to tell. The other, the implied author, serves to comment on the story, how the story is told, and the person who tells it. And, finally, as in "First Attempts" and "Welcome to High Culture," the implied author is the mature poet reflecting upon his youth, and the narrator speaks in the voice of the young poet himself, who learns by his misdeeds. To use Booth's subtle distinctions concerning distance, these two voices are separated by their places in time if not always by moral value. The implied author seems to be interested in the young narrator's behavior but too tired to live it again.

The poem's title aptly prepares us for the "hard" learning the narrator must do in its reference to Rimbaud, whose debauchery is legendary, and by its position in *Midquest* as a "fire poem." The story told by the narrator recounts "the artificial fevers, wet / With Falstaff beer":

I walked the railyard,
Stumbling the moon-streaked tracks, reciting line
After burning line I couldn't understand. (58)

The narrator tells of problems with his parents ("My folks thought I was crazy"), the youthful certainty of how much he knew ("Four things I knew"), and his disposition during high school ("The senior prom / I missed, and the girls, and all the thrilling sports").

The implied author has something to say about this story and makes mature, if damning, judgments—as the implied author of the essays does—about the youthful narrator and the hard work that must be done to educate *this* poet. The poem begins in the voice of the implied author: "That decade with Rimbaud I don't regret. / But could not live again. Man, that was *hard.*" During that foolhardy decade, says the implied author, "I formulated esoteric laws / That nothing ever obeyed, or ever will." Even lines from Rimbaud were, then, elusive: ". . . what they meant, or even what they *were,* / I never knew." The mature poet/implied author concludes that the youthful narrator was

Kind of a handbook on how to be weird and silly.
It might have helped if I had known some French,
But like any other Haywood County hillbilly
The simple thought of the language made me flinch. (58)

As for his teachers, the implied author reflects, "They stood up for health and truth and light, / I stood up for Baudelaire and me" (59). And we are led to the next portion of this growth of a poet's mind with this, again, in the voice of the implied author: "The subject gets more and more embarrassing" until after naming the places where his "growth" took place— "Mayola's Chili House, / Annamaria's Pizza, Maitland's Top Hat, / the Pickwick, and that truly squalid place, / The Duchess"—the narrator confides, "Finally / They kicked me out, and back to the hills I went." Eventually, perhaps acknowledging a general lack of common sense, the narrator and implied author seem to become one, at least in values: "I watched the mountains until the mountains touched / My mind and partly tore away my fire-red / Vision of a universe besmirched" (60–1). Then he returned to book-learning and started his "Concordance to Samuel Johnson, / And learned to list a proper footnote, got down / To reading folks like Pope and Bertrand Bronson, / And turned my back on the ashes of Paree-town" (61).

No doubt, this tale only in part sides with the sensibly voiced implied author. In spite of his judgments, he merely "could not live again" the life the narrator describes. The very behavior the implied author seems unhappy to note seems just as necessary in the end as the bookish behavior he seems to favor. The growth of the poet's mind in "Rimbaud Fire Letter to Jim Applewhite," recorded "for terror and symbolism," suggests by its strategy of story-telling that "growth" is a process that requires all the false steps that, when recorded and analyzed, show the distance not only in time, but in moral conviction, between the narrator and the implied author. As the poem ends, these two voices seem to speak in unison, narrowing dramatically the distance between the two in this poem. Narrative distance in the poem underscores the very symbolic process of maturing as a poet.

DISTANCE AS CHARACTER IN THE KIRKMAN TETRALOGY

Jess is the first-person narrator of each of the Kirkman novels. But Jess, like the narrators of the essays and poems by Chappell that deal with the growth of a poet's mind, is not always one person.[4] Often Jess is the young man narrating the novels' events. But on specific occasions and for specific reasons, Jess is also the mature poet looking back on his life. These two characters are not always in agreement, nor do they always live in the same place and time. Chappell skillfully uses distance to manipulate not only his readers, but his characters as well.

Clearly, when the implied author appears in the novel, Chappell intends to signal something. If we read the Kirkman novels as the story of Jess's education, we see that the distance between the narrator Jess and the implied author diminishes, as we've seen in "Rimbaud Fire Letter," when the narrator Jess and the implied author share moral conviction and, thus, experience the world similarly. Not surprisingly, this convergence occurs more often at the end of a novel than at the beginning, as though the process of the novel is the process of closing that gap. As Jess learns more and develops into the poet the implied author *is* all along, fewer and fewer intrusions by the implied author are necessary. This convergence is clearly shown in *I Am One of You Forever,* in which the process of Jess's education as a poet is begun, and culminates in the very last utterance of the novel: "'Well, Jess, are you one of us or not?'" (184). The answer "yes" is implied by the title and entitles Jess to narrate the remaining novels in an effort to understand his teachers.

The opening sections of the quartet of novels provide excellent opportunities to demonstrate how these two voices, Jess the narrator's and the implied author's, contend under the identity of the first-person narrator. This interaction works in two directions, across individual novels to suggest, specifically in *Forever* and *Brighten,* young Jess's growth, and across the entire tetralogy to suggest that the implied author's comments on actions in these stories is intended to guide the reader's judgments about Jess; it is as if Chappell is educating not only Jess, but the readers who read the books in the order in which they were written. As a result, we might expect the implied author to do more work, provide greater amounts of guidance in the early novels (*Forever* and *Brighten*) than in the later novels (*Farewell* and *Look Back*). This pattern suggests that toward the end of the first two novels, young Jess has learned enough to receive the approval of the implied author and in the later books the implied-author-as-poet and Jess (and in judgments at least we might extend this to the reader) are most often in agreement, seeing this particular world similarly and accepting its boundaries. While Jess the poet learns in the last two books, distance in time and place lessens and most of the learning to be done is moral education.

Distance from the event in *Forever* is evident in the very first sentence: "Then there was one brief time when we didn't live in the big brick house with my grandmother" (1). The novel begins *in medias res,* with the implied author in the midst, it seems, of telling other stories about his family and his upbringing, intruding in that implied sequence to tell *this* particular story. Likewise, *Brighten* is a recollection in which the distance is quickly established. The second sentence of the novel's opening section, "Moon," begins: "Those winter mornings were so cold that I felt I would ring like an anvil if my father touched me" (3). We see here the implied author recollecting the particular winter morning when the event occurs from among all winter mornings he might recall. He recalls these mornings from a time and place distant from the event itself.

In *Farewell,* Chappell uses a variation on this strategy. In this novel, a frame device is employed to distance the immediate event, Annie Barbara's imminent death, from Jess's recollection of stories told to him by his women-teachers. In this novel, Joe Robert and Jess are near enough in time, place, and moral value (we must keep in mind that the boy Jess is more like the boyish Joe Robert than the older, more mature Jess is) that fewer intrusions are necessary. It is Joe Robert who voices the purpose of the novel: "We will listen to the wind whisper and tell again the stories of women that your mother and grandmother need for you to hear" (5). Chappell may well have used this strategy to create the balance he needed in telling the growth of a poet's mind, asserting in this way that women's ways of knowing are as important to the poet's education as men's ways, the subject of *Brighten.*

Look Back chronicles Jess's final effort in obtaining his education as poet. Joe Robert is dead but, like Virgil Campbell of "At the Grave of Virgil Campbell," he continues to challenge Jess's inventiveness. The novel, employing a frame device, opens and closes in the here and now: the grown Jess and two comrades (Ned and Tod) are in the graveyard at night, as a storm is threatening, to exhume Joe Robert's bones. The implied author is not a presence here. In fact, the judgment-maker at the end of the novel is Jess, the poet: "my father was the fox" (278). Though this novel goes on to play more rhetorical games with Jess—and thus with the reader—than the other three novels, Chappell has closed the distance between Jess and the implied author. Finally, they are the same moral person, in the same place and time, and the story told within that frame tests the accuracy of Jess's moral judgments about the Fox's secret life. From the perspective that this novel continues to tell the growth of a poet's mind, Joe Robert, even after his death, contributes to Jess's moral development.

When Chappell distances the implied author from the narrator, as he does to greatest effect at the beginning of *Forever* and *Brighten,* he allows the implied author to speak with authority and to guide our judgments as readers. In these first two books of the series, for instance, the location where events take place is different from the place the implied author (the mature Jess, the poet) inhabits and, as the following passage from the text shows, time is distant too: "*At this time* my mother was visiting her brother in California" (*Forever* 1, my emphasis). In order to manipulate his characters as well as his readers, Chappell lessens the distance between implied author and narrator so that time and place converge until the narrator places himself alongside his father: "So my father and I had to fumble along as best we could." Chappell closes the distance between Jess and Joe Robert to influence the reader's reaction: on the one hand, we feel with Jess his desire to be close to his father and, on the other, we sense that it might be easier for the young boy to get close to his father at this time and in this place than it may be later, for instance in *Look Back,* where Jess seems to barely understand Joe Robert.

Clearly, the voice of the implied author looking back to this place and time from another place and time is different from the voice of the narrator who exists in the same place and time as Joe Robert. But Chappell wants to close the gap between the moral Jess and the moral Joe Robert, and the novel's ending suggests that that job has been accomplished. By moral judgment as well as by the implied author's continuous reminders, Jess the twelve-year-old boy, and Joe Robert the boyish father eventually experience the world similarly. Only initiation into the world, including introduction to its various outlandish characters and to Joe Robert's way of perceiving them, needs to be done before the boy and the boyish adult will come to see things similarly. We find out in *Look Back,* however, that the mature Jess does not in every way understand Joe Robert. But this is a moral distance rather than a distance in time and place, indicating that Chappell would have us read that book as the book in which the last efforts to educate Jess must take place. Certainly, this view of Chappell's use of distance requires that readers accept many of the fantastic elements in the book, elements that "The Overspill" introduces in microcosm (and that other chapters in *Forever* and *Brighten,* including well-known chapters titled "The Beard" in *Forever* and "Moon" in *Brighten,* take to their logical consequences). The convergence of time, place, and moral value between Jess and Joe Robert signals the divergence of these same elements of narrative distance between Jess the narrator and Jess the implied author until they, too, merge in recognition of the fantastic, that Joe Robert has all along been the Fox, at the end of *Look Back.*

Once connected in time and place and by the necessity that they "fumble along" in Jess's mother's absence, the implied narrator makes certain that we see why they get along, son and father: "We meet now on freshly neutral ground somewhere between my boyhood and his boyishness" (2). This is spoken by the grown Jess who, from the distance of time and in the voice of the wise authority, leads the reader into a greater understanding of the relationship between young Jess and his father. Jess is initiated into the world of boyish men, where wild imaginings are possible and pranks inevitable. The adult in the group, Jess's mom, needn't know or censor this way of acting and, we find out before chapter 1, this way of thinking: "We were clumsy housekeepers, there were lots of minor mishaps, and the tagline we formulated soonest was 'Let's just not tell Mama about this one.' I adored that thought."

Any number of intrusions by the implied author might be cited as guidelines used by Chappell to direct his readers' opinions. "The Overspill" details Joe Robert's effort to give his wife a welcome-home gift, "a small but elaborate bridge across the little creek that divided the yard and the garden" (3). From the distance of the grown Jess recalling the event, we are told the gift must be "something guaranteed to please a lady," even though young Jess wasn't told "what we were building." Judgments of value are made: "He must have been a handy carpenter," "the completed bridge appeared marvelous." These are the recollections of mature Jess, the implied author, and stand out as such because they are juxtaposed with judgments made in the voice of young Jess, who is closer in time and place (and eventually in moral values, at least at the end of this novel) to Joe Robert:

"When I walked back and forth across the bridge I heard and felt a satisfactory drumming." Young Jess is so close to the event that his observations are greeted with the reservations we usually employ in hearing the judgments of a young boy. Only the more mature and distant and, therefore, the more reliable observations of the implied author guide us truly. Clearly, young Jess is correct in assessing the symbolic nature of the bridge, but we must implicitly know so because the speaker of the section's first sentence has *selected* this tale as the one to tell us, and we trust that speaker as mature and reliable. We see the young boy's unwitting insight that it will take the distance of time and place for him to truly understand that "in crossing the bridge I was entering a different world, not simply going into the garden." We recognize this as the voice of young Jess and understand that the implied author, mature Jess, Jess reflecting on this experience across time and space, now recognizes the significance of this bridge to his growth. The boundaries of this world, and Jess's experience in it, are far from restricting.

In fact, the effects of such distancing in the Kirkman tetralogy are multiple. First, Chappell is thus able to separate the voice of Jess from the voice of the implied author, creating a distance in time, place, and moral values between the two that serves as an aid to Chappell as he renders Jess's growth. By creating this distance, Chappell helps his readers make correct judgments—or, in any event, the same judgments as those made by the mature Jess, Jess the poet—about the process of that growth. Second, such distancing enables us to envision two times: the time when Jess is young and the time when Jess is a mature poet telling these tales. Third, it provides Chappell with two rhetorical strategies, which enable him to manipulate time and place. For one, we are continually reminded, by how they are told and arranged, that these stories are selections only, chosen from many that might have been told and, as selections, promise only to belong to the time between childhood and adulthood. And, for another, this distancing makes it possible for Chappell to effectively posit a thesis, which the remainder of the novel supports.

CONCLUSION: CHAPPELL AND AUTOBIOGRAPHY

Chappell is well aware that writers of autobiographical pieces are often accused of self-interest and conceit. He is also aware of the technical dilemma this places him in: if these are not autobiographical works, yet if they are intended to portray the education and growth of the central character and thus are written in first person, Chappell must devise a means of narrating these tales that permits him to at once deny that the "I" and Chappell himself are identical beings and yet permit Chappell the author and his audience to share knowledge that the characters, including the narrator, do not possess. Thus he finds it necessary to address this problem in defense of the accusation of autobiographical, even confessional, writing. He employs three different tactics in doing so, two of which are simple denials. The third, however, the subject of this essay, requires an analysis of Chappell's use of point of view in several of his essays, poems, and novels that deal with the growth of a poet's mind.

Chappell's recent interview with George Hovis gives us the opportunity to reflect upon one of these denials. In it, Chappell explains why in *Look Back All the Green Valley* Jess Kirkman is given the pen name Fred Chappell:

> That confusion [between Chappell and his narrators] was beginning to become a real issue with me, because I don't like to be autobiographical. . . . There's no hard and fast dividing line between what you imagine and what you observe. What you observe, as in the Wordsworth line, you "half perceive and half create." . . . I thought that by reversing the ordinary expectations, where the real writer has a pen name—let's do it where the pen name has a real writer. That way we would establish a primacy of the imagination in the way this little universe is set up in these volumes. . . . And it would help answer that pesky question that I always get asked when I give public readings, "How much of this is real? Is that a real poem, or did you just make it up?" (69)

Chappell explains here his effort in *Look Back* to rid himself of accusations of writing autobiographically by establishing that the world of the novel is an imagined place, mostly separate from the real-life world Fred Chappell lives in. All observations, he argues, are a mixture of perception and imagining. This effort at explaining the link Chappell makes between Jess and himself would account for the events in the Kirkman novels if they existed apart from other of Chappell's work, but of course they don't. In a sense, as they elaborate the growth of the poet's mind, the poems and personal essays seem connected to the Kirkman novels, not to mention to *It Is Time, Lord*.

Chappell argues more convincingly and less defensively about the autobiographical elements of *Midquest* in the second of his denials when he places himself, as he does other writers whose works he criticizes, in historical context (see Bizzaro, "Teacher"). Chappell took the opportunity to dispense with any possible complaint of "self-conceit" in his poems when he was asked, long after writing some of the poems in *Midquest*, to write a preface to it, a kind of explanation of what he set out to accomplish. In that preface, Chappell seems to have had the accusation of self-concern in mind:

> Though he is called "Fred," the "I" of the poem is no more myself than any character in any novel I might choose to write. (And no less myself, either, I suppose.) He was constructed, as was Dante's persona, Dante, in order to be widely representative. He was reared on a farm but has moved to the city; he has deserted manual for intellectual labor, is "upwardly mobile"; he is cut off from his disappearing cultural tradition but finds them, in remembering, his real values. He is to some extent a demographic sample. (x)

But he is also to some extent Jess Kirkman.

The third tactic, the one this essay addresses, is Chappell's skillful and complex use of first-person narrative in his essays, poems, and stories when he addresses the growth of a poet's mind. Chappell insists upon separating his narrator from himself as author—especially when he addresses his education in *Plow Naked* and *A Way of Happening*, Ole Fred's education in a number of poems from *Midquest*, and Jess's education in the Kirkman novels—and thus introduces complexity to the narrator's descriptions and judgments. On the one hand, we know, because many of the events described portray the "mouthpiece" as immature (e.g., the childlike fantasies of what it would be like to be a successful writer, the sophomoric debauchery) that the narrator is sometimes unreliable. But on the other hand, judgments made (e.g., that childlike fantasies are correctable, that debauchery is not something a poet must or even can get "good" at) portray yet another voice entirely, somewhat cranky but certainly more reliable than the other voice we hear. Chappell claims to be neither of these voices or, in any event, they are no more Chappell, to paraphrase his denial in the preface to *Midquest*, than any other character he might create in any novel or poem or, we might add, any essay he might write. We learn much about Chappell the writer by how he deals with the dilemma these contradictory voices create for him, especially his insistence that he does not intend to identify either/any of these voices with himself.

The problem Chappell chooses to address by employing these three tactics, since he does not "like to be autobiographical," is what Keats labeled "the wordsworthian or egotistical sublime," which, in his oft-cited letter to Woodhouse, Keats says "is a thing per se and stands alone" (I, 387).[5] Chappell understands in the preface to *Midquest* that the only way around the "egotistical sublime" is for the author to make his work *representative* and not *idiosyncratic*. For Chappell seems to be aware of what Wordsworth acknowledged in his famous letter to Sir George Beaumont about *The Prelude*, then unpublished, that it is "a thing unprecedented in literary history that a man should talk so much about himself" (Wayne 72). For whatever reason, Chappell prefers not to be accused of having talked "so much about himself." With Chappell, however, we find the accusation (I hesitate to call it a *problem*) of having written autobiographically made all the more complex by his efforts, arguably unprecedented, to write about the "growth of a poet's mind" in three genres: poetry, essay, and novel. No doubt readers who assume Chappell's writings to be autobiographical do so because they do not read for distance, as described in this essay, and thus attribute to autobiography what should be seen as artistry.

NOTES

1. Unfortunately, a quartet of nonfiction works parallel to *Midquest* and the Kirkman tetralogy has not yet been written by Chappell.

2. In *Season of Youth*, Jerome Buckley lists "the principle characteristics" of the *bildungsroman* (p. 17), not all of which apply to the life of Jess Kirkman.

3. Admittedly, I will keep in mind the interrelationships long agreed upon concerning genres. For instance, Bakhtin writes in "Discourse on the Novel" that "The novel, and artistic prose in general, has the closest genetic family relationship to rhetorical forms." Chappell presents an interesting dilemma for the contemporary critic because his nonfiction and his poems often appropriate tactics usually associated with novels, connecting them in a familial relationship as well. This essay is interested, then, in what Chappell can teach us about genre as well as about narration.

4. A more conventional reading of these novels might argue that we all have voices in our heads that speak to each other, what Lev Vygotsky calls "inner voice." Saying so, however, does not adequately explain strategic uses of these voices, such as Chappell's.

5. Keats could not have referred to *The Prelude* in his letter to Woodhouse cited above. *The Prelude* was published nearly thirty years after Keats's death. But Keats acknowledges elsewhere *Tintern Abbey*, Wordsworth's other autobiographical poem concerned with the "growth of a poet's mind," and no doubt considers that poem an example of the egotistical sublime.

WORKS CITED

Bakhtin, Mikhail. "Discourse on the Novel." In *Critical Theory since 1965*, ed. Hazard Adams and Leroy Searle. Tallahassee: Florida State University Press, 1990.

Bizzaro, Patrick. "The Critic As Teacher: A Review of Fred Chappell's *A Way of Happening*." *Asheville Poetry Review* 6, no. 1 (1999): 101–3.

Booth, Wayne. *The Rhetoric of Fiction*. 2nd ed. Chicago: University of Chicago Press, 1983.

Buckley, Jerome Hamilton. *Season of Youth: The Bildungsroman from Dickens to Golding*. Cambridge: Harvard University Press, 1974.

Crane, Resa, and James Kirkland. "First and Last Words: A Conversation with Fred Chappell." In *Dream Garden: The Poetic Vision of Fred Chappell*, ed. Patrick Bizzaro. Baton Rouge: Louisiana State University Press, 1997.

Jauss, David. "From Long Shots to X-Rays: Distance and Point of View in Fiction Writing." *Writer's Chronicle* 33, no. 1 (2000): 5–14, 17.

Keats, John. "Letter of May 3, 1818, to Woodhouse." In *The Letters of John Keats*. 2 vols. Cambridge: Harvard University Press, 1958, I.

Morgan, Robert. "*Midquest* and the Gift of Narrative." In *Dream Garden: The Poetic Vision of Fred Chappell*, ed. Patrick Bizzaro. Baton Rouge: Louisiana State University Press, 1997.

Wordsworth, William. "Letter of May 1, 1805, to Sir George Beaumont." In *Letters of William Wordsworth*, ed. Philip Wayne. London: Oxford University Press, 1933.

‹ SIX ›

Metanarrative and the Story of Life
in the Kirkman Tetralogy

J. SPENCER EDMUNDS

A novel does not assert anything; a novel searches and poses questions.
—MILAN KUNDERA

Want me to feed you some more questions?
—FRED CHAPPELL

IN AN INTERVIEW with Philip Roth, later printed as an afterword to *The Book of Laughter and Forgetting*, Milan Kundera spoke of Laurence Sterne as one of the "greatest experimenters of all time in the form of the novel," a writer whose experiments were "amusing, full of happiness and joy." As he lamented the current, unimaginative state of the novel, Kundera explained that writers such as Sterne understood the novel as a *great game*. They discovered the *humor* of the novelistic form. When I hear learned arguments that the novel has exhausted its possibilities, I have precisely the opposite feeling. In the course of its history, the novel has *missed* many of its possibilities. For example, impulses for the development of the novel hidden in Sterne have not been picked up by any successors.[1]

Given society's increasing fascination with and consumption of legal thrillers, forensic crime-solving dramas, romantic tearjerkers with rosy endings, and other novels with layers of knots slowly untied with each suspense-laden page, surely Kundera's assessment harbors some truth. In Fred Chappell, however, we find a true successor to Sterne, for in Chappell's Kirkman quartet we witness his unflinching commitment to stretch the boundaries of narrative, to recognize the novel as a "great game," and to introduce knotty questions rather than to ease tension by delivering answers.

A life's work in themselves, these four Chappell novels chronicle the lives of the Kirkman clan. Chappell devotees know, however, that the larger architecture of Chappell's grand accomplishment also consists of four collections of poetry that are structurally—indeed thematically—aligned with the novels. Written between 1985 and 1999, the novels share a common strategy of metanarrative that marks them as uncommon, a strategy that might be overlooked by the "superficial skimmer" but which the "eagle-eyed reader" surely savors.[2] Each of the four novels has its own metafictive flair, with the first and the last novels emphasizing the strategy most. In the end, by challenging traditional narrative structure, by creating self-reflexive passages that raise issues of storytelling, by juxtaposing the real and the unreal, by embedding stories within stories, by pitting different kinds of narrators against one another, by blurring the line between writer and narrator, and by weaving characters through and across four novels in a variety of quirky scenarios, Chappell employs metanarrative to craft a narrative that is more like the unpredictable, helter-skelter story of life than the artificial construct of Realism.

I AM ONE OF YOU FOREVER

I invent stories, confront one with another, and by this means I ask questions. The stupidity of people comes from having an answer for everything. The wisdom of the novel comes from having a question for everything.

—MILAN KUNDERA

First in the Kirkman quartet, *I Am One of You Forever* ends with a question—"Well, Jess, are you one of us or not?"—to which the title presents one potential answer (184).[3] By ending with a question, Chappell reemphasizes the novel's repeated efforts to pull against our hard-headed, perhaps modern, insistence on answering every question rather than appreciating, indeed cherishing, the unexplainable mysteries of being, of life-threatening yet life-affirming thunderstorms, of human communion, of unending, billowing beards. In chapter 6, "The Storytellers," by contrasting Uncle Zeno's and Joe Robert's narrative strategies, Chappell weaves a layer of metanarrative that similarly begs us not to pen narrative into orderly, verifiable units of information. Instead, and against Joe Robert's finer sensibilities, Chappell invites us to recognize Zeno's expansive, wandering narrative, or story, as a reflection of the larger, intertwining, often unanswerable story of life.

When Uncle Zeno drifts into the narrative like the rest of the relatives who fade in and out of the novel, Jess wastes no time in beginning to describe Zeno's odd narrative power. Deeming Zeno a "presence" more than a definable character, Jess explains that Zeno "told stories, endless stories" and that "these stories worked on the fabric of our daily lives in such a manner that we began to doubt our own outlines" (97). Able only to remember scattered details about Zeno, "a frayed cuff, a nibbled husk," Jess describes Zeno in terms that make us immediately identify him as a natural narrator: "He was a voice" (97).

Further exploring this narrative power, Jess characterizes Zeno's yarns, first noting that they always begin with six words—*That puts me in mind of*—that cause us to surrender to "the power that beginnings have over us; we must find out what comes next" (98). But while Zeno's narratives begin predictably, Jess explains how Zeno steers his narratives toward less predictable terrain, rapidly veering away from what many expect from narrative. Oblivious to pursuing concrete or didactic ends, for instance, "Zeno had no discernible purpose in telling his stories." Not concerned with chronology, Zeno "would begin at the beginning, in the middle, or at the end." Defying the notion of a unilinear plot, he would "stretch his stories in two or three directions at once." Unwilling to provide resolution, "he would leave [a story] suspended in midair like a gibbeted thief or let it falter to a halt like a stalled car." Moreover, Zeno did not craft his stories to please the audience. In fact, says Jess, "he took no interest in our reactions. If the story was funny our laughter made no more impression upon him than a distant butterfly" (98). Indeed, Zeno was content with an audience of "mica rocks and horse nettles" (111).

When Zeno's first narrative begins "That puts me in mind of Lacey Joe Blackman," we recognize the added layer of narrative, the story within the story, which I once heard Chappell refer to as a "nesting story" (98). As good as any of Chappell's yarns, both its content and its narrative strategy nonetheless quickly initiate conflict between Zeno and Joe Robert as storytellers. Specifically, when Zeno leaves his tale hanging, literally with a bear swinging in a tree "just . . . a mite . . . slow," Joe Robert finds this ending entirely unsatisfactory: "Just a mite slow? I don't get it. A bear is not hanging in a tree to be keeping time. What does he mean, a mite slow?" But as Jess notes, making one of his most insightful assessments of Uncle Zeno, "that was the end of the story. . . . He only told stories, he didn't answer questions" (102).

Described as "unable to keep his hands off things," Joe Robert is an altogether different storyteller. "Stories passed through Uncle Zeno like the orange glow through an oil lamp chimney," Jess tells us, "but my father must always be seizing objects and making them into swords, elephants, and magic millstones" (103). Never mind that Zeno had no interest in his audience or in surprising endings, Joe Robert was "entranced by mischief and effect" (105) and "loved to end his stories with quick, violent gestures intended to startle his audience" (103). In fact, even when Joe Robert managed to begin leisurely, Jess explains that he inevitably "careened into wild gesticulation and ended with a . . . loud noise. 'Wham' he would shout. 'I've gotcha!'" (105).

Reading "The Storytellers" and encountering Zeno and Joe Robert as narrators always makes me think of a commentary by Raymond Carver that appeared in the *New York Times* in February 1981. In the essay, Carver explains that he jots his favorite credos about writing on three-by-five cards that he tapes to his wall. One of his favorite cards says NO TRICKS, for, as he explains, "writers don't need tricks or gimmicks. . . . At the risk of appearing foolish, a writer sometimes needs to be able to just stand and gape at this or that thing in simple amazement."[4] And while Zeno's narratives seem consistent with this credo of anti-trickery, we get the sense from Joe Robert's "whams" and "I've gotchas" that the three-by-five card on his wall would more likely read TRICK OR TREAT.

Joe Robert's suppertime story of the haunted shotgun well illustrates his shortcomings as a storyteller. After creating a tale so perplexing that none of the family could "follow it at all," he ends by slamming his fist on the table to simulate the blast of the haunted shotgun. Sure enough, the family is startled—not by the tale itself, but by the bowl of butter beans Joe Robert knocks into his own lap. Of course, as the butter beans settle, Zeno suddenly offers a counternarrative, a gothic tale that quickly builds suspense and as quickly ends: "Anyhow." We expect the response: "Anyhow?" Joe Robert cries. "What kind of climax is that?" (104).

Increasingly jealous of Zeno's narrative power, which he cannot well

emulate, Joe Robert nonetheless believes vindication is within reach when
Zeno begins, then suspends, the soon to be controversial story of Buford
Rhodes and his dog Elmer.

> My father leaned over the table toward him. "Well, I've got your num-
> ber now. I don't know . . . any Lacey Joe Blackman . . . but it happens
> that I do know Buford Rhodes. Hired him one time to do some house
> painting. I know right where he lives, down there on Iron Duff, and I
> can drive right to his house. That's what I'm going to do, Uncle Zeno,
> and check your story out." (106–7)

As Joe Robert embarks on his fruitless search for verification and Zeno
heads to the woods to tell stories to the "blue daylight and the sweet green
grass" (110) we understand that the former sees narrative as something to
squeeze until it provides answers and the latter sees it as something to whisper into the wind. Unlike Jess and the others, who "didn't care whether the
story was true," Joe Robert wanted "to see if Buford Rhodes had ever met
and talked to Uncle Zeno." In fact, Jess tells us that "the idea that he could
actually track down Buford Rhodes and talk to him seemed to give my
father a gleeful satisfaction" (107). But when Joe Robert fails, first to find
Buford himself and then to find a check he once wrote to Buford for house
painting, his failure seems to suggest that we should not come to narrative
with the desire to verify the truths in texts as much as we should relax,
enjoy ourselves, pick up fiction where we find it, and make of it what we
may.

Chappell truly seems to be having fun intertwining stories and talking
about storytelling at the same time when he has Joe Robert, exasperated,
tell Cora she should remember Buford Rhodes. "You ought to remember
him," says Joe Robert, "Zeno has got him down exactly. He was some kind
of character." "All I ever meet are characters," Cora responds. "I don't believe that normal human beings show up in this part of the country" (112).
"This part of the country," populated only by "characters," might be called
the land of fiction. And moments later, contemplating the relationship between the real and the fictive world, Jess is suddenly overcome by a "wild
thought and a goosy sensation":

> What if Buford Rhodes had ceased to exist upon the earth because
> Uncle Zeno told stories about him? What if Uncle Zeno's stories so

thoroughly absorbed the characters he spoke of that they took leave of the everyday world and just went off to inhabit his narratives? (113)

Here, Jess appears on the verge of expanding his father's hunches about Homer and Zeno into a theory of narrative that explains Buford's disappearance. Following Joe Robert's earlier insight that both Homer and Zeno were seemingly going through life without leaving a verifiable trace behind, Jess now concludes: "Homer and Uncle Zeno did not merely describe the world, they used it up" (113).

Armed with this new theory, Jess listens and watches closely after supper as Uncle Zeno resumes the story of Buford Rhodes, now narrating the hilarious "switch off" by which Buford, having been replaced by his dog Elmer as schoolteacher, agrees to take Elmer's place as dog. When Zeno, as we might guess, stops short of full resolution, Joe Robert once again shows his finite mind: "But what I want to know," he says, "is where does Buford live now? I've been looking for him all day." "But of course," Jess says, reiterating a message found throughout the book, "there was no answer" (115).

As "The Storytellers" winds down, its narrative only increases in multi-layered complexity, beginning with Joe Robert's outburst in response to Zeno's narrative antics. For when Joe Robert announces "Well, now I'll tell a story" (116) what follows is a story within the larger story, the subject of which is, generally, the larger story and, specifically, the tension over narrative arising from the story of Buford Rhodes:

Once upon a time there was a pretty good old boy who never did anybody any harm. . . . It happened that he fell in love with a fine mountain girl and married into her family and they lived there in the hills and he worked the farm for them. That was all right, everything was just fine. Except that in this family there was an army of strange uncles who were always dropping by. This good old boy—let's just call him Joe—got along O.K. with these strange visitors. . . . But there was this one weird uncle—we'll call him Uncle Z—he couldn't figure out to save his life. Truly he couldn't. And it began to prey on his mind until he couldn't make himself think about anything but this Uncle Z. . . . I'm sorry to tell you, Uncle Zeno, that I don't know the end of this story. But I think that this good old boy started worrying so much that he finally just went crazy and they carried him off in a straitjacket. (116)

Voicing his anger, Joe Robert quite properly offers a narrative that displays the disruption of expectations at the center of his dismay: a story that begins "once upon a time" but defies the proper resolution. At the same time, however, by speculating about his own dive into insanity, Joe Robert engages in an imaginative act nourished by the open-ended narrative: he creates his own ending. Having had his say, Joe Robert storms off to the front porch.

As if rising to the narrative challenge, Uncle Zeno offers a variation on Joe Robert's narrative, that is, a story within the larger story, the subject of which is, generally, the larger story and, specifically, an earlier prank of Joe Robert's that, as far as we know, Zeno did not witness:

> That puts me in mind of, Uncle Zeno said, Cousin Annie Barbara Sorrel's that lived down toward the mouth of Ember Cove. Had a right nice farm there, about a hundred acres or so, but didn't have nobody to work it, her oldest son dying when he was eight and her other boy, Luden, gone off to California on a motorcycle. But she had her a son-in-law, Joe Robert his name was, and he was a fair hand at farming, she didn't have no complaints to speak of, except that Joe Robert was ever the sort to dream up mischief. . . . Well it happened one time that her boy Luden had sent Annie Barbara a present, which was a box of fancy candies he'd bought in St. Louis. (117)

Jess's reaction seems appropriate:

> This was too much. Uncle Zeno was telling a story about us. I knew what he was going to say; I'd lived through those events, after all. His story focused on my father, and that fact disturbed me. My father didn't seem to get along too well with Uncle Zeno as it was, and perhaps he wouldn't be happy to hear that he was now a character in the old man's stories. (118)

Jarred by the sudden realization that Joe Robert might soon join Buford Rhodes and other characters extinguished by Zeno's narratives, Jess runs to the porch.

Out in the night air, in darkness "as dark as the dreams of a sleeping bear," Joe Robert has not yet evaporated, though his admission that he felt like "he'd lost a lot of weight in a hurry" feeds Jess's imaginative speculation (118). As the "indistinct mutter" of Zeno's narrative continues in the background, Joe Robert sets up the story's ending when he grudgingly accepts Jess's invitation to come back inside for apple pie:

> Finally [my father] rose slowly from the chair. But when he took a step he walked directly into the darkest shadow and I couldn't see him at all and at that moment Uncle Zeno's story concluded and all the night went silent. (118)

Here, Chappell offers his final, masterful convergence of three narrative threads: on the simplest level, we find the end of this chapter, the story of Zeno's visit; next, we find the end, though probably only a suspension, of the story Zeno is telling; and finally, because Joe Robert steps into a consuming darkness as Zeno's narrative about him tapers off, we find what Jess perceives as the untimely end of Joe Robert based on the theory that as Zeno tells stories he uses up the world. Without answering questions or providing resolution, all three narratives quietly drift off into the silent darkness.

As we read *I Am One of You Forever*, we might also consider how Chappell's narrative strategy reflects the story of life if we think about how many people actually read the novel, cover to cover, in one sitting. We know the answer: not many. In turn, I suggest that the narrative that makes the chapter "The Storytellers" not only raises issues of narrative itself but also cleverly approximates the act of reading. For just as this chapter, indeed this novel, involves a narrative that is at various moments interrupted by other narratives, temporarily suspended, intertwined with other threads, and returned to, so when we read we suspend the narratives of our lives, enter into fictional narratives, ponder how they perhaps overlap, put the book down to eat a snack, read some more, and then exit the fictive world and resume our life stories without necessarily reaching resolution or ending the novel.

Ultimately, just as *I Am One of You Forever* ends with a question, Chappell likewise exits "The Storytellers" quietly and without resolving Zeno's various mysteries. With such an exit, Chappell accurately captures the way life continuously presents unanswerable phenomena and irresolvable tension and, like the novel, leaves us hanging like the bear swinging in the tree. If life is full of questions we can't answer, Chappell seems to ask, why should narrative be any different? True to his apparent credo, Chappell thus initiates the quartet with *I Am One of You Forever*, a novel that is nonlinear, periodically bewildering, and passionate about raising questions rather than delivering answers, a novel in which Zeno's narratives and Jess's commentaries on them highlight the complex narrative web that both life and fiction perpetually weave with, through, and around us.

BRIGHTEN THE CORNER WHERE YOU ARE

In a world built on sacrosanct certainties the novel is dead.
—MILAN KUNDERA

Unlike *I Am One of You Forever*, which is structured in such a way that individual chapters might stand alone as stories, *Brighten the Corner Where You Are* targets a different task: to narrate in successive chapters a day in the life of Joe Robert as, of all things, a high school teacher. The destination of the comic tale is a late afternoon meeting with the governor to discuss a potential appointment as an educational adviser, but no such day in Joe Robert's complicated life would be complete without first hunting for a rare devil-possum, splashing into a creek to save a drowning girl, hiding out in an infernoesque boiler room, and negotiating with a billy goat atop the school building for an audience of peers and students. And while the strategies of metanarrative are less pronounced and less plentiful than in the previous novel, amid the chaos of *Brighten* Chappell once again finds a way to propel the narrative and, at the same time, weave threads of metanarrative into the larger fabric of the story that call attention to the craft and process of storytelling.

Chappell first makes reference to the narrative act when Joe Robert stops on his way to work and plunges into a creek to save a young girl who is floundering in the water. Seeking refuge, Joe Robert and the girl wind up at Virgil Campbell's store, where the two older men must undress and warm the soaked girl: an uneasy task for this duo. As if to distract them from the delicate dilemma at hand, Virgil wanders into a story he hopes will successfully divert the attention of all parties involved, but the story does not escape the critical commentary of Joe Robert filtered through Jess's voice as he retells the story:

> And so Virgil began the story of the flat land tourist. . . . It seemed no fitting time for a windy, my father thought, but then reflected that here were two big rough men who must strip down the little girl and get her warm and save her life and that they must put her at her ease and themselves, too. Even Virgil paid little attention to his story as it went though its quaint convolutions and ridiculous coincidences, laboring toward a supremely silly denouement. (44)[5]

Here, Joe Robert, the master of storytelling himself, evaluates and criticizes Virgil's narrative structure for its "quaint," "ridiculous," and "silly" characteristics, a series of modifiers we find comic since they likewise describe Joe Robert's narrative antics in "The Storytellers." But in Joe Robert's commentary, we perhaps also perceive Chappell's own distaste for unimaginative, formulaic strands of narrative by writers who pay "little attention" to the craft of writing and who, in turn, produce writing well defined by Joe Robert's evaluatory modifiers. Having himself at this point planned and written most of a highly structured architecture of four books each of poetry and fiction, Chappell surely does not fall into the classification of one who has given "little attention" to his story, a fact that Chappell expresses later in Joe Robert's discussion with Sandy Slater in the boiler room. "Folks get the wrong impression," Joe Robert tells Sandy. "Everything that happens to me is according to a plan I've been working on for years, a plan audacious in scope yet bold in its simplicity. Everything you see me do is but a necessary stage in the completion of this grand design" (97). In language that clearly calls attention to the "grand design" of his books, Chappell thus cleverly embeds comments about his own narrative journeys in the dialogue of a fellow spokesman.

Perhaps the most comic series of scenes in *Brighten* occurs when Joe Robert undertakes a heroic attempt to rid the school of a pesky goat, the party loving "Bah-ah-ah-chus." As the situation progresses from bad to worse on an already miserable day, Joe Robert finds himself perched atop the schoolhouse trying to persuade the likewise perched goat to evacuate the premises peacefully. More than merely a comic digression, however, the scene offers Chappell another opportunity to experiment with metanarrative, this time offering self-reflexive statements that seem like authorial reflections on the work in progress. Trying to reason with the goat, for example, Joe Robert says:

> So up to this point, I think we must count your appearance here at Tipton High School a fine success. It has been dramatic and educational and you have shown a real flair for acrobatic comedy. But I am going to suggest that our rooftop tryst now marks the natural high point of the episode and that if you choose to prolong your visit in this exhibitionist way, our good old mountaineer tradition of hospitality might feel some sense of strain and our sentiments of welcome might well turn into an annoyance and finally into rancor. . . . I'd like for you to consider the possibility that it might be best to take a final bow and let me help you down from here and return you to the place where you belong. (144)

Couched in this clever exchange, we can almost hear Chappell the critic sizing up the situation as he writes at his drafting table, analyzing the plot structure of the "episode" in progress, trying to gauge when he has used up his "flair for acrobatic comedy" and is in danger, thus, of wearing out the "hospitality" of his readers if he doesn't get the "exhibitionist" goat to "take a final bow" and leave the stage. Moments later, when Joe Robert pauses to evaluate how his rooftop predicament has evolved, the language evokes the sense of Chappell taking a similar pause to assess the questionable progression of the plot:

> My father looked then for the first time and saw . . . what seemed to be almost the whole personnel of the school—teachers, students, lunchroom cooks, and all: a good two hundred people at least, and all looking at him in silent speculation. Good Lord, he thought, how did I get into this fix? But he knew how it happened and he didn't want to think about it. If I get this goat down from here, he thought, I expect a four-star ovation and a job offer from the Clyde Beatty Wild Animal Circus. (145)

Again, if we consider how the sentences streaming across the page might simultaneously perpetuate the plot and reflect the thoughts of a writer pausing to take stock, we may be prone to hear the words "Good Lord . . . how did I get into this fix?" issuing from Chappell's mouth, with his own remedy to follow: don't "think about it," just "get this goat down."

Chappell's final metafictive flourish in *Brighten* occurs when Joe Robert, having finally quit his teaching job at the end of a toilsome day, attempts to explain how he reached this decision to a reporter curious about the series of events that ultimately brought him to his knees. When asked why he quit his job, Joe Robert initially responds, "Well, it's kind of complicated" (188) an answer that tapers off and is replaced with Jess's narrative commentary on Joe Robert's attempt at an explanation:

> But he did his level best to try to shape his story into a logical sequence. Sometimes it was comprehensible to him, while at others it seemed as slambang silly as a comic strip. It made sense to fish the little girl out of the creek, but why had he fooled around half the afternoon with that goat? The more he tried to explain them, the lamer his motive appeared, and he saw that he was portraying himself as a creature of mad impulse, someone whose helpless destination was the interior of a spacious butterfly net. And once his story was told, it was told; there was no way to untell it, no way to make himself look good. He ended with a mumbled brief statement: "And that's why I did it." (188)

In a general sense, while we can never presume to read Chappell's thoughts, we imagine that as he wrote *Brighten,* indeed the entire quartet, he "did his level best to shape the story into a logical sequence," even if it was "comprehensible" at times and "slambang silly" at others. More specific to this particular text, however, Chappell's clever and comic commentary again suggests a pattern of careful self-evaluation, as if he agreed with Joe Robert that "it made sense to fish the little girl out of the creek" but wondered in the aftermath of writing the chapter "Bacchus" why he "had fooled around half the afternoon with that goat." But like a writer committed to his text, flaws and all, Chappell notes that "once his story was told, it was told; there was no way to untell it."

FAREWELL, I'M BOUND TO LEAVE YOU

> The novelist teaches the reader to comprehend the world as a question. There is wisdom and tolerance in that attitude.
> —MILAN KUNDERA

Farewell, I'm Bound to Leave You takes as its touchstone the impending death of the family matriarch, Annie Barbara Sorrells. In a larger sense, however, Chappell uses the novel to explore the powerful voices of women through a series of narratives that chronicle their vast voices and experiences. For this reason, the novel is most similar in structure to *I Am One of You Forever*, as both involve a chain of episodes that are virtually self reliant, though they are also obviously linked to the larger work and to the entire project. Moreover, as he did in "The Storytellers" chapter from *I Am One of You Forever*, in *Farewell, I'm Bound to Leave You* Chappell primarily concentrates his strategies of metanarrative in one chapter, "The Wind Woman." In this novel, then, "The Wind Woman" becomes for Chappell a place to examine the process by which writers are exposed to sensory stimulation and, lured by the muse, respond with creative writing.

In a letter to me dated October 6, 1997, Chappell wrote to share his belief that "The Storytellers" was "the most important in the cycle" and was "a companion to 'The Wind Woman' in *Farewell*."[6] And while "The Wind Woman" does not offer the dueling narrators of Joe Robert and Uncle Zeno, it does, instead, explore the revelatory awakenings of a person coming to terms with being tapped by the writerly spirit. Put simply, the episode involves Jess and his mother's visiting the Wind Woman, though their arrival is delayed by several "duty calls" to see the Fire Woman, the Cloud Woman, Aunt Priddy, and the Happiest Woman, among others. Along the way, Cora notes that she saw Jess "writing poetry in one of [his] notebooks" and tells him "if you ever take a notion to write about our part of the earth . . . then you must meet the Wind Woman, for you'll never write a purposeful word until you do" (104).[7] When Jess's curiosity is sparked, Cora confesses that she never had what it took to stand up to the Wind Woman, having visited her once but been too embarrassed by her own simplistic love poems. As Cora explains to Jess, "I visited her just once, a long time ago. But I was too shy to begin, and when she pressed me, I went away" (112). Recognizing, however, "the difference between a young woman writing lines of affection and a poet writing true things to be known and seen in the world," Cora has greater faith in Jess and knows that he "must call on the Wind Woman" (105).

As the conversation continues, Jess expresses his desire to skip the visit, but Cora seems convinced of its necessity and of Jess's talents. In part, Cora's own experience has taught her that because she "never opened her mind to the Wind Woman," over time the "passion" she felt was calmed by "marriage" and by "family" until she "laid [her] pen aside" (105). For, as she explains, "it is passionate affection or sorrow that makes most of us poets, and when those feelings are smoothed down by the hand of time, we all become like one another again and see and know the same things. But when our passions are high, we are different from one another and see all things more furiously" (105). *Seize this opportunity*, she seems to tell Jess, *before your poetic drive withers and fades.* And with these instructions, of course, Chappell milks the meandering yarn for a dose of theoretic probing on the nature of poetic inspiration, the importance of listening to the windy muse, the essence of capturing a youthful and energetic creative spirit, and the romantic longing for such a spirit long since gone.

When Jess and Cora reach Wind Mountain, Chappell emphasizes the essentially individual nature of an encounter with the Wind Woman, as Cora begs off the visit in the name of fatigue. In a symbolic act, the head-wind has picked up considerably, and Cora can no longer fight the wind and the steepening slope to continue the now seemingly epic quest. "This is as far as I go," she tells Jess. "You'll have to go on by yourself" (112). And when the reluctant Jess asks "Are you sure about this?" Cora prods, "Go on, Jess" (113). Fighting against a wind now "full of mutterings, not animal, but not quite human," Jess marches on until he reaches the unimpressive little house perched atop the wind-encircled mountain—its shingles "warped and split," its steps "chewed and sagging," its chimney leaning "three ways at once." Moreover, no one answers his knock at the door, though Jess notes that the wind "was fresher now with green smells . . .and the muttering in it had turned to human language" (113). Motivated primarily by his understanding that his "mother would be dissatisfied" if he balked, Jess nonetheless enters the house, verifies by a brief tour that it is indeed lived in, and decides to tarry so that he might "mollify his mother," if nothing else (114).

Of course, in a chapter that forecasts a young poet's meeting with the muse, we are expecting more from "The Wind Woman" and from Jess than a leisurely nap to appease his mother, and Chappell ultimately delivers just when it appears that nothing will happen atop the mountain:

When I closed my eyes for a moment, the wind swelled up all around the cabin and inside it, making a great music of speaking voices and voices singing and instruments playing and the sounds that the horses and cows and dogs in the fields make and the trees and the birds and stones in the woods. The commotion in my head was frightening and intoxicating. I was lost in bewilderment. (114)

This spirit of epiphany sparked by the awesome power of nature, here embodied by the polyphonous wind, descends certainly in part from the legendary Transparent Eyeball image made famous by Ralph Waldo Emerson. In his generative essay "Nature," Emerson explained how a man encountering the unparalleled power of nature suddenly has his senses cleared, his spirit elevated, his sense of self minimized, and his understanding of how the universal current circulates in, around, and through all things enlarged. As in Jess's case, the sensation Emerson relates is overwhelming. Emerson writes:

> Crossing a bare common, in snow puddles, at twilight, under a clouded sky, without having in my thoughts any occurrence of special good fortune, I have enjoyed a perfect exhilaration. I am glad to the brink of fear. . . . Standing on the bare ground,—my head bathed by the blithe air and uplifted into infinite space,—all mean egotism vanishes. I become a transparent eyeball; I am nothing; I see all; the currents of the Universal Being circulate though me; I am part or parcel of God.[8]

In "The Wind Woman," then, Chappell seems to employ a variation on Emerson's theme, for while the similarities between the two are evident, in Jess's case we witness how his particular elevation of consciousness functions not primarily to awaken him spiritually but rather to help this young writer understand the implications of that vocation and of the creative process of translating life into literature.

In the aftermath of the initial barrage of bewildering sensations, Jess slowly begins to recognize the sounds and images he is encountering. As Jess explains, "the different sounds, gradually sorted themselves out, and I could understand what some of the voices were saying" (114). Shortly thereafter, when Jess hears "the wild, desolate, heartbroken voice of a woman crying away away away," we hear two voices we will encounter as the novel continues: Aunt Chancy's crazed wail over the loss of Frawley Harper and the soft moan of Jess's dying grandmother at the novel's end. And when

Jess hears a man singing "I see a blackbird fighting the crow / But I know something he don't know," we glimpse a voice from Chappell's poem "Remembering Wind Mountain" timelessly spinning in the windy middle of this novel. As the chapter winds down, Jess is beginning to feel "swarmed with the hurt" of the wind noises, including "houses and barns, ropes and straps, gunshot and sword slash, iron and calico, jubilation and lamentation, country and city, old age and childhood, birth and death," but he is suddenly saved when "all went silent except for that single round, silent tone of the moon . . . that sound was a mercy and a marvel" (115).

His head cleared, Jess now gathers his thoughts:

> Now I understand, I thought. This journey was for me to come here to this cabin and let these sounds come upon me. I can't figure them out by myself. The Wind Woman will teach me how to layout these sounds in proper fashion. I will wait here for her to come and beg the favor of her aid. I will wait here as long as it takes.
>
> And that is the last sight I have of myself at that time—sitting alone in the cabin up on Wind Mountain with my eyes closed and patient to consort the sounds of the hollers and slopes and valleys below into music. (115)

Not surprisingly, this image of Jess taming a multitude of voices into music resembles an image painted by Chappell in *I Am One of You Forever,* where Jess finds Uncle Zeno in the middle of nowhere reverently listening to the story of a tree. In this secluded environment, which Jess calls "the best setting for his stories," he finds Zeno "sitting on the tree, giving audience to the history of its regal life and calamitous downfall, a story I couldn't hear" (110). In turn, we understand how "The Wind Woman" is less a tale about a "duty call" than a metaphor for the writer's transformation from an inability to hear to a state of patient and dutiful listening for the stories that surround us. Such a listener, Chappell seems to suggest, learns how to sort through a cacophony of sensory stimuli and, ultimately, to write creatively about the nature of human experience.

With a narrative thread that explores the archetypal retreat into solitude for poetic inspiration, in *Farewell, I'm Bound to Leave You* Chappell once again employs metanarrative to probe the process of writing. In "The Wind Woman," the italicized interchapter placed literally and figuratively at the center of the novel, Chappell takes us on an epic quest to the small, still place in the middle of nowhere that is paradoxically teeming with the chaos of life, a place we might consider the calm epicenter of all literary production, where the voices of all characters and sounds and images intersect and reside, waiting patiently to be summoned to life by those who come searching to sort the chaos into order. And while Chappell sends the poet Jess to Wind Mountain alone, we understand that he seeks there the Wind Woman, the muse who can help the neophyte turn the voices of mayhem into the music of poetry, a woman who, like Uncle Zeno, is there and not there, her physical presence invisible but her guiding voice surely spinning in the wind.

LOOK BACK ALL THE GREEN VALLEY

Sterne and Diderot understood the novel as a great game.
—MILAN KUNDERA

Of the four novels in the Kirkman quartet, certainly *Look Back All the Green Valley* employs the most self-evident strategies of metanarrative, and, for this reason, the novel shares the most similarity with the first novel in the series, *I Am One of You Forever.* Like *Farewell,* however, the death of family drives *Look Back,* for as Cora faces her impending death from the confines of a nursing home, her children face putting business in order as they prepare to bid their mother farewell. As part of this process, Jess agrees to clean up one of his father's many secret workshops and, in so doing, braves the convoluted wake of Joe Robert's demise. To make matters worse, a cemetery mix-up has left no space for Cora to join Joe Robert in eternal rest. In turn, this lack of a plot drives the plot, and over the course of the novel Jess and Mitzi must find a joint resting place for their dearly beloved and arrange to unearth and relocate Joe Robert. Along the way, Chappell's deftly chimed tones of metanarrative cause his story to resonate with the polyphony of a fine symphony.

The novel's initial, italicized pre-chapter hints that Chappell will not wait long before he revisits the territory of narrative itself as a topic. At the gravesite with family friends who have agreed to help disentomb Joe Robert's corpse, Jess suddenly perceives the presence (or does he?) of "an old man with white hair," whom we imagine will be none other than Uncle

Zeno (5).[9] Rather than having Zeno expound here, however, Chappell only teases us along, having Jess note, "I feel like I know who he is" (5). But as we enter "Trapped," the first chapter, Chappell wastes no time in dismantling even our most basic concepts of narrative and of the novel. Having left the comfortable confines of academic life in Greensboro, Jess tells of his return to Asheville to visit his mother, where from the uncomfortable confines of her rest home she displays her sickness-induced rancor and chides him on his choice of profession. "You're a dreamer," Cora exclaims. "If Susan didn't look after you, I shudder to picture the condition your affairs would be in. Making footnotes. Writing poetry nobody can understand" (12). When she pauses to ask the name of one of his books and Jess responds, "*River* was the first one," it comes as no surprise, since his novels and poems often seem to reflect Chappell's personal life. But when Cora asks, "And what was that strange name you signed to it?" Jess's response provides an unusual kink: "My pen name is Fred Chappell. If I signed those books 'Jess Kirkman' you'd have a conniption fit. Some dark family secrets are aired in those poems" (12).

With a few strokes of his pen (Chappell still writes in longhand), Chappell here unsettles many of our conventional footholds. Suddenly, the fictional character of Jess seems to have crossed into the *real* world—having taken Chappell's wife and job along the way—and relegated "Ole Fred" to the fictive realm of Jess's imagination. So is Fred Chappell the fictional character and Jess Kirkman the real person? If so, who wrote this book, and *River,* and the other ones? And whose family secrets are aired in the poems? Chappell's? Kirkman's?

In short, the chain reaction of gleeful uncertainty sparked by this imaginative inversion testifies that Chappell recognizes the perfect playing field the novel offers for the "great game" Kundera craved but found missing in the modern novel. Of course we know who wrote the novel in hand, but by engaging in such playful conniving Chappell jars our complacent consciousness and teases us into rapturous delight. Make no mistake, however; along the way Chappell's domain is also severely serious, as he inevitably raises issues of authorship, agency, the fuzzy connections between writers and their characters, and modern society's general disrespect for poetry and poets. *Pay attention,* Chappell seems to say, *I'm making my own rules, and I refuse to answer questions about how the game is played.* And if we are wise, we go along for the ride, suspend our incessant insistence on answers to all questions, and enjoy the experience of reading a story and delving into the theory of storytelling as we ride.

The Kirkman-posing-as-Chappell playfulness pervades the novel, as narrator Jess repeatedly speaks of his poetic works in progress, his laborious translations of Dante, his academic career put on hold in the name of family business. Many a time, Jess pauses to scribble would-be lines of poems in his black writer's notebook, which he calls his "staunch comrade," as he sits in Asheville's cozy cafés. In one scene, Jess's explanation of the contents of his notebook sparks a digression on his current project.

> Some notes I could consider important. Here were suggestions for my fourth book of poetry, to be called *Earthsleep*. This volume would be centered around the last of the Pythagorean elements I was employing in my scheme. Earth was my theme, and my connective tropes were gardens and graves, intimate engagements with dirt. Two poems were to be about ideal gardens, one that Susan dreamed of, and one I would dream up myself as a utopian proposition for a poet friend, George Garrett. (20)

Again, we cross familiar terrain from Chappell's biography via references to his wife Susan and to University of Virginia creative writing guru and author George Garrett. And, of course, we recognize how Chappell highlights the larger architecture of *Midquest* by making reference to *Earthsleep*. But we must also perceive another kind of playfulness here, as Chappell creates the illusion that Jess is writing the still unfinished *Earthsleep*, the last volume in the quartet of poetry, even as Chappell has completed the narrative we hold in our hands, the companion in the quartet of novels. Chappell perpetuates the illusion of *Earthsleep* in progress when Jess ventures into his father's secret workshop and finds his father's note in the margin of Shakespeare's *Twelfth Night:* "See *Fred Chappell's* scheme" (66). Although he cannot find copies of his books "*River, Bloodfire,* and *Wind Mountain*" in the workshop, he nonetheless seems proud that his father "grasped [his] plan of organizing each volume around the pythagorean elements" and shares that he is currently "at work on the concluding volume, *Earthsleep*"(66).[10]

In a final twist, the Kirkman-as-Chappell play suggestively probes the issue of a society that has collectively deemed poets maniacs or idiots and that believes poetry is a pesky waste of everyone's time. In fact, as Jess wonders why his father would have read his books but never said a word to him about them, Cora's commentary offers an explanation.

> "Poetry," she said, and with that word she canceled the topic. The term *poetry* now had for her the force of malediction. *Poetry* explained my wayward and drifting existence to her; it was the vice that had brought me low and made me crazy. How could she take seriously the ravings of a prodigal son who wrote poetry? No wonder I wanted to be Fred Chappell instead of Jess Kirkman; no wonder I chose a phony name, the silliest in the telephone book. Fred Chappell showed that in my heart I, too, was ashamed. (175)

Indeed, Chappell shows how the shame over having a poet in the family has shaped Jess's appraisal of himself, his mother's feelings, and even his sister Mitzi's cool assessment of his vocation. In fact, when Mitzi asks whether Jess is writing "another Fred Chappell book" (84), to which Jess responds, "Guilty as charged, Your Honor," she replies, "I'll never figure out what you think you're up to. Never. You're just like your Daddy that way" (84). In turn, as we contemplate these passages written by the poet laureate of North Carolina, it seems difficult to overlook how Chappell uses these exchanges of dialogue both to develop the dynamics among the characters and to make a gentle plea for a wider acceptance of poets and poetry.

Beyond the playful strategy of Jess-as-Fred, another delightful tactic of metanarrative that links *Look Back All the Green Valley* to *I Am One of You Forever,* and by connection to Uncle Zeno's quirky yarns, appears when Jess attempts to hunt down Joe Robert's harem of would-be one-night stands. With his map and list of names in hand, Jess seems sure that some answers to the mystery of his father's secret life will be uncovered when he finds Susan Louise, or Julia Mannerling, or Betty Uprichard, or Mrs. Mawley. Here, we find a clever revisitation of Joe Robert's unsuccessful attempt to hunt down Buford Rhodes in "The Storytellers," a quest that at the time seemed critical in order to give finitude to Uncle Zeno's otherwise infinitely baffling narratives. When the inquisitive Jess explains his quest to Mitzi on the phone, stating "Tomorrow I'll go over to Hardison and see if I can track down any of these names. . . . If they're real people, somebody will know about them" (89), we surely hear echoes of Joe Robert's commitment to locate Buford Rhodes: "I know right where he lives, down there on Iron Duff, and I can drive right to his house. That's what I'm going to do, Uncle Zeno, and check your story out" (*Forever* 106–7). In this instance, Mitzi is quick to point out Jess's resemblance to Joe Robert, stating "Jess if you try to trace down what's drawn on that map, you'll be the very same kind of little boy our daddy was" (89). And when—like father, like son—both Joe Robert and Jess fall short in their quests, Chappell again seems to reemphasize thoughtful respect for the realm of the unanswerable rather than an unnatural insistence on answers. For Chappell seems to make clear that, while no one may ever fully unlock the mystery of the thirteen ladies or find Buford Rhodes, we can nonetheless witness how they inspire the imaginative impulse that creates narratives. In fact, as Jess orders himself— "restore your mind to sanity"—he pauses to reflect on the power of the mysterious women: "here were the names of women posted in the crannies of hollers and the elbows of creeks. . . . They were not mere compass points; they had stories attached to them, and the ones my imagination constructed were spicy narratives indeed" (92).

Look Back is also similar in metanarrative strategy to *Forever,* and particularly to "The Storytellers," when Chappell uses Jess to comment on styles of narration, most commonly to remind us of the flawed nature of Joe Robert's narrative enterprises. In Jess's conversation with his mother at the nursing home, Cora recalls a time on a European tour when Joe Robert filled in for a missing tour guide and had the bus howling with laughter as he "devised colorful chronicles" along the way. But Jess seems unconvinced of the story:

> I didn't believe her. Time after time, I had heard my father attempt to tell stories; time after time, he failed miserably, starting off as suddenly and loudly as an Atlas rocket and almost immediately plunging to piteous human ruin like Icarus. . . . My father could shoe horses, build bridges, plumb toilets, and design futuristic aircraft, but whenever he tried to construct a story, he unfailingly banged his thumb on the punchline. (16)

Later in the novel, after Jess finally hears the complete story of the ruined bridge from Aunt Ora and Uncle Gray, a story that we know initiates the quartet in "The Overspill," the conversation turns to a comparison of Uncle Zeno and Joe Robert. The family remembers how "Uncle Zeno must have been one of Joe Robert's rare defeats," for while Uncle Zeno was known far and wide as a "legendary" storyteller, Uncle Gray recalls that when Joe Robert "tried to tell a windy, he'd get so tangled up, it was like he'd wandered into a laurel hell. He couldn't even tell the stories of his own pranks and antics. He tried to tell me how him and Johnson Gibbs put some banty eggs in a box of chocolate candy one time. I never did understand what all went on" (207). As in *I Am One of You Forever*, these exchanges suggest that not everyone who can tell a story has the capacity to create engaging, intelligent, imaginative narrative, and we are reminded again of the difference between Zeno's calm, meditative musings and Joe Robert's "whams!" and "I've gotchas!"

The final strategy of metanarrative in *Look Back All the Green Valley* occurs when Chappell writes passages that drive the plot but seem also to harbor authorial commentaries on the narrative process itself. In these instances, which resemble similarly suggestive sections of *Brighten*, we quickly recognize how the writer's and character's voices appear to merge as we read the words across the page. Having created a sizable amount of work for himself with the events of the first half of the novel, for example, Jess pauses to create a checklist:

> Okay, let's see: I needed to organize the picnic for Sunday afternoon, to telephone the New Briar Rose ramblers, to have a look at the home places of the Irelands and the Hillyers, to establish a strategy for choosing the gravesite, to figure out how to comply in short order with the reburial regulations, and to lay the groundwork for the whole scheme.
>
> In order to get the groundwork laid, I'd have to interview my mother again, and I decided to do it immediately. Time was short and all the gears had to mesh or J would be driving back and forth from Greensboro to Asheville for months to come. I could live with that necessity, but the uncertainties and anxieties would do my mother no good. For her peace of mind, we had to get things settled. (169)

Here, Jess's grocery list of duties could just as easily be Chappell's notes of plot-related items to address during the construction of the novel. For as

Chappell put the story together, surely he had to "organize the picnic," to "establish a strategy for choosing the gravesite," and to "lay the groundwork for the whole scheme." After all, when the weight of finishing a quartet of novels and volumes of poetry was on your back, "all the gears had to mesh." In a similar fashion, Jess's comments upon encountering his father's Fugio notebooks might also approximate Chappell's frustration as he nears the completion of the Kirkman saga. "I was becoming so entangled in so many puzzles, I began to feel physically constrained" (93).

Chappell's tendency to weave a narrative thread that perpetuates the plot and simultaneously approximates writerly self-reflection also appears in *Look Back* as characters from the larger quartet make their way back into the final novel. As if Chappell feels pressure to bring each member of his supporting cast back onstage for a bow, many appear in turn, but the sentences fall into place in a way that makes us think of Chappell's narrative process. In the scene that sparks the title of the novel, for example, Jess is lured into reminiscence when "a voice that seemed distantly familiar" comes across the airwaves crooning "Look Back All the Green Valley." The woman's voice is none other than that of Aunt Samantha Barefoot, a realization that sends Jess into a dreamy meditation:

> I turned off the radio, wanting to hold warm these memories as long as possible. I had been trying to remember the old days, thinking I might stumble upon clues that would help unravel the knotted puzzles of the present dilemmas that faced Mitzi and me. Aunt Sam's music had opened another sluice gate and I needed to examine the flow. (110)

As we read these sentences, we can envision Chappell perched at his writing desk, "trying to remember the old days" when he started his grand project, hoping all the while that he might "stumble upon clues that would help him unravel the knotted puzzles of the present dilemmas" associated with bringing the Kirkman saga to a finish. In a similar fashion, Chappell gathers members of his ensemble cast at the fairgrounds near the novel's end to read Joe Robert's will and to announce his parents' eternal resting place. Looking across the crowd of guests, Jess notes:

> Many I did not recognize, but many I did—more than I had expected to distinguish, considering the changes that decades wreak on face and

figure. . . . Cousin Earlene Lewis came alone, invited by Mitzi for old time sake. . . . I thought I recognized in one wiry form that feistiest woman, Ginger Summerell, but she was on the arm of a gentleman who didn't look sufficiently cowered to be her spouse. If I could only recall the faces and the episodes they belonged to, this was the story of my youth unfolding and a larger tale, too, than that very small one: the chronicle of a period of mountain culture of rare and striking flavor. (251)

Again, the language here evokes a sense of Chappell meditatively pondering the weight of bringing his life's work to a close: recognizing and remembering characters long since written about, trying to "recall the faces and episodes they belonged to," realizing that as he places the words across the page he is watching "the story of (his) youth unfolding and a larger tale, too," namely the one he spent his adult life writing.

As Chappell brings the Kirkman quartet to a close, we are no closer to answering whatever questions we may have collected along the way: we will never know the length of Uncle Gurton's beard; we will never be able to clock Uncle Zeph's prayers; we will never know what Jess, Johnson Gibbs, and Joe Robert heard in the marvelous thunderstorm; we will never know where Joe Robert is after being absent from his grave; and as we float together off the last page with a mysterious figure and disappear "into the rain," we will never know whether Uncle Zeno was ever there or not. But if we have learned anything along the way, we have not only come to value the unanswerable mysteries of being, we have also come to respect another entity without boundaries: the power of narrative freed from conventional constraints. In the end, as Chappell would have it, we should revere the collection for its magnificent aesthetic value as an art object, and particularly for its innovative strategies of metanarrative, rather than feel unsatisfied that *Look Back* did not untie the knots that its predecessors so craftily cinched together.

What a journey!
—LAURENCE STERNE
Still, some questions remained unanswered.
—FRED CHAPPELL

In the latter stages of Laurence Sterne's *The Life and Opinions of Tristram Shandy*, the narrator pauses to comment on the progress, or lack thereof, he has made during his attempt to tell the story of his life:

I am now beginning to get fairly into my work; and by the help of a vegitable [*sic*] diet . . . I make no doubt but I shall be able to go on with my new uncle Toby's story, and my own, in a tolerable straight line. Now,

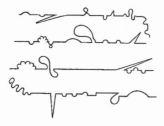

These were the four lines I moved in through my first, second, third, and fourth volumes. In the fifth volume, I have been very good,—the precise line I have described in it being this:

Having mapped out his path thus far, Sterne then makes projections about his future plans to reign in his digressions, noting that "if I mend at this rate, it is not impossible—by the good leave of his grace of Benevito's devils—but I may arrive hereafter at the excellency of going on even thus:
————————————————" (454).[11]

Without question, Sterne's self-reflexive comments and typographic innovations point to the larger game of the novel—an oddball narrator's attempt to tell his life story, even as he is perpetually diverted by a series of comic digressions, such as his attempts to chart his [lack of] progress. Like Sterne, who recommended at all costs "to let people tell their story their own way," in his quartet of Kirkman novels Chappell spins his yarns by following his own understanding of what the narrative process itself means to writers, characters, and narrators, rather than what literary convention might otherwise prescribe.[12] And like Sterne's narrator, Chappell's own Jess Kirkman, with the help of narrative theorist Uncle Zeno and other so-called relatives, propels the narrative along and, at the same time, probes the theories on which storytelling is grounded, or ought to be. In turn, as we examine Sterne's diagrams above, we should not be surprised to see how Chappell's and his cast of characters' narratives closely resemble Sterne's and Shandy's curvy, wandering, unpredictable ones, rather than the conventional, predictable, formulaic strands represented by the (yawn) straight line.

In the end, then, we understand how Milan Kundera was perhaps right and wrong at the same time. For while multitudes of writers churn out endless pages of unimaginative fiction, others, like Chappell, have followed in Sterne's footsteps by creating clever, playful fiction that teems with the creative chaos of life. For surely the novels in the Kirkman quartet are like the story of life: rich, complex, unpredictable, painful, rapturous, enlightening. Much in the way that stream-of-consciousness writers attempt to capture presynthesized, unedited thought processes, or cubist painters attempt to capture unrefined visual perceptions, in the Kirkman quartet Chappell crafts a narrative that, unlike the artificial construct of realism, more truly approximates the stories that make up our lives. After all, the story of life is a series of narratives—like Zeno's—that intermingle, overlap, are discontinuous, repeatedly and unexpectedly start and stop, do not often consider their audiences, and do not always answer questions. And if life is full of questions we can't answer, Chappell seems to ask, why should narrative be any different? Moreover, at times the novels even reflect accurately the way readers so often engage with narrative, as we repeatedly interrupt or enrich the story of our lives by picking up a book, entering that story, suspending that story, and resuming our own without reaching the ending, whether or not it eventually provides resolution. Ultimately, in novels that are variously nonlinear, riddled with the unexplainable, and prone to relish questions rather than to worship answers, Chappell's deft metanarrative highlights the multiplicitous nature of story itself and awakens us to the complex narrative web that both life and fiction perpetually weave with, through, and around us.

That puts me in mind of the time I wrote a paper on metanarrative in *I Am One of You Forever* and presented it at the Southern Writers' Symposium at Methodist College. Later I sent the paper to Fred at his request, and we exchanged letters on the topic and eventually discussed it over lunch when he visited my class at Elon College. Later still, Patrick Bizzaro asked if I might expand the paper for his forthcoming book of essays on Chappell's fiction. Though I gladly accepted, my work was initially delayed by the birth of my first child, Spencer. And then when I finally set aside some time to finish the project, a tulip poplar and a cherry tree crashed into my bedroom during a violent thunderstorm in Greensboro.

Anyhow.

NOTES

1. Milan Kundera, *The Book of Laughter and Forgetting* (New York: Penguin Books, 1981), 237. The quotes that precede my analysis of each novel all appear on page 237.

2. Ann Charters, ed., *The Story and Its Writer* (New York: Bedford Books, 1995), 1458. Herman Melville used these terms in his essay on Nathaniel Hawthorne's *Mosses from an Old Manse*. Melville's original essay, excerpts of which are reprinted by Charters, appeared in August 1850 in the New York periodical *Literary World*.

3. Fred Chappell, *I Am One of You Forever* (Baton Rouge: Louisiana State University Press, 1985).

4. Charters, ed., *The Story and Its Writer*, 1525.

5. Fred Chappell, *Brighten the Corner Where You Are* (New York: St. Martin's Press, 1989).

6. Chappell was writing to share his comments after having read a conference paper on metanarrative in *I Am One of You Forever*, which I had presented at the Southern Writers' Symposium and mailed to him afterward at his request.

7. Fred Chappell, *Farewell, I'm Bound to Leave You* (New York: Picador, 1996).

8. Stephen Whicher, ed., *Selections from Ralph Waldo Emerson* (Boston: Houghton Mifflin, 1957), 24.

9. Fred Chappell, *Look Back All the Green Valley* (New York: Picador, 1999).

10. Initially published separately, Chappell's four collections of poetry, *River, Bloodfire, Wind Mountain,* and *Earthsleep,* were later published in one volume, *Midquest* (Baton Rouge: Louisiana State University Press, 1981). The four volumes are structurally and thematically aligned with the four novels of the Kirkman quartet.

11. Laurence Sterne, *The Life and Opinions of Tristram Shandy* (London: Penguin Books, 1985).

12. Ibid., 602.

SEVEN

The Search for Moral Order in *Moments of Light*

REBECCA SMITH

IN A 1970 response to a letter disparaging his novel *The Inkling* for its vulgarity, Fred Chappell retorts that astute readers might in fact see *The Inkling* as a religious book and defends himself as "a modern moralist."[1] This label describes well the author of the eleven narratives that make up his first short-story collection *Moments of Light* (1980), which present a chronological history of human moral development, from the beginning to modern times. We find within this collection human beings at their moral best and at their moral worst; in between, we find those struggling to bridge the gap between their dream of moral order and the chaos of the fallen world. Throughout the stories, music recurs as an emblem of characters' search for the music of the spheres, or a universal moral harmony, as they ply their art to impose an order on the disordered world.

The first story, "Three Boxes," presents a parable of humans' introduction to choice, the basic component of moral consciousness. That the three men are naked and of "indeterminate color" suggests they live prior to racial prejudice, a detail rendering the moral failure of the volume's final story all the more poignant. Without the trappings of materialism or competition, these men represent pure intellectual and moral innocence. Having no complicating sense of past or future, they find complete satisfaction in their journey of unknown destination. But the end of their innocent enjoyment of nature's music in the wind, bird song, and rippling water is foreshadowed by a leaf twirling in the clear river, portending the moral complexity that will soon face them and the characters in the following stories.

When the three men discover three boxes on the far side of the river, they enter a world of covetousness and moral detachment suggested by the objective, detached narrative style. The first man to swim the river, seeking the material goods hidden in the boxes, muddies the water, leaving a "yellow stain" representing both the origin of different races and a disrupting of the natural universal harmony that humans struggle to reestablish in the rest of the book. The first swimmer remains white, and as soon as he owns the wealth he finds in the box, he is unable to see his brothers on the far shore and so turns his back on them. His figure becomes grotesquely distorted by the burden of the material world; his eyesight is impaired. Immediately, the two remaining men covet the first man's possessions and risk their own safety to explore the other boxes. The second swimmer takes on the water's yellow stain, to represent the oriental race, and leaves the water behind him (which will stain the skin of the last swimmer) black. The material wealth of each box diminishes; the second swimmer finds not gold but paper money, implements of work, civil order, diplomacy, and a tranquility of spirit that obscures his face, suggesting that utter serenity blinds us to our fellow human beings' needs. Again, a diminution of the man's stature symbolizes the burden of material gain. And Chappell's allegory of the distribution of wealth becomes even more poignant as the final man receives his color and embraces the material world.

When the first two swimmers are unable to see the third remaining on the shore, the air around him becomes cold, and darkness threatens. The third man's swim in the black water is "a kind of death." His skin becomes black, and he has "no choice" but to open the last box, which emanates "no light" and reveals to him only "misery"—chains, scars, hatred, diseases, pests, but also patience to endure the suffering of slavery and oppression. The now-black man, seeing the disparity among the three boxes, asks God humanity's ultimate theological question: why is there no justice in the world? If God is omnipotent, can't He make the world fair? God's answer opens the way for the actions of all the following stories: humans, He says, must create justice. Justice can be fashioned only out of injustice, and not in the abstract but only from real, physical suffering. Then, lightening the black man's palms and soles, God explains: "It is for you to remember that when you are oppressed and beaten down by men of other color, that it is themselves also they crush into the earth. . . . For I tell you now forever, that until oppression of you shall quit not one step toward victory shall have been taken by a single person."[2] What better statement could Chappell—or any writer—create as a guide to moral responsibility?

Significantly, only the man carrying the box of suffering and injustice away from the river's shore finds music, the gourds and bones of early African music, and only he walks tall and erect under his load. He has a mission, a purpose that will take him outside himself, and he is thrilled to have the gift of justice to take to his comrades. Only he feels a "warm candle-flame," a moment of divinely revealed light that leads him to understand the morally ambiguous truth that injustice must exist to lead the way to justice, that the gift of justice is "the one thing in the whole world worth knowing that can be learned in the world, and is not divinely revealed" (14). In the following stories, the characters who confront some of mankind's most frustrating dilemmas thus become Chappell's experiments in human strength. Can they create justice from the suffering of their fellow man? Will they allow the music of the spheres to play a harmony all people can enjoy?

The hope of moral engagement and harmonious existence falls quickly into despair in the second story, "Judas." This first-person account of Judas's betrayal of Christ recounts humanity's choosing material gain and a secular moral order over a transcendent order that yet, Christ implies, must be grounded in the physical world because it must guide the physical world. The excitement that the black man of "The Three Boxes" feels when challenged to spread the gift of justice is lost to Judas's petty obsession with Christ's difference from his own moral system. By associating with whores, thieves, lepers, and others whom Judas deems "useless refuse" (16), Christ overturns the secular order that Judas values, and Christ's holier-than-thou certainty of a transcendent order incenses Judas because that order is incomprehensible to him. Judas represses his intuitive sense that Christ is right and shies away from Christ because of this main objection: "he engendered an insupportable feeling of responsibility" (17). We leave the betrayer in a state of dissatisfied guilt and darkness, uneasy in his awareness that he has failed in his moral obligation. Judas botches mankind's gift of choice, of responsibility for justice. His secularly formed prejudices preclude his thinking outside their boundaries, and his reasoning with the rules of a secular order leaves him emotionally and morally bankrupt. But without Judas's treachery Christ would not have been crucified and hence not resurrected, so we must recognize that this story, despite its darkness, signifies the oppositions—and their potential reconciliation—that form the core of this book.[3]

The third story jumps to the eighteenth century, the first of three consecutive stories set during the Age of Reason. The first, "Mrs. Franklin Ascends," takes place in the new Eden, the United States, in 1762, upon Benjamin Franklin's return from a trip to London, and so presents the possibility that the New World will give rise to a new Adam and a perfect moral order. Deborah Franklin has deliberately overspent during her husband's absence, creating disorder in their financial accounts so that her husband can set them straight—exemplifying again the book's emphasis on people's search for order. This story presents no weighty moral dilemma such as Judas's betrayal of Christ: the main moral failure here seems to be Benjamin's failure to recognize his wife's exasperation with his scientific investigations. But Ben Franklin is pursuing a transcendent kind of order, the music of the spheres, and this story is the first to focus on man-made music as a path to universal harmony. Benjamin arises during his first night home to play the armonica, his new musical invention, creating tones from the rubbing of glasses. Deborah hears the tones in a kind of half-dream and ascends to the attic to find Ben; she believes that they have died together and gone to heaven. He is, she thinks, "unleashing the music of the spheres" (28). This story leaves us with hope for a harmonious universal moral order.

But the order of the first eighteenth-century tale turns quickly to chaos in the succeeding story, "Thatch Retaliates," when the New World fails to live up to its Edenic potential. Toby Milliver, newly arrived from England, believes most ardently in this New World myth: "He saw the colonies as a fresh beginning, a place where the old mistakes did not have to be repeated . . . *Reason* was . . . to be the guildmark of America, for every man is first guided by self-interest and can only injure his affairs with unreason. Therefore, injustice and prejudicial opinion and baseless cruelty could never importantly take root here, for each man's personal welfare was posed against them." Milliver's faith in humanity's moral development is corrected by his friend Prescott's perception that "the Old Adam [is] still heartily at work in every man and that a new-found landscape [can] hardly be a panacea for all the ills of human character" (34). The reference to Mr. Tidrow's owning slaves in Williamsburg suggests such a flaw, and the remainder of the story quickly verifies that Milliver's idealism is only that. For the title character of this tale is none other than Blackbeard the Pirate (Edward Teach, whom Chappell fictionalizes as Edward Thatch), "one of the arrantest villains that God has ever made to creep upon the earth" (39). The drunken Blackbeard kills Toby Milliver, supposedly mistaking him for another man. Man at his moral worst senselessly destroys man at his moral best.

"Thatch Retaliates" recalls "Judas" in that the secular order Judas embraces is shown to be absolutely corrupt in the Bath, North Carolina, society: Governor Eden (note the irony of the name) is in league with Blackbeard, leaving the community no hope of ridding itself of evil. Amazingly, Milliver, the most optimistic character in the entire collection, never loses his faith in the human spirit, nor is he the story's only good character: James MacCollum and William Jameson befriend Milliver and Prescott; bystanders do the right thing by taking the injured Milliver and Prescott into their home for aid; and Prescott, himself in pain from being pistol-whipped by the demonic Blackbeard, pulls himself to the dying Milliver's side, crying, "He is my responsibility in this place. I cannot have it on my conscience that I did not go to him" (47). Thus while Prescott epitomizes the ideal of moral accountability that Chappell's collection of stories explores, he cannot save Milliver or the town from the dark forces of evil. This story ends with "a little more of the relentless American nighttime" (48) entering the room when Milliver's foot topples a candle during his final death jerk, extinguishing the moment of light that seems to have shone in Milliver and the other generous-of-spirit characters.

This darkness comes between two stories offering clear hope for a harmonious world. Chappell seems to have arranged the stories in this collection to create a rhythmic cycle of hope and despair rather than a perfectly chronological series. "Thatch Retaliates" takes place in 1718, prior to the previous story's time of 1782. After "Judas," "Mrs. Franklin Ascends" offers the hope of a better world; "Thatch Retaliates" then shows a descent into moral depravity. True to the movement of the collection, the next story answers with an ascent of enlightenment.

"Moments of Light" moves from America to England, centering on the 1792 convergence of art and science in the meeting of composer Franz Joseph Haydn and astronomer William Herschel, both German immigrants to England. Having discovered the planet Uranus eleven years earlier, Herschel is presently working on his "grand treatise on the construction of the heavens" (51), a scientific metaphor for the music of the spheres that Annie Dillard notes in the foreword as the central notion of Chappell's collection. Since late-eighteenth-century thought no longer considers the artist and the scientist antipodal but rather sees "the advancement of learning and the refinement of the senses" as complements (50), Haydn and Herschel are expected to meet. Haydn, on whom the story focuses through its limited omniscient point of view, dreads and delays the rendezvous, for he finds the new celestial discoveries disturbing. They present a rift in the world order that he knows. The disorder he observes in his earthly surroundings likewise unnerves him: he is bothered by discovering "butchers with more gracious manners than counts . . . and carters who had a broader knowledge of the world than princes" (51). As any artist, Haydn seeks in his music the order he finds missing in his environment, and through this fellow artist Fred Chappell presents his most overt statement on the power of art to soothe humanity's troubled existence in a world that seems at best morally neutral, resistant to our attempts to understand and perfect its flaws.

Haydn is pleasantly surprised to find that the scientist Herschel appreciates and understands the arts' contributions to humanity's knowledge: "We must never forget how much our present state of scientific knowledge is indebted to the writings of the ancient poets," Herschel asserts (54). Amazingly, this world-renowned scientist does not discredit the notion of the music of the spheres, either, and Haydn in turn recognizes the astronomer's admirable pursuit of "new moments of light" in the heavens (56). The musician soon experiences his own moment of light when he learns from Herschel that astronomy is not the glorious, inspired calling he assumes, but a profession of tedious, hard work and physical discomfort. This new enlightenment prepares Haydn for the truly transcendent experience he enjoys when looking through the scientist's telescope.

What follows represents a veritable marriage of art and science. This story in fact encapsulates the moral dilemma that has characterized the twentieth century in such controversies as evolution versus creationism, and science versus the arts. Haydn is physically transported by the sight of the stars to an alien city where he hears, literally, the music of the spheres emanating from a fountain as well as from a dragonfly music box floating in the void of space. Haydn learns, in his out-of-body experience soaring through the interstellar spaces of the heavens, that "if music and poetry are not mindless, but instead the appreciable workings of personality, then this drama of light [is] intelligently assertive in the same way" (63). His epiphany creates in him a "flight of genius" that soon leads to his oratorio *The Creation,* whose musical description of chaos transfixes his audience, and to his accepting Beethoven as a music pupil. The absolutely positive ending of this title story, with Haydn pointing his baton toward heaven at the end of a performance of his oratorio and giving credit to a greater spirit for his music, "Not from me. . . . From thence comes everything" (70), seems to reinstate an Edenic purity and hope for a universal moral order. From the music of the spheres comes the glorious music of Haydn and Beethoven, a bit of heaven come down to earth. Haydn's epiphany represents the demise of humans' intellectual innocence and the birth of a new hope, hope in a beauty that man admittedly cannot fully discern. Only art can articulate this mystery, as humanity uses and reflects the music of the spheres in its own musical creations.

The next story, which introduces modern-day (mid-twentieth-century) narratives, presents another kind of artist figure, the writer Mark Vance, and introduces the focus on individual fragmented personalities that seems to characterize the second half of *Moments of Light.* This story ends the same way that it begins, with Mark tossing and turning on his bed, trying to write a long, philosophical poem on human suffering, trying to order with words the disorder he observes about him. The story chronicles Mark's two-day journey of encounters with misery and his attempts to soothe humanity's wounds of despair. The suffering he sees when he ventures from his room explains the story's title, "The Thousand Ways," for through its examples, the story suggests that human beings misuse their own and others' lives in a thousand different ways.

Although the story centers on the failing of human moral action, it also presents two of the book's most earnest characters, Mark Vance and George Palinopolous, a Greek immigrant working hard at a grubby local grill. George forfeits his daughter's chance to attend a good college when he makes a moral decision—to help his brother-in-law out of drug-related trouble. George feels an essential debt to humanity for his success in America, a debt that he repays by customarily giving Mark his supper free of charge. George's moral responsibility is paralleled by the actions and sensibility of the main character. When he chances upon a young boy sent out by his mother to wander the streets while she has a sexual encounter, Mark gives the boy, Joe Starret, all the money in his pocket. Mark also wants to save his girlfriend Norma Lang from her self-imposed turmoil. Living in squalor, neglecting her personal hygiene, and drinking excessively, Norma chastises Mark for his moral rectitude, the prudishness that causes his outrage at Joe's mother's negligence and her alcoholism, part of her unhealthy lifestyle that apparently has led to a serious, incurable sickness. Mark's final confrontation of the day solidifies his sense of the world's need. Back at his hotel, he befriends a teenaged girl who shoulders responsibility for her stumbling father, whose drunkenness she denies. He is aghast when this fourteen- or fifteen-year-old, attracted by his kindness, kisses him quite sensuously. Sexual innocence is lost to both this girl, Edwina Tumperling, and Joe Starret, the children whose names he records when he returns to his philosophical poem at the story's end. Mark Vance seeks to order through his art the chaos he has witnessed, but despair overwhelms him. His ending call of "help" portrays him as an artist lost because he discerns too keenly others' suffering and lack of moral accountability. This story's continual juxtaposition of light and dark imagery intensifies its message that the light of moral decency lingers always just beyond the fringes of our failures.

The very short first-person narrative that follows shows us, possibly, a young Mark Vance, a boy just facing the fact that we cannot escape our accountability to other human beings. "January" is the genesis for chapter 1 of Chappell's novel *It Is Time, Lord*, which is set in the 1940s, so the 1962 setting of "The Thousand Ways" strengthens the argument that the young narrator of "January" is indeed a childhood version of Mark Vance. "January" is in many ways a cold story, its style providing little narrative reflection to give the reader a sense of the teller's emotions. Rather, the objective, childlike language (simple words, short paragraphs) creates an innocent narrative voice recalling a simple scene: a boy's inadequately clad young sister follows him to a cold barn, where unnamed men worry that the child will freeze to death; the father appears suddenly and carries the girl back home with the boy following; the waiting mother wonders what the children were doing out in the cold. The boy's denial of responsibility for the three-year-old innocent, "I told her not to come with me," rings hollow when he offers it to the strange men in the barn. He doesn't even bother to repeat his excuse to his reprimanding father. "January" presents in little more than two pages a boy's moral coming of age, his learning about the ambiguity at the heart of human relationships. He did tell his sister not to follow him, but he knows he is still responsible, and he realizes that telling his father the truth, ironically, will not absolve his culpability. As the lonely boy looks heavenward, a spot emerges to obscure his view of the moon, a symbol of enlightenment and humanity's spiritual life. This young boy's moment of light has darkened his world, for he has moved, unwillingly, from the innocence of childhood into the adult world of accountability, a world that weighs heavily on the adult Mark Vance in the previous story.

The next story reiterates the loss of innocence presented in "January," this time through a sexual coming of age. "The Weather," unlike the other stories in *Moments of Light,* is published only in this collection, and Chappell explains that he wrote it as a link between stories.[4] "The Weather" is the most sensual of all the narratives. Full of color (golden skin, licorice-black hair, streams of sunlight), misting rain, the smell of alfalfa, kisses redolent of bittersweet chocolate, "The Weather" recreates both the emotional and the physical intensity of an adolescent boy's first sexual encounter. The child of "January" has become an adolescent; in the barn of the previous story, he loses his sexual innocence at the hands of an older but still puerile Rosemary McKay, daughter of a local drunkard. Like "January," this story is told as a memory, but in "The Weather," the adult narrator speaks overtly to an unnamed but specific listener, a current lover. His openly nostalgic, now-experienced voice speaks philosophically at the end of the story to this lover and the reader, creating a bridge between the physical enjoyment he remembers and its spiritual parallels that form the basis of this collection's theme of moral responsibility:

> So that is what I meant when you suggested we make love and I replied, "No, you make love and I'll just lie here." For a moment it seemed to me that by imitating lassitude I might recapture the lassitude of innocence . . .

But it doesn't work that way, does it? Innocence is not recaptured in an awkward dance of the body simple. Let us do then whatever we please; we shall always remember and always forget.

Like the rest of the stricken world. (110)

This reminder of time's passage recalls the collection's movement through centuries of human moral development and reminds us that moral passivity will not suffice. When we forget our accountability, we become one with the ill-fated world.

"The Weather" leads to the fine story "Broken Blossoms," the last of four narratives that might be seen as a "portrait of the artist as a young man" series, culminating, in reverse order, with the artistic anxiety of Mark Vance in "The Thousand Ways." "Broken Blossoms" makes clear that the dreaming boy must wake up to the practical world where people are accountable, as Annie Dillard explains in her introduction to the collection, not only for what they do know but also for what they do not. As the first-person speaker describes his boyhood fascination with stamp-collecting as part of his awakening to a world outside himself, we realize that the voice here is a learned, retrospective voice, that of a poet looking back at his coming of age. It is reminiscent of "Moments of Light," for art and science converge when the young boy forsakes chemistry experiments and cryptography in favor of writing romantic nature poetry. He sets his poems on a fantasy planet inhabited by butterfly-like creatures "whose method of communication was a music composed of tones beyond the range of human hearing" (122), similar to the heavenly harmonies Haydn hears when transported through Herschel's telescope in the earlier story. The adolescent's poetry ensues from an imagination that dominates his mind, rendering him practically useless as a farm boy. Finally, he recognizes the danger of living totally in a world of self-centered dreaminess, a state of existence rendered as moral indifference on the part of adults in other stories in this collection.

The boy's first epiphany turns out to be a misleading one, but his final awakening brings him fully into adulthood. Looking for exotic stamps, he explores without permission keepsakes that his parents have stored in an old trunk, which he opens with a claw hammer. Realizing for the first time that his parents were people with interests and dreams of their own before his birth, he vows to become a better son and convinces himself that his destiny lies not in stamp-collecting but in diving even more deeply into his fanciful introspection. His practical father, ever frustrated with the son's inadequacies, ironically orchestrates the young poet's awakening to the world of moral responsibility. He sends him on a walk with the farmhand Harmon Cody, who illustrates symbolically to the boy the entire meaning of existence by blowing to smithereens a box of blasting caps the boy luckily did not disturb as he rambled through the forbidden trunk. "You see, honey, you're going to have to take better care. Happened you hit one of those caps a lick up in your attic, you'd been blowed to pieces. Blowed half the roof off" (132). The boy's poetic sensibility has already led him to recognize the fragile juxtaposition of life and death as he contemplates the apple tree into which Mr. Cody places the caps, a tree stunted by a lightning strike so that its missing half, seared with a firescar, offsets a side yet blooming with pinkish-white, bee-laden flowers. Mr. Cody's shot obliterates another portion of the tree in an eye-opening act of violence reminiscent of the violence it takes to open Flannery O'Connor's characters' eyes to their own shortcomings. Remembering this scene, the adult narrator describes his epiphany as a physical undressing, allowing the world "so long closed away" to rush in upon him and change him forever: "And in this same moment that someone who is myself is born again, someone who is myself also dies. From this instant I can date my awkward tumble into the world." Like most of us, he regrets his fall into the world of knowledge, wishing that he could have spent his life in a warm dream of innocence, never hurting anyone, so that he could say at the Judgment Day, "'*I slept and never woke. . . . I am so innocent I might never have existed*'" (133).

This wish encapsulates the definitive statement on moral accountability that Chappell makes in this collection of stories. To live as human beings, we must act—not only on our own behalf but on others' as well. We cannot remain indifferent to the consequences of our actions, a fact that haunts Mark Vance in "The Thousand Ways" because he cannot make everyone see that basic tenet of human existence. The last two stories in *Moments of Light* continue Chappell's critique of the failings of human responsibility.

"Children of Strikers" is a dark story whose sensuous imagery enhances its picture of human suffering in a world gone awry. Two children, a girl and a boy, find by the edge of a stinking, black chemical river—no doubt inspired by the paper mills of Chappell's Canton, North Carolina—a severed baby doll's foot—a perfect symbolic blend of innocence and sordid experience. The boy argues that the smooth edge of the stub indicates that an adult, not a child, must have cut the doll's foot as practice "before he went and kilt a real baby." Such an assumption strikes the reader as amusing, until the omniscient narrator's descriptions of the "strained" faces of unshaven men and crying women, of strangers "saying hard wild sentences" and "banging tabletops" in rooms of "unguessable violence" suggest the real possibility of domestic disorder in the milltown shanties (137). The toy foot, representing a fallen innocent, makes the children who find it face unaware the pain caused by moral irresponsibility.

The final story of Chappell's distinguished collection returns overtly to the motifs of journeys, music, and race introduced in the opening narrative, "The Three Boxes." The racial discrimination suggested when the dark-skinned man of the first story is left with chains, scars, cotton sack, mule harness, and endurance has come to ironic fruition in "Blue Dive." In the ending selection, a black bluesman just out of prison travels on a Greyhound bus in the 1960s or '70s to find a nightclub, The Blue Dive, where the owner once promised him a job. Stovebolt Johnson is on a journey of moral redemption, trying to make a living after serving time for his moral failings. The story begins on a hopeful note, with Stovebolt gazing frequently at the horizon and in fact being welcomed at his first stop, the house of a kind-hearted couple who enjoy his guitar playing and give him food. B. J. and Darlene represent the best of human moral potential, but their goodness is overshadowed by the selfish materialism of The Blue Dive's new owner, Locklear Hawkins. Mr. Hawkins, who is, like the other characters, African American, will not risk hiring an ex-convict even though his patrons clearly love Stovebolt's live music. "In my plans there is no room for any Rastuses or any Sambos," he explains. "And there's no room for anybody named Stovebolt" (165). The denigrating racial stereotype intensifies Hawkins's rejection of his fellow human being, for he colludes in the stereotyping of his own race. Through Hawkins's complicity, Chappell implicates us all as conspirers in the world's evil.

Annie Dillard suggests in her foreword to *Moments of Light* that Hawkins's rejection of Stovebolt parallels Judas's betrayal of Christ, a reading reinforced by the "one clear yellow star" lighting the sky as Stovebolt leaves The Blue Dive. Like the story "Judas," "The Blue Dive" shows us what happens when justice is left in mankind's hands, as God explains in "The Three Boxes" that it must be. We see in the end allegiance to self out-weighing responsibility to others, as in the opening story when the first two men become literally blind to their fellow travelers upon opening their own box of material goods. But the conclusion of this final story also provides a ray of hope for humanity's continuing moral development: when the tip of a wild cherry tree blowing in the wind brushes through the light of that one yellow star, Stovebolt is confident that it is "never going to brush that light away" (166). The universal transcendent order will not abandon us despite our moral failings. Stovebolt continues on his way, as we all must, with his music grounding him in the world's often unfathomable beauty.

In an essay titled "A Pact with Faustus," published in a special Chappell issue of *Mississippi Quarterly* cited earlier, Fred Chappell speaks of his early fascination with the magic of music, his passion for the drama of its har-monies. His comments elucidate his choice of music as the art that is suc-cessful, in *Moments of Light*, at helping humans to satisfy their longing for order. I want to cite once more Annie Dillard's discerning introduction to Chappell's first story collection, as she offers her interpretation of the role of art in human survival as well as in these stories: "[Man] casts his spiritual longing [for order] into the very teeth of the matter—and comes up with art. . . . art, the heavenly harmonies translated into the soul's own lowdown blues."[5] Fred Chappell's art, with its well-crafted symmetries and delights, forms his action against the disharmony he sees in the world about him. In *Moments of Light*, his moral and artistic imperative is this: our actions and our art make a difference in this imperfect material world.

NOTES

1. Alex Albright, "Friend of Reason: Surveying the Fred Chappell Papers at Duke Univer-sity," in *Dream Garden: The Poetic Vision of Fred Chappell*, ed. Patrick Bizzaro (Baton Rouge: Louisiana State University Press, 1997), 226.

2. Fred Chappell, *Moments of Light* (Los Angeles: New South, 1980), 9–13. References to the text are in parentheses.

3. Dabney Stuart, "'Blue Pee': Fred Chappell's Mythical Kingdom," *Iron Mountain Review* 2 (spring 1985): 13–21, discusses these stories' concern with the harmonizing of polarities.

4. James Everett Kibler Jr., "A Fred Chappell Bibliography, 1963–1983," *Mississippi Quarterly* 37 (winter 1983–84): 79.

5. Annie Dillard, foreword to *Moments of Light*, by Fred Chappell (Los Angeles: New South, 1980), vii.

EIGHT

Myth and Mundane in *More Shapes Than One*

TRACI LAZENBY

The mythic world is only important because of the physical world, and the physical world is only important because of the mythic world. Here, at least, you get to experience the heroic myth of the mystic experience, because death is real here.
— WIM COLEMAN AND PAT PERRIN, *The Jamais Vu Papers*

WE MAY THINK of human experience as being divided into two realms: the mythic and the physical. Certainly Fred Chappell's works depict two such realms, separated by an "infinite black ditch," across which inspiration flows primarily in only one direction (*Midquest* 8). But the interaction between the two worlds is not necessarily from the sensory to the mythical; inspiration and meaning continue to inform the physical world, regardless of whether we take note of them. However, as the stories in *More Shapes Than One* show, life loses some aspect of its meaning when this inspiration is neglected. In fact, the Truths, which can take many different shapes, and which *More Shapes Than One* contemplate in detail, are these: What is the cost of a life without attention to either realm of experience? Indeed, is it even possible to live such a life? How does one live a life that integrates both? The answers to these questions take many shapes in this collection of stories, but they might be distilled to two precepts. The first is that we transcend the physical world not by denial of the sensory or by entering an emotional or spiritual vacuum but by building relationships with the people and world around us. The second is that we participate in the mythic, one might even say in the divine, by carrying inspiration through to creation.

In the first two stories of the collection, "Linnaeus Forgets" and "Ladies from Lapland," the main characters are themselves alien observers of microcosms, upon which each of them has more or less effect. Linnaeus finds himself in the role of supernatural observer in relation to the world within the mysterious plant sent to him by Gerhaert Oorts, "in which the mundane and the fanciful commingled in matter-of-fact fashion but at a feverish rate of speed" (13). He has assumed the perspective of a deity, uninvolved in the activities taking place on the plant but unable to resist the temptation to watch them. He finds that "There was too much movement; the distraction was too violent" (12). While he does not take any of the actions of which he is capable—burning the plant, for instance—and does take the action that allows the life on the plant to rejuvenate after its journey to him—watering and caring for the plant—he remains outside of its residents' awareness. With the addition of only one letter, plant becomes planet, and the transformation in Linnaeus's perspective becomes even clearer.

To the residents of Lapland, Maupertuis is similarly alien and has the potential to be as uninvolved an observer as Linnaeus. The reactions of the women of the country to him are, from the beginning, as they might be to the missionary he imagines himself to be. Maupertuis is charmed by them, as Linnaeus is charmed by life on the plant, but Maupertuis is an alien who is *observed* by the inhabitants of the world that he watches. While Linnaeus is like a god unknown, Maupertuis is like a god who is intimately involved and charmed by his power only because it marvels at him. In his first meeting with the women of Lapland, they "reached out to touch him, tugging like curious children at his hands and waistcoat and breeches," and it is this attention that draws Maupertuis to them (21). Following their cunnilingual session, the first of the two Lapland sisters looks at him "with an expression of submissive adoration" (25). Their reaction to his departure is equally telling, as is his decision to take some of the women with him. While life on Linnaeus's plant is "self-determining" and remains so as the botanist watches, Maupertuis decides that the women who will accompany him back to Paris will be those whom *he* chooses, and there will be "no violence, no lamenting, no unseemly display; they were to abide compliantly by his decision" (12, 27). Unfortunately for the women, Maupertuis proves to be a false god who spends only half an hour in contemplation before deciding to abandon his worshipers when they reach their destination (29).

Each of the men has an opportunity to partake of a point of view outside of the ordinary, and each has a store of knowledge that is larger than or different from that of the people whom he observes. The differences in their reactions to these opportunities lie not merely in the morality of each character but in the degree of emotional involvement each allows himself with the natural world and with the people he encounters. Linnaeus considers the criticism he receives regarding his theories of the sexual properties of plants and concludes that "to describe his system of classification as immoral was to describe nature as immoral, and nature could not be immoral" (7). While his observations of plants retain scientific objectivity, they are not completely detached, as he imagines a plant whose sexual makeup is one in which "twenty males or more [are] in bed with the female" (8). Further, Linnaeus has genuine relationships with the people in his life, customarily spending two hours "gossiping, teasing and laughing" with his family over dinner, or spending an hour counseling a student who has personal problems (5, 4). Linnaeus is a man who was deeply involved in the emotional and physical content of his life before discovering the lives being led on his plant, and his involvement in his own life continues during the episode with the plant. On discovering the animals living on the plant, "tears streamed on the botanist's face," and he orients himself by checking his physical surroundings (11). After closer inspection, he is moved to "mingled fear and astonishment," and "he also felt an admiration" (12). His first reactions to the rejuvenated plant are physical, in the form of sensory confusion between smell and sound, and following the procession to Flora, Linnaeus loses consciousness, he is overcome (9, 16). While Linnaeus chooses not to affect the life on the plant, that life affects him profoundly and emotionally.

Maupertuis, on the other hand, begins his adventure without the connection to genuine physicality that Linnaeus enjoys. His relationships, such as the one with Mme. Du Chatelet, lack emotional substance or truthfulness (20). While Linnaeus has been, to a degree, prepared for his encounter by his love for his wife, his children, his students, and his work, Maupertuis does not appear to have any emotional involvement with his student and lover or with anyone else. This pattern continues in his sexual encounters with the women in Lapland, in which the physical atmosphere he creates not only lacks emotional sincerity but is physically false, including a chandelier made of reindeer antlers, gauzy curtains, and rouge on his cheeks (22). The other potential love in his life, his work, is abandoned to his crew as soon as they arrive in Lapland, and his dedication to his purpose seems as ephemeral as his dedication to his acquaintances in Paris or to the ladies of Lapland (27). The falseness of society in Paris allows Maupertuis to remain emotionally detached from every aspect of his life, before, during, and after his trip to Lapland.

Linnaeus's emotional and sensory involvement with his life results in a reaction to the supernatural that, despite his later inability to consciously remember the episode, affects him on the level that we would expect a brush with the supernatural to affect him—in dreams and in writing. His nightmares about Siegesbeck cease, and his writing becomes infected by metaphor—both products of the subconscious, where we react most strongly to the mythic and the supernatural (18). Maupertuis, on the other hand, is unaffected by his term as deity, perhaps because he has failed as a caretaker of the people whose lives he has taken into his hands. The sexuality that Linnaeus observes among plants as being carried on with an air of transcendence, "in high and winsome delight," is distorted by Maupertuis, degraded to a smudge of false color on the inside of a lady's thigh (18). His life continues to be as superficial as it was before his trip. Paris society's adulation of him, and its lack of concern for the women of Lapland whom he abandons, draws into focus the superficiality of that society as a whole, rather than excusing Maupertuis (30).

While Linnaeus and Maupertuis play roles that can be discussed as godlike in their widened perspective, the protagonist of the next story in the collection, "The Snow That Is Nothing in the Triangle," plays the part of a would-be Christ. While jailed by a political regime whose motives he cannot understand, Feuerbach has a vision that tells him that "If one man dies, the others shall be freed" (37). Like Linnaeus, Feuerbach experiences a confusion of the senses when this revelation occurs, and the visual image of snow falling becomes linked to the sounds of the turnkeys shuffling through the prison's corridors (36). Whether the flaming letters of the message come from a supernatural source or from Feuerbach's subconscious, they seem to him to be the sort of inspiration that "must have come in antique time to Plato, to Euclid, to Aristotle" (37). His vision of the flaming words proves to be true, as the prisoners are freed after the death of one man. Feuerbach's mistake is in "the further corollary, that he Karl Wilhelm Feuerbach must be the man to die" (37). Despite his two attempts at suicide, Feuerbach is not the sacrifice that the forces in power will accept. It is his friend Klaus Hornli whom the regime accepts as its sacrificial "one man" who dies, not by his own intent, but as a result of the conditions in the prison. Feuerbach's experience of the mythic pattern is genuine yet distorted; he receives the instructions, but he is not the one who must act on them.

Likewise the charges for which they have been imprisoned are impossible for Feuerbach to understand. As geometricians, anarchy would be impossible. The definition of anarchy offered by Feuerbach points out, "Anarchos, meaning without a ruler, there can be no construction without a ruler" (35). A ruler is one of the primary tools of Feuerbach's vocation, and he defines himself in large part through his vocation. He sees mathematics as receiving approval from nature, as Feuerbach points out to his students: "Here in the snowflake nature reaches out to us as if it were reassuringly, gentlemen, suggesting that the mind makes no mistake in intuiting intimations of a high and eternal order, an order that, though we can but guess at it, is as certain and apprehensible as the Pythagorean theorem" (36).

The order in the universe is as geometrically correct as the hexagram of the snowflake, "varying but unvarying" (36). Like Linnaeus in his views on the morality or immorality of nature, Feuerbach sees the necessity of unraveling the apparently random order of variations in nature, rather than dismissing it as anarchic. The regime inside the prison runs counter to this ordered disorder in its refusal of Feuerbach as victim and in its misunderstanding of the impossibility of an anarchic geometrician.

Feuerbach's tragedy is in being deeply involved in his life, emotionally and physically, while living under the control of powers that work against him and against nature as he perceives it. Like Linnaeus, Feuerbach sees nature as the proof of his scientific work, and, also like Linnaeus, he is genuinely involved in at least one emotional relationship, with Hornli. He is like the ladies of Lapland, though, in that the forces that act upon him, in the form of King Maximilian Joseph, are unintelligible because they act in ways counter to nature and deleterious to the people whose lives they govern. Like Linnaeus, he is affected by his encounter with the mythic, and his reaction is appropriately opposite that of the botanist. While Linnaeus gains artistically from his experience of the supernatural because it is consistent with the nature he observes, Feuerbach has found the supernatural to be senseless because it contradicts his observations of nature. Linnaeus is relieved of his sleeplessness and nightmares; Feuerbach's life becomes an unending nightmare of incoherence. He is left without the faith and beauty of his work, so that nothingness begins to preoccupy him, until he changes from the Pope of the Theorems to merely Feuerbach, the nihilist. The two characters begin with vital similarities and have predictably opposite results from their encounters with true and untrue governing forces.

Feuerbach, in his rush to make the sacrifice his vision demands, fails to realize the truth expressed so succinctly in the final line of Milton's Sonnet XIX: "They also serve who only stand and wait." This poem plays an important part in "The Adder," in which John Milton's work, and this sonnet in particular, is attacked by the satanic forces of *Al Azif,* a book that "first . . . poisons, then . . . devours" other books (102). While Feuerbach fails in his overwillingness to act for the common good, *Al Azif,* or *The Necronomicon,* actively works against the common good by polluting and then consuming *Paradise Lost,* with its message of the *felix culpa,* and Sonnet XIX, with its equally comforting message about mankind's relationship to the divine.

The creative impulse, like dreams or other messages from the subconscious, seems to come to us from outside ourselves; certainly Milton thinks of his "one talent" as having been given to him by God. Sonnet XIX begins with his lament that he has been unable to enlarge upon this gift from his Maker, like the servants in the parable. Creation is one of the ways in which we participate in the divine, and its destruction of creations makes *The Necronomicon* evil. We are cued to its satanic force by its attack on Milton's work, and, more strongly, by the emotions that reading it prompts in Robert, the story's protagonist. "I began to think how I secretly longed to possess this volume for myself, how indeed I had burned to possess it for a long time, and how my ridiculous rabbit-faced Uncle Alvin was the only obstacle in my way" (118). The battle fought inside the safe at the bookstore is nothing less, then, than the powers of creation against those of annihilation.

The turn in Robert's thinking follows the pattern in the stories already discussed here. At the beginning of the story, Robert is fully involved in his emotional relationship with his Uncle Alvin. He looks forward to their lasagna lunch and enjoys their involvement in the same profession, as dealers in rare and used books (98). When he reads *The Necronomicon*, however, his feelings toward his uncle reverse. Wholly engrossed by the book and by possessing it, he becomes detached from his uncle and from everything else in his physical world. While Linnaeus comes to value the creative urge following his encounter with the supernatural, and Feuerbach moves away from involvement with the creative and physical worlds following his brush with counterfeit supernatural goodness, Robert's state of mind becomes limited, monomaniacal, during his surrender to the nihilistic power of *The Necronomicon*. As Robert loses sight of the individual and the mundane in his lust for the mythic, if destructive, power of the book, his unassuming, rabbit-faced uncle rescues him from his surrender (118). Likewise, it is an unassuming housefly that carries the poison of *The Necronomicon* into the rest of the world, when Robert unthinkingly shoos it out the window after it consumes part of the bright ink in the book (120). The forces of annihilation remain in the world, the supernaturally destructive interacting with the mundane details of everyday life just as the supernaturally creative do.

The same destructive and Lovecraftian powers are considered in more depth in "Weird Tales," linked to this story in part by the remaining incorrect word, *weird*, in Robert and Uncle Alvin's last consultation of Milton's Sonnet XIX. The events in this story certainly are weird, progressing from Crane's good-natured drunkenness and Lovecraft's disapproval of Crane's drinking to catastrophic movements in time and space and encounters with supernaturally destructive powers. Like Feuerbach, Croydon attempts to force the mythic; but however well-intended, their attempts cannot be successful, because *wyrd* is a part of the mythic forces that act upon mankind but cannot be directly manipulated by mankind. Croydon rejects the mundane, the emotional, and the individual to pursue the mystic exclusively, and he becomes possessed by the dark knowledge he gains in the same way that Robert momentarily loses himself to *Al Azif.* Locked in his apartment, he becomes lost in the snow, literally consumed by the same Substantive Nothing that Feuerbach imagines and names (67).

The effects of Croydon's mysterious and supernatural disappearance on his friends also contain a sort of message from Chappell. Loveman, the single witness to Croydon's demise, "did not want to answer questions; he did not want anyone to know what he knew" (68). He goes to his room to "reaffirm his sanity," and he, along with the public that has been notified of Croydon's disappearance by the newspapers, seems largely to forget the entire event (68). While Linnaeus has the ability to "deeply forget" his encounter with the supernatural, Loveman and the public seem merely to put the event, despite its drama, from their minds, a sort of intentional ignorance of the presence of these forces.

Crane's and Lovecraft's reactions to the disappearance are opposite and have partially opposite results. Crane does not express his knowledge in any way but decides instead to face his preternatural predators on their own terms by going to Mexico, the land where they were worshiped. He has begun to live as if the forces of destruction hunt him, in "a state of haunted terror, wild and frightful, dependent on alcohol to keep his fear manageable" (69). Unfortunately, his attempt to confront Dzhaimbu is doomed, not only by Crane's drinking, but also by his humanity. His decision to go to Mexico echoes Croydon's experiment in that it moves the supernatural into the physical world as if the supernatural could be controlled or manipulated.

Lovecraft, rather than arranging a standoff with Dzhaimbu, adds a mythos to his creative works that represents Dzhaimbu, releasing him, through his art at least, from the mental torture that Crane endures (69). Perhaps Lovecraft has been better equipped to find this as a solution by his dreams "of vertiginous geometries and cyclopean half gods, vivid dreams that would have been anyone else's sweat-drenched nightmares" (59). Lovecraft has encountered the terrifying before and has exorcized it by writing. While Crane's reaction to his vicarious contact with the mythic is inappropriate, Lovecraft fights it as he does his dreams, in the only way that people can fight the forces of annihilation: by creating. Both men die, in the end, Crane by suicide and Lovecraft supposedly of colon cancer. Whether Lovecraft is actually only a subtler victim of Dzhaimbu is somewhat irrelevant, because the quality of his last years stands in contrast to Crane's. While Crane has been of little use to himself or to anyone because of his inability to fight the destructive forces he has met appropriately, Lovecraft has used those same forces creatively (69).

The power of Dzhaimbu is contrasted by the power of the Owners in "After Revelation," the last story in the collection. Like Dzhaimbu, the Owners appear to be elemental forces, although they are at the opposite end of the spectrum. While Dzhaimbu gives humankind a voice by "in-flict[ing] upon them unspeakable atrocities," the Owners are beings for whom "benevolence would be an accidental quality of [their] personali-t[ies]" (63, 190–1). Nonetheless, close interaction with them results in at least physical death, as Larilla's death shows. She spills out of her body, out of the physical and into the world of myth, as a result of her Owner's ministrations (195). Unlike Croydon and Crane, who are devoured by the destructive power they encounter, Larilla's death is caused by her expan-sion, by a continued becoming rather than by a ceasing to be.

George, the narrator of the story, survives Larilla, and while he does not understand the events taking place around him, he is fully involved in them. He and Larilla have been occupied by the mundane aspects of life, from his work as an outlaw scientist to his composition of a musical work for her to her humming while brushing her hair (186, 187, 190). Larilla's revelation has come to her in the way that transcendence often comes— "Maybe [her Owner] told her things. . . . Perhaps he made love to her" (196). While George's emotions for her have been genuine, and he mourns her death, the greatest effect of her death on him is that it prompts him to begin his own mythic quest. Like Larilla, though perhaps to a lesser degree, he has balanced an involvement in the mythic and the physical. He realizes, at story's end, that "it was no good sitting in a room and waiting for the answers to rise from within myself" but that he must begin a search for the knowledge that has caused Larilla's expansion (197).

Not all of the characters in this collection come to that realization be-fore it is too late. Mr. M in "Miss Prue" realizes only after he has died that his life could have been more meaningful. After twenty years of weekly conversations with Miss Prue, Mr. M commits suicide, perhaps having no-ticed that his life is without contact with the "other things" that I have been calling mythical or supernatural (151, 153). He and Miss Prue have had conversations apparently limited to trivial matters for twenty years, without any physicality and without belonging to the "world of animal flesh" (151). Though they have "*swilled* nuance," their relationship has been limited to nuance and delicacy rather than having been allowed to grow into one in which a true union could develop (153). Heartfelt communication and phys-ical sex have been ways in which characters in the other stories in *More Shapes Than One* connect with the elemental forces that move human existence, and Mr. M and Miss Prue have avoided these as possibilities. As a result, Mr. M finds himself unhappy, undead, and unnamed, after his death, as he has been emasculated, like Wisdom the cat, during his life (150). He and Miss Prue have managed to remain detached from one another in the most intimate of senses throughout their acquaintance by ignoring the parts of physical existence that form bridges to the mystic.

The possibilities available to the partners in a relationship are again examined in "Alma." The drover in the story, Dingo, lives with no one other than the women he drives like cattle, and yet he remains distant from them, divided by his view of them as livestock. The narrator of the story, on the other hand, "had me my own woman one time. I lived real close to her and that has made me think things apart" (169). Fretlaw's intimacy with his own woman, Alma, has changed his thoughts about women and prompts him to vow to release any women he finds in the future who are being used as livestock (185). This promise to himself comes as a result of his interaction with the mythical, which he finds in his relationship with Alma, whose name means either nourishment (Latin) or soul (Italian). For Fretlaw, Alma seems to mean both. Like George in "After Revelation," he has found some nourishment and some part of his soul in this woman with whom he has "lived real close," and she has changed his vision of his future.

The union that Fretlaw and Alma form not only allows them to prosper but prompts Alma to suggest that they "have us a youngun" (182). Fretlaw objects at first, hesitant to risk Alma or to be away from her, and perhaps also a little frightened at the creation in which she will take part. She explains to him that "the youngun is the woman's chore," and that she will go to a place where "they kill a man that tries to get too close" (182, 183). Childbearing is a contact with the mythic that women experience in a more profound way than do men, at least physically, and Fretlaw is excluded from it except for the "things we needed to do together" (183). He is not taken to the island in the middle of Weeping Lake but watches Alma be taken by the Guardian Women with all of the reminiscences of Avalon that an island full of women invokes (183).

Nonetheless, Fretlaw is affected by even this distanced contact with the mythic figures of the Guardian Women and by the supernatural event of childbearing. He has lived intimately with Alma, and he is "a little bit proud . . . as well as scared and sad" as he watches her leave. When she does not return from the island, he returns annually for eight years to their appointed meeting spot (184). He has not only recognized in this woman—whom he found being treated as if she were livestock—humanity like his own, but he has become proud of her, for her courage in continuing to the island despite her fear and his own. She has been the link for him to creativity in its most profound sense, the reproductive, and in its more day-to-day senses while they build their life together. He is able to partake of this contact with the mythical through her because of their emotional and physical togetherness, and the fact that he has lost her does not diminish the effect of their intimacy on him. Like George in "After Revelation," Fretlaw has lost the woman he loves, but even the loss has had a positive effect on his opinion and has inspired him to take constructive action.

The effect that romantic union can have on men, specifically on artistic men, is the subject of "Barcarole." Like Klaus Hornli and Karl Feuerbach, and like Linnaeus and Maupertuis, Rudolf Zimmer and Jacques Offenbach serve as a contrasting pair. Their contrast lies in the degree of soulful involvement each has in his life and in his work, as if each is a version of what the other could have been. Even their physical appearance is similar—at their first meeting, "it might be not two men but one man reflected as in a mirror"—despite the fact that Jacques is "extremely tall and thin" while Zimmer is "a short man" (44, 45). Both are musicians, although Jacques's works feature the cancan and Zimmer's lone creation is a soulful waltz. The differences in the two men's music come from their differing life experiences. In fact, the two offer—in Offenbach's view, at least—an example of the effects circumstances have on our lives: "If circumstances had been a little different in one place and opportunities had come a bit later in another, Rudolf now might be enjoying Jacques's place and Jacques Rudolf's" (49).

Jacques is a part of the Viennese culture of pleasure and appearance, in much the same way that Maupertuis is a part of that same cultural superficiality in Paris. We are assured that in most cases Jacques "would not be so careless of his clothing, for he held it an article of faith that his dress was almost as important to his career as his music" (44). As a child, he has enjoyed the same sort of reverential attention, without the sexual content, from his sisters that Maupertuis receives from the ladies of Lapland—his sisters "sit around [Jacques] in a worshipful circle as he practiced on his cello" (46). He has married a woman who is mentioned only in regard to her beauty and wealth, and nowhere in the story does Offenbach have an emotional reaction to her or any thoughts of her (49). He has lived a life without sorrow, as "even his most egregious effronteries [are] rewarded" (49). His spirit has been untested, in this sense, allowing him to become what Chappell refers to as "autoerotic bankers" (his name, after all, is Jack Off-enbach), his interest and attention focused on being "swarmed over by the butterflies and gnats of the salons" (*Midquest* 3; *More Shapes* 44). His only sorrow has been his loneliness at being sent to Paris at the age of twelve, and he has since become distanced from that pain by the spoils of his success (48).

Zimmer, on the other hand, has lived intimately with his sorrow since the death of his lover Rosalie. Her loss to him has taken on the guise of the mythic, the tragic death of the perfect woman on the night before her wedding. Her death is the impetus for his composition of the waltz that has both haunted and comforted his counterpart, Offenbach. His poverty and poor health have taken their toll on him, as has his continued mourning for Rosalie. His waltz is written from the depths of his grief and cannot be repeated; to write another would require that he lose again something as precious to him as she has been (55).

During their final interview, before Zimmer's death, Offenbach experiences the same confusion of senses that Feuerbach and Linnaeus feel, when Mme. Holzer's cinnamon breath and the notes of Zimmer's waltz become connected in Offenbach's mind. This sensory confusion is repeated as Offenbach falls asleep, at story's end, with "the slow voices rolling over him forever the scent of cinnamon" (57). He has encountered the mythic in Zimmer and his waltz, and it leads him to remember the origin of the dance that has made him famous, that it is "the raw music of the streets" to which whores and factory girls originally danced "gay and defiant and full of a bitter courage" (57). It is perhaps this last that allows Offenbach to be soothed and to drift to sleep, as he remembers that he has been involved perhaps more fully in both the mythic and the physical aspects of life than he has realized. His music is, as Zimmer has pointed out, at its heart "a sad music indeed" (55).

If Zimmer has taken Rosalie as a vehicle for something outside himself that transforms his art, Arthur, the protagonist of "The Somewhere

Doors," has his Rosalie in Francesca. In the beginning of the story, we find that Arthur receives his stories not in the nightmares that occupy Lovecraft's sleep, but as "melancholy twilight visions of things distant in time and space, stories that seemed not entirely his, but gifts from a source at which he could not guess" (73). Following his conversation with Francesca, who comes to him dressed all in white in a car that makes only the slightest of noises on the dirt road, Arthur's stories begin to be more accepted by his editors and "the intensity of his visions flamed through . . . even if sensual nuance was lost" (75, 81, 82). Like Milton, he receives his "one talent" from outside of himself, and his efforts to increase what he returns is rewarded not only by the two doors and their promise of Utopia or Paradise, but by the note delivered with them, thanking him for his efforts (89). Like Zimmer, Arthur has improved his artistic creations through contact with a woman who seems celestial, perfect.

Arthur meets the same resistive force in the person of Ugly Dick that Robert and Uncle Alvin find in "The Adder." Ugly Dick's distorted innuendoes about the possibility of a sexual relationship between Francesca and Arthur, and his erroneous reference to the myth system of which Arthur's name makes him a part, link him to *The Necronomicon.* At their first meeting, he tells Arthur that he understands his position, that "she let you have a piece and you think you're Sir Galahad or something" (84). Of course Francesca and Arthur have not had a physically intimate relationship, and his concept of her is not reductive in that way. The exchange between them, when Arthur asks if she is married, lacks the purely hormonal quality that Ugly Dick implies (79). Ugly Dick's disregard for the details of Galahad's story, and his suggestion that both he and the Arthur character in this story are less than virginal, indicate at least a lack of concern about the sort of quest that an artist might undertake. Like *The Necronomicon,* Ugly Dick attempts to change the creative power represented by Francesca in Arthur's mind to something senseless. Also telling is Ugly Dick's continued alteration of the name of the town where the story takes place, from Cherry Cove, N.C., to Cherry Cola, N.C., in the same way that *The Necronomicon* changes the lines of Sonnet XIX to words that nearly make grammatical sense, but ultimately have no meaning (83, 93).

Following his receipt of the fabulous doors, Arthur resolves to live his life as he has in the past, without pressuring himself to chose between the doors. At that point Arthur realizes he has a third choice, that the familiar, physical world of Cherry Cove is as available to him as are the ideal worlds behind the colored doors (90). At this revelation, Arthur's life takes on the "dignity of election," yet he wavers undecided at Farley Redmon's offer of a third interest in the Red Man Café (90–1). He has lived without real attachment in Cherry Cove, even though he remains constant at the café following the death of Redmon's son and Redmon's ensuing drunkenness (90–1). His involvement with his surroundings is merely an appreciation of their convenience rather than an emotional connection.

The moment he becomes connected to the land and, by implication, to the sensory and emotional aspects of his life, follows another interview with Ugly Dick at the moment when his decision about the doors is made. Like Offenbach, Arthur has been more deeply moved by the people and geography surrounding him than he has realized. He notices "a stand of silver-birch trees and beneath them a clump of knee-tall scarlet bee balm" and stops to admire them, realizing that he sees them every day without really looking at them, and he is overwhelmed (96). His decision is made, and he sinks to his knees, crying. The Somewhere doors offer him Utopia and Paradise, neither of which can "remember" and neither of which has sadness, since each exists outside of time (96–7). Like George in "After Revelation," Arthur realizes that without past, without memory, there is no future. "They were dreams that Arthur for a long time had been experiencing with all his senses except those of his body" (97). In his detachment from physical life, Arthur has already visited both worlds but has not experienced the physical world in which death and loss, like his loss of Francesca and her possible death, are real. The choice that brings him to his knees is one not to become the emasculated shade of a man whom we meet in Miss Prue's Mr. M.

The death of a loved one ties this story to another pair of stories near the center of the collection, "Ember" and "Duet." While Arthur has as one of his choices a movement into Paradise, Bill Puckett is run out of Paradise in a hail of gunfire after murdering his allegedly cheating girlfriend Phoebe Redd in "Ember" (122). Bill makes a turn at the crossroads that leads him across Burning Creek and up Ember Mountain, running from the men who wish to avenge Bill's momentary surrender to anger (123). He has loved Phoebe in a self-centered way, without the true attachment to her that would have made shooting her impossible. He has loved her in a way unlike that of the Owners in "After Revelation," who "can pay full attention to someone else" (191). His encounter with the mythical on Ember Mountain leads him to understand the gravity of his error in a way that he does not at the beginning of the story and makes of him the mythic jealous lover who cannot survive his own guilt.

The woman whom Bill meets at the top of Ember Mountain is the crone of death, just as Phoebe represents both the virginal (white) and the maternal (Redd) manifestations of the feminine trinity. Significantly, Bill notices the lack of dogs at the cabin, which were sacrificed to the Hecate form of this triple goddess, and the "granny woman" casts a shadow that "divided into three on the walls" (129). Her most dramatic link to this mythology is in her transformation into something that resembles decay, like "toadstools . . . on fallen timber" or "the bottom of a rotted oak stump turned up" (126). Bill has killed, or attempted to kill, both the Virgin and the Mother, and he has come inadvertently to the mountain to face the Crone.

Bill's encounter with this mythological woman leaves him with an understanding of what he has done and of what the results of that action will be. Phoebe Redd has been killed over and over throughout history, by at least twelve men other than Bill, and their punishment is that there is "no rest for us and no surcease, but only being driven miserable on the rocks and thorns until Ember Mountain perishes and time itself passes all away" (132). Bill's love for Phoebe has been insincere; he has been emotionally detached from her and remains so to the end of the story. His last words lead us to understand, though, that he has the rest of eternity to become more intimately involved in his feelings for Phoebe. His is the hell of isolation that we create for ourselves in this life or the next.

The protagonist of the other story in the pair, "Duet," makes a different choice from Bill's when he nears Ember Mountain. While Bill drinks "like a dog" at Burning Creek and proceeds up the mountain, Kermit Wilson in "Duet" takes three drinks from the stream, sits next to it and listens, and then decides not to climb the mountain (141). Following Caney Barham's death, his friend Kermit "figured I could climb if I desired, setting one foot before the other and feeling no strain, not today" (141). His choice, though, is to sit close by the border between life and death that Burning Creek

forms and listen to the stream's music, which engenders in him "purest sadness, sad but free and floating, sad but natural-feeling" (142). While Bill
Puckett has drunk long at the creek and then rushed past it and up the
mountain to a sort of judgment, Kermit is able to find the peace and appro-
priateness of his mourning, sitting intimately next to death. The mythology
of the mountain is drawn together at story's end, when Kermit's wish, if
his friend cannot be alive, is that Kermit be on "a grassy bald," like the one
where Bill and the other murderers gather, where he is sure that Caney will
be able to hear his songs (149).

His visit to the creek changes the darkness that Kermit has felt about
his friend's death, left from dreams that he cannot remember but whose
emotion stays with him after waking. The stream replaces them with this
feeling of peaceful mourning, as Kermit stabilizes himself in his physical
and natural world. The pain expressed by his subconscious in his dreams
is soothed, though not removed, by his communion with the creek. Like
Feuerbach and Hornli, as well as Offenbach and Zimmer, Kermit and
Caney have been linked, like twins. The loss of his friend affects Kermit
deeply, so much so that he is unsure if he will be able to sing at the funeral
until his trip into the woods to the base of Ember Mountain.

The depth and complexity of Kermit's attachment to Caney is indicated
by his reactions to the news of his death, including the above, as well as his
memories of Caney and the times they spent together. They have been
friends in the intimate ways that men are friends, hunting and fishing,
drinking and talking and singing (135). Kermit appreciates Caney not in his
perfection, as Zimmer remembers Rosalie, but for his idiosyncrasies. His
memories are "not drawn-out, put-together thoughts, but little bright pic-
tures," in the way that we remember the friends we love (137). These memories and his trip into the woods are a more genuine method of mourning
than Preacher Garvin's platitudes, and they certainly are more emotional
and intimate than "The Lord disposes. He giveth and He taketh away"
(138, 142). Kermit's choice of songs to sing at the funeral—"Peace in the
Valley" and "Roll in My Sweet Baby's Arms"—balances the spiritual with
the physical and acknowledges both aspects of Caney (142–3). Kermit recognizes in his friend a mixture of the mythical event that has taken him
and the equally important physical facts of the life Caney has lived.

It is out of this intense and genuine emotional attachment to Caney that the change in Kermit's music comes. While he has been a singer and guitar player with Caney for years, the sort who sit on the front porch randomly picking and singing together, his sorrow "would always be with [him] and [he] could call it to come whenever [he] wanted to sing" (145). From this sorrow, he sings the rendition of "Peace in the Valley" that silences the church during the funeral service and he sings "Roll in My Sweet Baby's Arms" to his dead friend at the graveside. The experience of Caney's death has initiated Kermit into sorrow, and it is from that knowledge of mythic sorrow that his music comes. Like Zimmer or Linnaeus or Arthur, Kermit's artistic ability comes to him from outside himself or from so deeply within himself that he is unable to name its source.

The role of the subconscious as a factory of creativity surfaces most magically in "Mankind Journeys through Forests of Symbols," the third of three stories written in a resoundingly North Carolinian voice. The dream in Deputy Bill's subconscious materializes on Highway 51 and can only be moved by being written. In the same way that Lovecraft's dreams are defused by the creation of his horror stories, Bill's poem disperses the tangible dream his subconscious has invented. Bill, the "slow and earnest thinker," is far from the scholar or artist that the word "poet" draws to mind, spitting tobacco juice as he does through the beginning of the story (157). Nonetheless, he has received the poem, in the way that Arthur receives his stories, and there is no solution to the physical problem of it except to write it.

The price of writing can be high, though, as Zimmer's waltz illustrates, and as the sheriff's admonition to Bill acknowledges: "'Look here, Bill,' Balsam said, 'you're a deputy sheriff of Osgood County. I don't have to tell you what kind of responsibility that is. Sometimes the job is dirty and dangerous, but you know that when you put on the badge. I never expect to see you back off from the job, boy. Never'" (166). Writing the poem causes Bill's face to turn ashen and his hair gray (167). Building a bridge between the world of myth and the mundane is "dirty and dangerous" work, but it is also necessary for some people and can cause those poets to become fearless, as Bill proves to be by tasting the Secret Formula left behind by Dr. Litmouse (168).

As Dr. Litmouse exclaims following his taste of the poem, mankind journeys through forests of symbols, sometimes recognizing them as familiar, sometimes allowing them to inspire awe, and sometimes passing by them blithely. Joseph Campbell, in the interview that became *The Power of Myth,* says: "No, mythology is not a lie, mythology is poetry, it is metaphorical. It has been well said that mythology is the penultimate truth— penultimate because the ultimate cannot be put into words. . . . Mythology pitches the mind beyond that rim, to what can be known but not told. So this is penultimate truth."[1] Chappell begins his book with an epigraph from Milton's *Areopagitica,* from which the title of the collection comes. Truth may take on more shapes than one, and many of those shapes are hinted at or alluded to by the myths in our lives. Chappell's characters in *More Shapes Than One* illustrate the importance of myth as part of our lives being actively lived and in which we are actively engaged.

Our intuitions of the transcendent come to us subconsciously, in dreams; as inspirations, in poetry or stories or music; or in communion with nature, which would include genuine relationships with other people. They cannot come while our lives are lived as neatly and primly as Miss Prue's, or as falsely as Offenbach's, or as compassionlessly as Maupertuis's. It is only while we are busy in the dirty and dangerous business of living our mundane lives, loving and hating, drinking and eating, arriving early and arriving late, grocery shopping and washing the dog, that we accumulate the spectrum of feeling and experience that complete myth and symbol's pitch, carrying us beyond penultimate to ultimate truth.

NOTE

1. Joseph Campbell, *The Power of Myth* (New York: Doubleday, 1988), 163.

{ NINE }

The Shape of Truth
Men and Women in Fred Chappell's
More Shapes Than One

ROSEMARY COX

IN THE FOREWORD to his translation of *Les Fleurs du Mal,* Richard Howard maintains, "Baudelaire's poetry concerns us much more, and much more valuably, by its strangeness than by its familiarity: its authentic relation to us is in its remoteness" (xxi). The same may be said of Fred Chappell's collection of strange tales *More Shapes Than One.* Actually, the link to Baudelaire is not so remote. In one of the stories, "Mankind Journeys through Forests of Symbols," while attempting to ascertain the cause of a massive dream that is blocking Highway 51 between Turkey Knob and Ember Forks, Dr. Litmouse the scientist, whose name is a pun on "litmus," cries out from a vision the first four lines of Baudelaire's definitive sonnet "Correspondances":

La Nature est un temple ou de vivants piliers
Laissent parfois sortir de confuses paroles;
L'homme y passe à travers des forêts de symboles
Qui l'observent avec des regards familiers. (160)

Nature is a temple where the living pillars
Sometimes allow confused words to come out;
Man passes there, across forests of symbols
Which observe him with familiar looks. [my translation]

In this poem, Baudelaire outlines one of the major tenets of *symbolisme,* a movement in French poetry which came to prominence in the 1880s expounding, among other ideas, the philosophy (Platonic in origin) that elements in the natural world have analogies or "correspondences" in the realm of the ideal. Baudelaire expresses the belief that "everything, form, movement, number, color, perfume, in the spiritual as well as in the *natural* is significant, reciprocal, converse, correspondent." Baudelaire continues, "We arrive at this truth, that everything is hieroglyphic, and we know that symbols are obscure only in a relative way, that is, according to the purity, the good will or the native clairvoyance of souls." The function of the poet is, thus, to act as a "translator, a decoder [*dechiffreur*]" (quoted in Bertocci 53).

Certainly in *More Shapes Than One*, Chappell is not trying to apply to fiction the principles of French symbolist poetry, though, for the record, this subject has intrigued him since his senior year in high school ("A Pact with Faustus" 13). Rather, the connection between the complex metaphors of symbolism and Chappell's fabulous worlds is the synesthetic relationship these images have to the stark reality of existence. As a headnote to his collection of stories, Chappell quotes from Milton's *Areopagitica:*

> For who knows not that Truth is strong, next to the Almighty. She needs no policies, nor stratagems nor licensings to make her victorious—those are the shifts and defenses that error uses against her power. . . .
> Yet is it not impossible that she may have more shapes than one.

As Milton claims, the truth can take many forms. Baudelaire's poetic correspondences thus find their fictional counterpart in Chappell's stories, as the title of this particular story, "Mankind Journeys through Forests of Symbols," suggests by drawing a parallel to Baudelaire's lines. Readers should not endeavor to explain the massive dream blob on the highway, for example, but should, instead, look beyond the phantasmagoric to see what it can reveal about their own, very real, lives.

If the most significant aspect of the fabulous is its relationship to reality, what, then, is the reality, the truth, behind the stories in *More Shapes Than One?* Chappell himself poses a similar question in his essay "Fantasia on the Theme of Theme and Fantasy": "There is a point at which a reader will say to the writer, 'I have given you enough leeway; I have allowed you a great many liberties in the matter of verisimilitude. Now you must satisfy me that my confidence has not been misplaced. What is it that, after all this preparation, all these preliminaries which violate the laws of physics and the idea of causality—what is it that you desire to show me?'" (186).

There is no one definitive answer to this question, for *More Shapes Than One* embraces many verities: the symbiotic relationship between humanity and science, the crucial importance of self-acceptance, and the vital acknowledgment of the creative impulse. One inescapable truth, however, deserves closer consideration: though we all live on the same planet, men and women inhabit totally different spheres, separated by fear and superstition, yet inextricably intertwined by desire and the need to belong. From the lecherous exploits of Maupertuis in "Ladies from Lapland" to George's unrequited longing in "After Revelation," virtually all of the relationships between men and women in *More Shapes Than One* are flawed in some way, yet women seem invariably to hold the key to enlightenment, even if that enlightenment is still an enigma.

Taking this view of women in the stories of *More Shapes,* "Ladies from Lapland" poses the greatest difficulty of interpretation. If one views the stories as a progression of male/female relationships from the physical to the spiritual, then this story qualifies as the most literal, with its emphasis on sex and the elemental, animal nature of human desire. Both Maupertuis and the women he seduces are distorted by passion. Maupertuis is basically obnoxious, not only in the subtle way he disguises rape but also in the callous manner in which he treats his colleagues. He is hungry for power and fame; bent on pleasure, he shirks work and takes credit for the labor of others. The ultimate injustice is that, in the end, he is glorified: "His accomplishment was universally bruited, and his face was known everywhere, especially after the broad dissemination of the famous engraving taken after the painting by Tournieres" (29). Even Mme. Graffigny does not condemn Maupertuis when she learns of his true exploits so much as to degrade Laplanders. She praises Maupertuis for his ability to "please even in frozen climates" and arrogantly concludes, "Ah, mon Dieu, how can one be a Laplander?" (30). As a typical Parisian, Mme. Graffigny thus speaks for her society which not only condones Maupertuis's conduct but actually promotes it. Only Clairaut—whose name suggests clarity—sees Maupertuis for the hypocrite that he is. Maupertuis's attitude toward women further accentuates his odiousness, as exemplified by the carnival aspect he adopts

in the seduction scene with his gaudy costume and painted face, the sump-
tuous surroundings, and the mocking names he gives to his Lapland par-
amours—"Choufleur" and "Doucette." These titles may sound romantic on
the surface, but they reveal that Maupertuis considers a woman nothing
more than a "cauliflower" or a sweetmeat to be enjoyed—used and then
cast off. For him, conquest is all: "He looked at the Lapland women and
thought that here, too, was a terra incognita from which he could learn
things unknown in Europe" (21).

The women Maupertuis beguiles are really not much better than he
is—we may pity the Lap women because Maupertuis takes advantage of
their innocence and ignorance, but we hold them in contempt for not having more sense, for not putting up some resistance to Maupertuis's advances—although, ironically, this somewhat tarnishes his victory. While
they may not deserve what they get, they are certainly instrumental in
bringing about their own ruin and unhappiness. The same is true for Mme.
Du Chatelet who is so enamored of the two principles Maupertuis introduces to her—sex and Newtonian science—that she perishes from the consequences.

With all of this death, debauchery, and deceit, it is unclear how women
function in any redemptive capacity in this story. But that is precisely the
point Chappell makes. Without the guidance of a strong female character,
Maupertuis degenerates into a rogue. His attitude toward women—and
life—remains superficial. The women, too, suffer from their own failure to
fulfill their proper function in life, as the four Lapland ladies exemplify in
their pathetic, grotesque situation in Paris. Alienated from their rightful
environment, they become misfits, both figuratively and literally with
"fashionable gowns that in no way could contain their capacious hips and
upper arms"; they wear "monstrous high piled" wigs that "would not sit
straight and kept sliding down over their eyes," and because "no shoemaker
stocked a last to fit them . . . they flopped about in soiled carpet slippers."
Their "splendid Lapland teeth" have become "ruinous" (30), yet another
symbol for wasted talent and potential.

While the ladies of Lapland may fail as purveyors of insight and inspiration, the mysterious Francesca from "The Somewhere Doors" aptly fulfills
her role as mentor. Like a goddess, she suddenly materializes on the bridge
over the Little Tennessee River, where Arthur Strakl stands contemplating

the water before dawn on a September morning. Eerily omniscient, she startles Arthur with her intimate knowledge of the details in his bizarre science-fiction stories, and she reveals the purpose of her journey to find him: he will eventually be presented with two doors, a blue door opening into a natural paradise and a violet door leading into a wonderful "world of great cities" (180), from either of which there is no return. Arthur is immediately captivated by her presence—she is beautiful—yet he is simultaneously rebuffed and frustrated by her evasiveness. When the government agent "Ugly Dick" appears at Redmon's Café two years later, informing Arthur of Francesca's real identity and hinting at her possible criminal connections, Arthur remains steadfast. She may not be what she seems, but for Arthur the allure is the same. To him, Francesca represents an ideal—albeit one that he will never possess, a fact reinforced by her eventual suicide.

One could interpret the conflicting emotions that Francesca arouses in Arthur as characteristic of the sublime contradictions of the mythical White Goddess, a figure with whom Francesca shares many qualities. Dressed totally in white—from her "white silk party frock with a wide square collar" to her "white pumps of patent leather" and "shiny white silk" hair bow (75)—Francesca echoes the pale, bride-like loveliness of the White Goddess. But that virginal beauty masks another, darker identity, just as the White Goddess, as Robert Graves describes her, can "suddenly transform herself into sow, mare, bitch, vixen, she-ass, weasel, serpent, owl, she-wolf, tigress, mermaid or loathsome hag" (*White Goddess* 24).

Francesca admonishes Arthur to "keep writing your wonderful stories," to "keep on imagining the kinds of things that only you can imagine" (80), suggesting that she comes to represent Arthur's Muse, as, indeed, she continues to provide incentive and inspiration for him to write in the lonely and trying years that follow their singular encounter. Here, again, is a parallel to the White Goddess for, according to Robert Graves, the White Goddess is the ultimate source of creative literature. Graves notes, "I cannot think of any true poet from Homer onwards who has not independently recorded his experience of her." He further maintains, "The test of a poet's vision, one might say, is the accuracy of his portrayal of the White Goddess and of the island over which she rules." He continues, "The reason why the hairs stand on end, the eyes water, the throat is constricted, the skin crawls and a shiver runs down the spine when one writes or reads a true poem is that a true poem is necessarily an invocation of the White Goddess, or Muse, the Mother of All Living, the ancient power of fright and lust—the female spider or the queen-bee whose embrace is death" (*White Goddess* 24).

Unlike the traditional White Goddess who seems bent on the destruction of those who come under her spell (one recalls Keats's La Belle Dame and Coleridge's lady dicing with death in *Rime of the Ancient Mariner*), Francesca provides Arthur with the impetus for a more meaningful life. In a world full of poverty, mistrust, and war, Arthur chooses to ignore the information Ugly Dick gives him about Francesca (alias Sheila Weddell) and continues to believe in her because she believes in him and his talent for writing science fiction. The eventual appearance of the colorful doors confirms Arthur's faith and leads him to the ultimate realization that the choice he has made to live in the real world and to value it for itself is the best and only choice a person can make. Revisiting the bridge, Arthur is overwhelmed by the sight of birch trees and scarlet bee balm which he really sees for the first time. Bursting into tears, he kneels on the gravel road, overcome with the knowledge that "He had already opened both Doors and visited both Somewheres. He was ready to fling open wide the third door, the entrance to the world in which he already lived. Much had passed him by. Oh yes. Yet much awaited him still" (97). Ironically, neither Arthur nor Francesca truly understands the "tangle of circumstance" (95) surrounding the Somewhere Doors, but how and why they arrive is immaterial. What is significant is the impact that they and Francesca have on Arthur. Like the legendary King Arthur, Arthur Strakl has pulled the sword of understanding out of this stone-cum-doors, under the guidance and inspiration of a Holy Virgin named Francesca.

It is perhaps in the story "Ember" that the weird most strikingly unveils the truth of the relationship between men and women. Having shot his cheating girlfriend Phoebe Redd, Bill Puckett flees from the inevitable pursuit of the law; making a wrong turn in his haste, he ends up abandoning his pickup truck at the base of Ember Mountain, which is legendary for its mysterious "ridges and hollers" (124). Attempting to climb to the summit through the blackest pitch of night, he stumbles into the cabin of an old woman who offers him some herbal tea and her advice. The cabin has appeared unexpectedly; there are no dogs to bark a warning; the tea is intoxicating, and the crone knows Puckett's story even before he tells it. And, after all, why shouldn't she know it? Has it not been played out—by both men and women—countless times throughout human history, as many old ballads demonstrate? "Banks of the Ohio" is a typical American example:

> I started home 'tween twelve and one,
> I cried, "My God! What have I done?
> Killed the only woman I loved,
> Because she would not be my bride."

> And only say that you'll be mine
> In no other's arms entwine,
> Down beside where the waters flow,
> Down by the banks of the Ohio. (Siegmeister 103)

But the old woman on Ember Mountain is more than just the voice of past wrongs. Puckett laments:

> I didn't want to look into her eyes, so it was her throat I saw, the red new-healed smooth place beneath her chin. Right then I recognized that wound for the first time as the place on her body where my .44 bullet had struck my deceitful Phoebe back in Paradise. It was the exact same spot. (131)

The old woman—Phoebe Redd in another guise—is an archetype, as biblical allusions and parallels to myth seem to suggest. As Adam is banished from the Garden of Eden, so Puckett is expelled from *Paradise*, all because of a woman: "Oh, Phoebe, I thought, oh Phoebe Redd. See what your *faithless* ways have brought on me" (124, emphasis mine). The twisted, primeval tree-stump image also evokes biblical associations. Puckett first sees the old woman sitting in her rocking chair, "remembering in front of her fire" (126), but when he looks a second time, she has metamorphosed: "this time it wasn't an old woman in her rocking chair but another kind of thing hard to tell about. All gnarled and rooty like the bottom of a rotted oak stump turned up" (126). Perhaps this is what remains of the Tree of Knowledge, hewn down and decayed from millennial human abuses.

On a mythic level, the transformation from hag to stump places the old woman, like Francesca from "The Somewhere Doors," clearly in the tradition of the White Goddess, this time replete with negative associations: Puckett will never escape her enchantment. The tripartite nature of the White Goddess is also exemplified in old Phoebe Redd: as she steps to the fire to stir up the embers, Puckett observes that "Her bunched-up shadow divided into three on the walls" (129). Graves equates the White Goddess with what he calls "the Theme," which he describes as "the antique story, which falls into thirteen chapters and an epilogue, of the birth, life, death and resurrection of the God of the Waxing Year." Graves notes that "the central chapters concern the God's losing battle with the God of the Waning Year for love of the capricious and all-powerful Threefold Goddess, their mother, bride, and layer-out" (24). Graves further discusses the qualities of the Triple Goddess as she assumes the characteristics of Goddess of the Sky, Earth, and Underworld:

> As Goddess of the Underworld she was concerned with Birth, Procreation and Death. As Goddess of the Earth she was concerned with the three seasons of Spring, Summer and Winter: she animated trees and plants and ruled all living creatures. As Goddess of the Sky she was the Moon, in her three phases of New Moon, Full Moon, and Waning Moon. This explains why from a triad she was so often enlarged to an ennead. But it must never be forgotten that the Triple Goddess . . . was a personification of primitive woman—woman the creatress and destructress. As the New Moon or Spring she was girl; as the Full Moon or Summer she was woman; as the Old Moon or Winter she was hag. (386)

Phoebe Redd is this ancient figure. She is timeless, as Puckett observes: "I couldn't place her age, the skin of her face being so smooth and ruddy" (128). She is omniscient, a symbol of the creative force in the universe. And without question, she represents *all* women, marred by the countless injustices that men continue to commit against her. Her pock-marked complexion is her testimony, as Puckett describes it:

> There were dents in her skin here and there, two in her forehead and one on her left cheek just below the eye and three dents in her throat, little pushed-in places like the thumbprints you'd leave in biscuit dough. The skin was smooth in the dents, smooth as isinglass. Wounds that

have healed over, I thought, old wounds. Except for one in her throat just under her chin: That one was healed but looked fresh, too, as red and rare as a scarlet flower. (130)

Phoebe may have been wounded, but her power over men is undiminished. Puckett bemoans his fate and that of the other men unfortunate enough to have crossed her: "I know how her revenge on us is everlasting and how we are to be scattered howling to and fro on the mountain. . ." (132). This is Phoebe in her role as destroyer, but she is also creator. Not only does she invite Puckett in out of the cold to sit comfortably in her chair and warm himself before the fire, but she arranges his wet socks and shoes to dry and plies him with soothing herbal tea. She takes an uncommon interest in Puckett's plight and understands him so well he cannot lie to her or refuse the tea. It is as if her shining, golden, cat-like eyes penetrate his soul. Having to face the truth of his actions and seeing the marks of other men's transgressions on her face brings him to an epiphany, and he swoons, not able to fully understand what he has learned, but more aware of the complexity of the relationship between men and women. Addressing the jury-like twelve men in the clearing, Puckett places guilt on himself and on all members of his sex: "I can see in your bitter faces and in the bitter shadows of your eyes how it is and how it is going to be, that we are the men who ever killed Phoebe Redd; over the years and generations and centuries it was us that left the marks of our pistol balls on her again and again" (132).

Phoebe's link to the legendary Triple Goddess and her association with the moon further connects her to Greek myth and provides a clue to her name. For the ancient Greeks, Phoebe was the name of several different deities. As the daughter of Uranus and Gaia, she was a Titaness, guardian of the moon and, according to some beliefs, the third guardian of the Delphic Oracle; as the daughter of Leucippus, she was courted by Polydeuces, the twin of Castor and brother of Helen of Troy; and as the daughter of Tyndareos and Leda, she was sister to Helen. The most common form she assumes in Greek mythology, however, is as an alternate name for Artemis, either because this Olympian goddess was associated with the moon goddess Selene or because her grandmother was the Titaness Phoebe. An interesting gloss on Artemis as moon goddess is that, according to Graves in

The Greek Myths, she is "the youngest member of the Artemis Triad, Artemis being one more title of the Triple Moon-Goddess" (85).

Phoebe Redd's affiliation with Artemis has important ramifications. For example, Puckett first mistakes the old woman's fire for that of a hunter; Artemis is goddess of the hunt. Though a virgin goddess and fiercely protective of her chastity, as the multiple-breasted Goddess of Ephesus, Artemis is an icon of fertility. Phoebe Redd, too, is a sort of earth mother, as Puckett implies when he observes her through the window of her cabin. She is "something alive that nobody would ever think could live, something that knew about me out here by the window without seeing me, something that was an old woman in a chair and was no old woman any way in the world" (126–7). Phoebe Redd's capacity to both heal and destroy is also consistent with the traits attributed to Artemis. Edith Hamilton says of the goddess that "In her is shown most vividly the uncertainty between good and evil which is apparent in every one of the divinities" (32).

Because Phoebe Redd drives Puckett to commit his crime, he believes he is blameless or at least justified—and perhaps, in a sense, he is. Shocked by the realization that the old woman is his own Phoebe Redd, Puckett cries, "I wanted to understand that; I wanted to try to make some sense, but it was too late" (131). Like the other men at the end of the story—like *all* men—Puckett will never understand women. Women are the ultimate enigma: they are men's ruin and their salvation at the same time. Puckett's attempt to strike out against this perplexity is futile, a fate he shares with all men: "there is no rest for us and no surcease, but only being driven miserable on the rocks and thorns until Ember Mountain perishes and time itself passes all away" (132).

"Miss Prue" is another story in this collection that demonstrates the idea that men are tantalized and tormented by the very women who could provide them with the key to a better life. But, like "Ladies from Lapland," this story presents a reversal, rather than an affirmation, of the redemptive influence of women. Too reticent and cowardly to confront the truth in life, Mr. M. must reappear as a ghost, after he has committed suicide with a drug overdose, before he can confront his formidable and *pru*dish lady friend with the knowledge that they have wasted their lives. Exactly why he takes his own life remains obscure. Miss Prue intimates it may be an illness, as she chides his forlorn outlook: "'Nonsense,' she said firmly. 'You have allowed this matter of your health to upset you unduly'" (153). Nevertheless, one cannot rule out the possibility that he has despaired of ever finding fulfillment in his relationship with Miss Prue. Their conversation over the predictable Thursday-afternoon tea is both poignant and pathetic:

> "How can you desire it to be different? We have been a fixed pair these last twenty years."
>
> "We might have been closer," he said, and what a world of cold this latter word implied.
>
> "How closer? How steadier? Few married couples are as close and steady as we have been."
>
> "Might we not have gotten married?"
>
> She flicked her hand at the question as if it were a tedious housefly.
>
> "That is not in our personalities, I think. We are a different sort, you and I." (152)

Her rejection, however, cuts even deeper into his soul when, with contempt, she accuses him of inaction: "You might have swept me off my feet, Mr. M. You might have carried me away like an impetuous bandit or a dashing pirate" (152). Her romantic notions echo the fantasies of many women, just as his downcast view beyond the hooked rug on the floor "through the crust of the earth to the shoals of mineral and the molten seas of fire" (152) represents the exasperated, bewildered, and angry response of all men (as Mr. M.'s name may signify: Mr. Man).

Not only does Miss Prue believe Mr. M. does not measure up to her expectations, she is irritated at his lack of consideration: "You haven't touched your tea. . . . I took the trouble, Mr. M., of beating biscuits" (153). From her shallow and self-centered perspective, he lacks understanding; as she states, "I believe that you never learned to appreciate some very important things" (153). Convinced that they have had the very best of relationships, Miss Prue confronts the cadaverous Mr. M.: "Haven't we enjoyed our company together? Haven't we had our Thursdays, our tea and our talk?" Mr. M.'s reply is prophetic: "'There are other things.' His voice was like the sound of wind in a ragged thornbush. 'I know now that there are other things, though I don't quite know what they are'" (153). Mr. M.'s uncertainty is troublesome. He later remarks, "'Lost?' It was the cry of the Arctic moon. 'Everything is lost. There is nothing'" (153). Mr. M. has encountered the "Beast in the Jungle," as Henry James would phrase it, and though he does not know what to make of his revelation, he has, at least, recognized that it exists—something that Miss Prue is incapable of or unwilling to accept.

Even though her name may imply "prudence," whatever judgment she is capable of is blotted out by her arrogance (she is certain Mr. M. will come to visit despite his death) and by her implacable independence. Like the enormous "emasculated" (150) cat on her hearth, Miss Prue's "Wisdom" is asleep. Is the "strange infection" (154) from which the cat suffers a brief disturbance in her way of thinking, doubt about the way she has chosen to conduct her life?

Unrelenting and unenlightened herself, Miss Prue is still, ironically, the catalyst for Mr. M.'s epiphany. He is compelled to visit Miss Prue once more not out of courtesy—"'No,' he said. 'It isn't manners. Not exactly'" (152)—but because of the unexplainable power that she exerts over him, the mystery that all women hold for men. He senses that something has gone amiss; her obstinate attitude has obliterated their potential for happiness. Thus, from the improbable lips of death comes one of the secrets of life: for existence to be meaningful, men and women must traverse the gulf of pride, or fear, or habit that separates us and "only connect!" as E. M. Forster suggests in *Howard's End* (186).

"Alma" means "soul" in Spanish, and that is precisely the focus of Chappell's story by the same name. In this pseudo-frontier, a "lubberland" so to speak, women are a subspecies to men. Treated even worse than stock animals, a group of women is tethered and "herded" by a drover, destined to be sold at Fort Ox 1 for the soldiers stationed there to "use up" (172). When Fretlaw, the narrator of the story, happens to meet up with this unscrupulous drover at the edge of his camp at Busted River, he declares that the captives are "the plumb sorriest string of women ever I laid eyes on" (169). Fretlaw continues:

> Most of them wouldn't make good buzzard bait when he got hold of them and he had took no pains to keep them up, never washing them down and hadn't put clothes on them and I could tell they'd been fed scanty, their ribs sticking out. The rattiest bunch you could think of, mud and dust and scabs and their hair all ropy and their eyes wild. (169–70)

Fretlaw's colloquial speech and the unperturbed manner in which he describes the situation, on the one hand, puts readers at ease, emphasizing the narrator's lack of pretension, making him "one of us." But is he an unreliable narrator? Fretlaw's easy tone and diction hold the reader in suspense, waiting to discover what other abnormalities and inhumane practices are the status quo in this warped society. The drover refers to the women as "shoats," and he tells Fretlaw he will "move them downwind if the smell bothers you" (170). He feeds them on jerky and old biscuit and takes them down to the river to be "watered" (171). This world is truly a male chauvinist's fantasy played out, with women reduced to complete subservience and men in total control. Women are considered useless except as scullery maids and bed partners. The drover Dingo (appropriately named after a type of wild Australian dog) maintains, "you can't teach them nothing; it's like they ain't got nothing to learn with. Dangerous, too" (172).

The subconscious desire to eliminate women also manifests itself when Fretlaw tells Dingo, "I've heard tell there's some people that raise them for food" (173). Accepting this as a rational statement, like a Swiftian "Modest Proposal," Dingo nonchalantly replies, "I can't think how starved I'd have to get before I'd eat a woman. They're my trade, you see, so I know how dirty they are" (173). The issue for Dingo is not ethics but hygiene.

Despite his references to cannibalism, however, Fretlaw takes an independent view of women, as he states from the outset: "I feel different about women than a lot of men do. . . . because I had me my own woman one time. I lived real close with her and that has made me think thoughts apart" (169). Fretlaw maintains: "The truth is, I never did really hold with woman trading. I know it's how things are and I suppose somebody will always be doing it but not me, never" (173). Fretlaw perceives that something is inherently wrong with the prevalent attitude toward women, making him vulnerable to the advances of one particular red-hair, Alma, who easily convinces him to overpower the drover and free the other women. The biblical implications are unmistakable: women are the evil manipulators, the corrupters and destroyers of men. But as men in the real world know and Fretlaw soon discovers, this view is all too simplistic. Despite Fretlaw's declarations, "I don't have no use for a woman" and "I better not get accustomed [to having one]" (174), Alma becomes his boon companion and indispensable helpmate. Fretlaw reluctantly realizes that the desire of all men for freedom is overwhelmed by their instinctive need for women—a need that is more emotional than sexual, as Fretlaw's ignorance about sex (which is almost *too* naïve) reveals.

Alma is certainly an ambivalent character. Sharing the contradictory destroyer/preserver qualities of the White Goddess with Phoebe Redd and Francesca, she is capable of revenge—and even murder—against Dingo, whom she perceives to be an enemy to all womankind. She instinctively knows that Fretlaw is "the better man" (177), she is diplomatic enough to let him "be the boss" (179), and she knows how to flatter and manipulate him to implement her plan to eliminate Dingo and free the other women. Yet she becomes the "nourishing mother" (*Alma Mater*) to Fretlaw. In this capacity, not only does she aid Fretlaw with domestic duties and give him invaluable advice about trapping animals and selling the pelts, but she opens up his soul, proving that men and women are capable of profound and enduring love.

By the end of the story when Alma leaves for the island in Weeping Lake to bear their child, Fretlaw is devastated, though he does not openly admit it. When they part, he sees her, for the first time, as an equal, in the sense that they both experience the same misgivings, fear, and joy about the prospect of parenthood and their impending separation. Fretlaw says:

> [B]ut mostly I looked at Alma, how small she seemed all of a sudden with the big boat in front of her and all the width of Weeping Lake around. And it come to me then that she was scared, too, just as scared as I was, and I felt a little bit proud, too, as well as scared and sad. (184)

Echoing the practice of some primitive societies where women would live in seclusion for the duration of their menses, the mysterious world that Alma enters, guarded by Amazon-like women "in armor and with spears and pistols and cutlasses" (184), symbolizes the enigma of pregnancy and childbirth, a world *from* which men are excluded yet *to* which they are inevitably linked in the cycle of procreation, life, and death. Fretlaw is not alone as he waits on the shore, returning each spring, hoping for a reunion with Alma—other men, grieving for their women who have vanished, experience the same sense of loss and exclusion.

Alma's disappearance is never explained. Does she die in childbirth? Does she fail to conceive, or lose the child and not want to disappoint Fret-

law? Or does she decide that a different way of life suits her better? Whatever the reason for her failure to return, her impact on Fretlaw is significant.
As Fretlaw puts it: "Whenever I hear them talking in the whiskey sheds
about women, going on about how dirty they are and how they're pizen
and more murderous than bobcats and copperheads, I just feel weary in my
bones" (185). She has given him a deeper understanding of women, changing his life forever. Thus, with Alma's guidance, the man who critic Bill
Christophersen claims "sounds like Huck Finn grown crusty in the territor-
ies" (20) demonstrates that he, like Twain's young hero, can transcend the
narrow mores of his society to acknowledge what is right.

A new vision of society is what George seeks in "After Revelation." As
the final story in *More Shapes Than One*, "After Revelation" is the most
allegorical statement of the theme that women, however inexplicable and
fascinating, can lead men to a greater understanding of themselves and the
world around them, but, all too often, this knowledge baffles, frustrates,
and confuses those who would achieve it. As George remarks, "A great deal
has been revealed to us, but it is revelation so pure that our minds and
senses cannot interpret it. We are not ready" (197).

The distinction between knowledge (as in scientific facts) and revelation
(as in true understanding) in this story is almost biblical as the title suggests, Revelation being the last, apocalyptic book of the Bible. George relates that civilization has twice destroyed itself from the abuse of
knowledge, or science, just as eating from the Tree of Knowledge in the
Garden of Eden brings a curse upon Adam and Eve. But the attainment
of true knowledge, or revelation, brings total fulfillment, "peace the way a
lamp brings a warm and pleasant glow into a dark room" (191), much like
the "Rapture" that some Christians describe. George's desire for this revelation, his longing for peace, transcends his desire for love or his feelings of
jealousy, and, like many Christians, he undertakes a pilgrimage to attain it.
Significantly, George associates his search for truth with images of the
woman he loves:

> I was stricken with grievous longing and driven on the roads under the
> starry night. I, too, must leave and go as a pilgrim; and even as I realized
> that fact and began to see a little of what lay before me, I thought,
> Wherever I roam tonight I shall see the slow strokes of Larilla's brush
> and hear her little song. (191–2)

THE SHAPE OF TRUTH · 165

George's awakening, like Mr. M.'s, indirectly results from his futile infatuation with a woman, though in George's situation, the widow Larilla is faultless. A woman of both innocence (she is young and beautiful) and experience (she is a widow), Larilla's death from an excess of happiness when her Owner calls on her (as the Owners have come for all of the human race) represents her attainment of a sacred knowledge that George, following her example, must begin to find for himself. Staring into Larilla's open grave, George laments, "the blank box of yellow pine told me nothing" (196). He is overcome with mingled emotions—mystery, longing, love, grief, frustration, the sense of being unfulfilled—but on returning to Larilla's cottage, surrounded by her lingering presence, he is convinced that he must continue the journey. Revelation is not the termination but the commencement of the quest for truth: "Everything had been revealed to us, and yet . . . After revelation, what then?" (197).

Chappell has said, "An author discovers soon enough that a fantastic premise is only what the ancient natural philosophers called a *lusus naturae*. Such a sport of nature is less interesting in itself than in the light it sheds on the normal order of things" ("Fantasia" 183). This is particularly true in this collection of stories where Chappell uses fantasy to reveal elemental truths in the relationships between the sexes, also a fundamental theme in his Kirkman tetralogy. Chappell's female characters are mysterious, exasperating, and judgmental, yet they serve as moral guides, provide the inspiration to go on living, and represent the ideal to which humanity can aspire. As the botanist Linnaeus discovers in "Linnaeus Forgets," we must allow ourselves to imagine worlds within worlds, to recognize the multilayers of reality even though once we confront them, like Hawthorne's Young Goodman Brown or Ethan Brand, we are changed forever. The truth does, indeed, come in "more shapes than one."

WORKS CITED

Baudelaire, Charles. *Les Fleurs du Mal*. Trans. Richard Howard. Boston: Godine, 1982.

Bertocci, Angelo Philip. *From Symbolism to Baudelaire*. Preface by Harry T. Moore. Carbondale: Southern Illinois University Press, 1964.

Chappell, Fred. "After Revelation." *More Shapes Than One* (New York: St. Martin's Press, 1991), 186–97.

———. "Alma." *More Shapes,* 169–85.

———. "Ember." *More Shapes,* 122–32.

———. "Fantasia on the Theme of Theme and Fantasy." *Studies in Short Fiction* 27, no. 2 (spring 1990): 179–90.

———. "Ladies from Lapland." *More Shapes,* 19–30.

———. "Mankind Journeys through Forests of Symbols." *More Shapes,* 155–68.

———. "Miss Prue." *More Shapes,* 150–4.

———. *More Shapes Than One.* New York: St. Martin's Press, 1991.

———. "A Pact with Faustus." *Mississippi Quarterly: The Journal of Southern Culture: Special Issue: The Work of Fred Chappell* 37, no. 1 (winter 1983–84), 9–20.

———. "The Somewhere Doors." *More Shapes,* 71–97.

Christophersen, Bill. "*More Shapes Than One*" [book review]. *New York Times Book Review,* October 6, 1991, sec. 7, p. 20.

Forster, E. M. . *Howard's End.* New York: Buccaneer, 1984.

Graves, Robert. *The Greek Myths.* Vol. 1. New York: Braziller, 1955.

———. *The White Goddess: A Historical Grammar of Poetic Myth.* Amended and enlarged ed. New York: Farrar, 1948.

Hamilton, Edith. *Mythology: Timeless Tales of Gods and Heroes.* New York: New American Library, 1942.

Siegmeister, Elie. *The Joan Baez Songbook.* New York: Ryerson (Vanguard Records), 1964.

{ TEN }

The Kirkman Novels

First and Last Concerns

PETER MAKUCK

FRED CHAPPELL'S seven novels seem to fall into two groups: a core group with a profound sense of place, recurring techniques, themes and characters *(It Is Time, Lord,* 1963; *I Am One of You Forever,* 1985; *Brighten the Corner Where You Are,* 1990; *Farewell, I'm Bound to Leave You,* 1996; and *Look Back All the Green Valley,* 1999) and a group less central to the concerns of his primary vision *(Inkling,* 1965; *Dagon,* 1968; and *The Gaudy Place,* 1973). It is the first group I am concerned with here, especially the four most recent novels, which share subjects and themes found in his poetic tetralogy *Midquest.* But something must be said at the outset about Chappell's remarkable first novel, *It Is Time, Lord,* a sourcebook for the Kirkman novels.

It Is Time, Lord seems a false start for what was to become, beginning with *I Am One of You Forever,* the story of Jess Kirkman's widely extended family. What links Chappell's first novel to the Kirkman books is, among other things, its first-person point of view, James Christopher's religious formation and interest in science fiction, James's uneasy relationship with his father, the character of Virgil Campbell, strongly religious grandparents, a house fire, a significant brother-sister relationship, and the importance of dreams. But James Christopher, unlike Jess Kirkman, is a man haunted by the past, death, the specter of nothingness, chronic loneliness, and the possibility that nothing matters: "I don't even know how to find out what is important" (39).

As the title *It Is Time, Lord* suggests, religion is central to the story of James Christopher. We learn that Christopher's grandmother lived long enough to see him ordained a minister and felt that her dreams had been fulfilled. On the other hand, his grandfather, whose attitude toward organized religion was at best equivocal, died before James was ordained. The grandfather's respect for the Bible, however, was "thorough and literal" (28). Growing up in the home of his grandparents, James, a former minister and narrator of the novel, mentally circles several real or imagined events in his past in order to exorcize demons. Did he burn his grandfather's house? Or is it a red-haired intruder, angry because his car has broken down and because James's grandfather refused him the use of a phone to call for help? The narrator's—and probably Chappell's—sense of the ambiguous and thorny nature of the past is impressively caught in a sermon from James Christopher's days as a churchman and is worth partial quotation:

> The past is an eternally current danger, in effect, a suicide. We desire the past, we call to it just as men who have fallen overboard an ocean liner call, because we must predict the future. But this prediction, which is most necessitous, we cannot achieve. We back into the future and are blind to what happens until it has already occurred. Then we only see it receding, metamorphosing with distance and distorted with memory's impure Doppler effect. As far as event is concerned, the mind is an isolated citadel standing in a desert. Miles of sand surround it. A starry sky stretches overhead. The face of God never leans toward it, and in the desert nothing moves. The citadel itself is peopled only with thin ghosts. . . .
>
> This is the kind of thing the past is: it is not unchanging. It grows up soon with weeds and underbrush like a dangerous trail. . . . The self is very precious, too; it is only with the self, open-eyed and sober, that we can accept Christ and the salvation of God. I do not trust another; I do not trust a book, a rock, a stream; I do not trust my friendly Doppelgänger who ranges my dreams and day-dreams: these are all traitors, and they will murder me with the Judas kiss of the unconscious. Sleep, the night, belong to the unconscious, but one must take care to cut it off, like an electric light, at dawn. (34–5)

The sermon is significant for a number of reasons. First, it sounds several themes that will be fundamental in Chappell's fiction and poetry: the lonely, dangerous struggle to understand the past, to find and/or create both meaning and some sense of God. The notion that the mind is a lonely citadel toward which the face of God never leans puts one in mind of Pascal, who wrote, "Every religion that does not affirm that God is hidden is not true." (In the Kirkman novels, Jess's father, a champion of science, charges the narrative with wicked comedy by taking on fundamentalist preachers who claim to speak to God and Jesus on a daily basis.) The sermon is also important for its sharp insights and the way it reveals character. James Christopher must have been as ineffective as Gail Hightower in Faulkner's *Light in August;* must have had members of the congregation shaking their heads and exchanging looks of astonishment. The sermon also reveals self-knowledge, the cleric's tendency toward morbid introspection. For James, unlike Jess of the later novels, the past leads to a form of suicide: self-destructive drinking and adultery; the unwise trust he puts in his Doppelgänger "Preacher," a whore master and drinking buddy.

The father in this first novel, David Christopher, is a prototype for Joe Robert Kirkman. Both are teachers embroiled with Bible-punching parents and the small-town school board over the teaching of science, and both lack an understanding of their sons. Like Joe Robert Kirkman, David Christopher goes for help to Virgil Campbell, an influential man and owner of "Bound For Hell Grocery & Dry Goods." (Campbell chose the name to defy and mock the local preachers who excoriate him from the Sunday-morning pulpits for his personal knowledge of spirits of the liquid variety.)

Though Chappell recycles material from his first novel into the Kirkman tetralogy, his thinking about religion and the father figure has evolved significantly by the time Joe Robert Kirkman appears in *I Am One of You Forever.* Joe Robert does not understand his son Jess's brand of woolgathering but, unlike David Christopher, he would never say, "I don't like the thought of turning a gun on a mewling baby, especially one over thirty years old." Nor would he attribute his son's problems to "reading too many novels . . . Stephen Dedalus . . . the boy with a golden screw for a navel. The search for a father. All that literary stuff. I've read it myself one time or another. It's hogwash. Bull shit" (58). Joe Robert Kirkman, by contrast, is boyishly irresponsible, playful, a trickster (associated with a fox throughout the books) with a taste for practical jokes. Though highly intelligent, he has little comprehension of his son's attempts at writing poetry and, by all accounts, is himself one of the worst storytellers in the family.

In *I Am One of You Forever,* written twenty-two years after *It Is Time, Lord,* Fred Chappell makes Jess Kirkman also feel the squeeze of childhood religion but gives him a more positive outlook than that of James Christopher. Jess, in fact, begins Chappell's self-portrait of the artist as a young man. The past for him is not a suicide, but mastering and shaping it is not without difficulty, even pain. Søren Kierkegaard, in *Stages in Life's Way,* makes a distinction between memory and recollection, asserting that memory is flat and indifferent, smothered with detail. Kierkegaard's idea is that experience can only be consecrated by an act of recollection, one which involves effort and responsibility, ideality and reflection, illusion and enchantment. "Hence it is an art to recollect" (30). A mature Jess Kirkman would implicitly agree and underscore the importance of imagination or of the fiction that makes one see the truth. While James Christopher is at a loss as to how to find out what is important, what is sacred, Jess Kirkman is not.

In the Kirkman novels, as in his poetic tetralogy *Midquest,* Chappell is redefining the nature of what ultimately sustains. Talk in the Kirkman family often fastens on religion, but for some members of the family organized religion does not wholly sustain. In *Farewell, I'm Bound to Leave You,* Jess tells us that it tickled him "to hear Aunt Sam declare that Preacher Andy Garvin had less true religion than a rooster fart" (116). Besides Aunt Sam's wicked humor, what we have here is the implication of the possibility that there exists true religion or a truly religious person. And Jess's grandmother, Annie Barbara Sorrells, qualifies as the latter (we never see her attending church, but she belongs to a women's Bible circle, and her daily ritual includes reading the Book). First, however, let's consider Jess's father Joe Robert.

Jess tells us that he has trouble describing his father's attitude toward religion, except to say that "he was tolerant" and that "ideas about divinity and the related mysteries, he kept private" (62). But Joe Robert's tolerance for valley preachers, the "Ugly Holies," has its limits. In *Farewell,* the dying Annie Barbara Sorrells believes that her son-in-law is not truly against religion: "Only he can't resist teasing anybody who seems dead certain about anything" (20). The absolute certainty of certain preachers galls him absolutely and moves him in these novels to some of his greatest practical jokes. In redefining the realm of the sacred, one must first point to what it is not, and Chappell endows Joe Robert with the gift of satirical observation: "'What are they so het up about?' he asked. 'If what they believe is correct, they've got it made. If they really believed what they said, they wouldn't have to say it so much!'" (62). In *Farewell*, he says, "All these homemade religionists read a different Bible . . . but it makes them all crazy in the same way" (160). One of his funniest anecdotes is about the contentious nature of absolutists and the result of a "theological ruckus":

> "They can't stand much more ruckus," he said. "There where the road starts up Turkey Cove is your Rainbow Baptist Church, and it's a nice white wooden church. You go up the cove a piece and there's a little old concrete block house which is your New Rainbow Baptist Church. A big chunk of them busted away in an argument over predestination. Another two miles is the True Light Rainbow Baptist Church, which starts off with a few concrete blocks and finishes up tar paper siding."
>
> "And if we'd won that baseball game?"
>
> "They'd of had them another fight. You'd go on up the mountain and find a pup tent by the road. The One True Rainbow Baptist Church of the Curveball Jesus." (*Forever* 63–4)

As delighted as he is by his father's and Aunt Sam's irreverent observations, Jess recognizes true religion when he encounters it. And even though he is critical of his grandmother's intellectual credentials (*Forever* 68), he instinctively knows the limits of the intellect in matters of faith and knows her to be possessed of a truly religious spirit. When Joe Robert pokes fun at the "hillside Holies," who always report personal conversations with God or Jesus, Grandma Sorrells shuts him up:

> "You ain't never had no vision," she said. "You ain't never had no talk with God. You ain't the kind that does."
>
> I felt a shiver between my shoulder blades. It was clear that she had had a vision, she had truly talked with God; she simply didn't noise the fact around, call attention to herself.

She goes on to tell Joe Robert that he has a good heart, but he is not yet ready for a meeting with the Lord because he is too immature, "too flibberty and not contrite" (*Forever* 67–8).

Shortly after this dressing down, however, Jess and his father share a frightening but transcendent moment and come to a sense of what cannot be put into words. After experiencing in the barn the closeness of an "apocalyptic" storm with hail and lightning and whispering voices, a storm that prefigures the fury of war, Jess, his father, and Johnson Gibbs (a young man) cannot speak to each other about what they have seen and heard: "We already realized, I think, that our hardest job would be not to talk about what had happened to us, to lessen it and cheapen it with clumsy words. We would have to find some way around it. For a space of time we had become men transfigured, and you don't talk about that. At least, you try not to" (72). Chappell seems to be suggesting that genuine prayer is something tremblingly private. It falls into the category of what Wittgenstein called the truths of silence—truths that, when spoken, are no longer true.

Champion of the modern scientific attitude that he is, Joe Robert Kirkman is thought by some to be irreligious, godless, but a number of times in the novels his verbal gestures betray a man who nonetheless struggles with belief, if not prayer. In the closing pages of *I Am One of You Forever*, he takes Jess fishing and they listen to the life story of John Clinchley, an old man who rents out boats. It is a story Job-like in its outlines. At the end of an overcast melancholy afternoon, in the chilly lakeside cabin, Clinchley concludes his story: "I kept thinking if they was a God in heaven, I wouldn't treat a yellow dog the way I been treated" (164). Joe Robert doesn't react. He simply pays the rental fee and thanks the man. He and Jess get into the car and drive off. Jess observes the gray, lonesome hills and valleys. It isn't until Joe Robert's *cri de coeur* (which ends the chapter) that we realize he has been prompted by Clinchley's story to ponder painful mysteries: "'O Jesus Jesus,' he said, 'I wish Johnson Gibbs hadn't got killed'" (165).

Another poignant example of Joe Robert's sympathetic, if not religious, good heart (which Jess imagines for his father, since the point of view is his) comes in the "Medal of Honor" chapter of *Brighten the Corner Where You Are*. A former student and soldier, Lewis Pruitt, has killed himself after returning from the war. Pruitt's parents come to the high school to present

Joe Robert with their son's Medal of Honor because he was often mentioned by the boy as being one of the best teachers. Joe Robert argues his unworthiness but finally accepts. Speaking to the mother, he says:

> "I thought the world of him. More than that."
>
> "More than the world." She looked into his face. "I count on more."
>
> But that wasn't what he meant, whatever he meant. The world was what my father knew, nothing more or less, better or worse. The world was plenty.
>
> "We all do," he said. (66)

The woman's grief is contagious, Joe Robert's lie is spontaneous, but his lie is perhaps a residue of hope from the depths.

Jess goes on to say that his father is not a praying man. In this respect, he is like his father "for he has learned from the death of Johnson Gibbs that prayer changes nothing." In "The Telegram," one of the most powerfully written chapters in *I Am One of You Forever*, we see the death-notice telegram, "yellow like an ugly pus," leaning against the sugar bowl for weeks, unopened. Each member of the family tries to hide or destroy it, but mysteriously it returns, an unending grief. Jess finally prays.

> I prayed that it would be removed from us. I have never prayed so earnestly since, with such guileless passion. I knew that all of us were praying, my grandmother continuously night and day. But the prayers had no effect on the telegram, and seemed not even to alleviate the dead feeling in our hearts. It was then I found out I could pray in despair and the despair might only deepen, that I could form the words and cling to the meaning of them even though my spirit had shriveled within me to a pinpoint. (95)

If Jess cannot believe in a personal God or traditional prayer, he can and does put his faith in the Word, or the words of stories.

In perhaps the most compelling and comic chapter of *I Am One of You Forever*, "The Storytellers," Chappell explores the epistemology of narrative and its implications. While prayer may have little effect on the world, perhaps storytelling does. One of the storytellers in question is Uncle Zeno (interestingly named after the Greek Stoic). Uncle Zeno isn't as colorful as some of the other eccentric uncles who periodically show up for extended visits at the Kirkman family home. He is "slight" and "unremarkable," given to frayed white shirts, a man who barely occupies the chair he sits in. But what is more significant, "He was a voice." And Chappell pays the highest respect to this voice by applying to it one final adjective stamped with a Faulknerian copyright: "inexhaustible." If the sound of the voice itself is "unremarkable," the effect it has upon hearers is not:

> [H]e told stories, endless stories, and these stories worked upon the fabric of our daily lives in such a manner that we began to doubt our own outlines. Sometimes, walking in the country, one comes upon an abandoned flower garden overtaken by wild flowers. Is it still a garden? The natural and the artificial orders intermingle, and ready definition is lost. (97)

The voice of Uncle Zeno has a divine quality. Jess and his father have the impression that Uncle Zeno isn't so much remembering or inventing his stories as "repeating words whispered to him by another voice issuing from somewhere behind the high, fleecy clouds he loved to stare at." And Jess is certain that his uncle's formulaic beginning (*"That puts me in mind of"*) will be sounded on Judgment Day. The power of the phrase is such that Time will stop, for the world of the imagination is everlasting and holds dominion (98).

Though comic, the story has serious implications about being and nothingness, about storytelling and the void that it fills. Uncle Zeno is variously described as gazing "into his Portable Outer Space" or "looking deep into his private void." John Barth once said that reality was a nice place to visit, but who would want to live there? Barth, however, is a writer who submits to interviews and answers questions about his methods. Uncle Zeno remains mute when Jess's father questions him. He "looked calmly into his vast inane, contemplating the nothingness that hung between stories" (115–6). It is finally the imagination—to echo Wallace Stevens in "The Noble Rider and the Sound of Words"—that enables Uncle Zeno to press back against the pressure of unredeemed reality, or what Jess senses as the threat of "nothingness." For Chappell and Stevens this mental process has something to do with self-preservation.

Narrative imagination is exactly what the other storyteller, Joe Robert

Kirkman, lacks. Uncle Zeno unintentionally arouses him to a state of com-petitive jealousy, so that he desperately visits Virgil Campbell's store to col-lect a few stories from the idlers and whittlers there. Even with their help, Joe Robert's stories, depending on props and violent closures, fail comically because he is so literal-minded. Joe Robert's imaginative blindness is evi-dent in his preoccupation with Homer's blindness. He wonders how Homer could have written about real soldiers and details of bloody battles he had never seen. He argues that the ancient Greek left no historical trace and probably never existed. In similar fashion, Joe Robert is upset by Uncle Zeno's storytelling because he suspects Zeno's stories are fabricated. When Uncle Zeno finally tells a story about Buford Rhodes, a painter who has worked for the family, Joe Robert decides to drive all the way down to Iron Duff to investigate the truth behind the story he has just heard—that is, to prove it a lie.

What intrigues Jess, the real storyteller, is the possibility that "Homer and Uncle did not merely describe the world, they used it up." Jess's father fails to locate even a trace of Buford Rhodes. Perhaps the man had vanished "*because* Uncle Zeno told stories about him" (113). The chapter ends with Jess's father sitting frustrated on the porch while Uncle Zeno, inside at the dinner table, begins telling a new story, one that involves Joe Robert and his theft of grandmother Sorrells's candy. Jess's fears figuratively come true and forecast his father's future disappearance:

> Finally he rose slowly from the chair. But when he took a step he walked directly into the darkest shadow and I couldn't see him at all and at that moment Uncle Zeno's story concluded and all the night went silent. (118)

Somewhere between experiencing this premonition of world-loss and the composition of the novel *I Am One of You Forever*, which is the antidote to world-loss, Jess has made discoveries about the salvific powers of the imagination. Unlike James Christopher, for whom the past was potentially suicide, or Lewis Pruitt, the broken veteran in *Brighten the Corner Where You Are*, for whom the past was literally suicide, Jess Kirkman sees the past as an unweeded garden ready for restoration, a way to nourish the future. In a wonderful scene that concludes the first Kirkman novel, Aunt Saman-tha, a famous singer from Nashville, performs "Come All You Fair and

Tender Ladies" at a family reunion. Finally it is Jess's turn to sing, and his father requests "The Green Laurel." Jess fights the suggestion "like a wild dog" because, though he loves music, he knows he is a poor singer. His voice, like Uncle Zeno's, is made for a related but different art:

> My face burned like a comet; I mumbled and choked, I couldn't sing then and I can't sing now. If I could sing—sing, I mean, so that another human being could bear to hear me—I wouldn't sit scribbling this story of a long time ago. (179)

Farewell, I'm Bound to Leave You, among other things, is about Jess's continued development as a writer. The title nicely prefigures Jess's leaving the mountains to become the poet he will have become (his non de plume is Fred Chappell) in *Look Back All the Green Valley;* it also suggests the Kirkman novels' central theme of death and loss and their relationship to poetry and song. Is music, as George Bernard Shaw asserted, "the brandy of the damned"? Are language and song merely sad narcotics that blunt the keen edge of human pain? Or do the voices of poets and singers prevent world-loss, shore against our ruin, and carry us and those we love into the future? Surely the mountain storytelling traditions Jess was raised with suggest the latter.

It is largely from the women in his family (with some prompting from Uncle Zeno's example) that Jess learns the techniques and metaphysics of narrative. The novel is framed by the italicized chapters of a deathwatch for Grandmother Sorrells. Without stories, an entire world would be annihilated with her. Dying, she thinks, "It is cruel how the power of time is a power only to separate" (21). But Jess will have an answer for separation, for the "away, away" of "Shenandoah" buried in the novel's title. He has heard the most engaging stories from his mother and grandmother and learns the Faulknerian lesson that the past is never dead. In "The Shining Woman," he is fifteen and has

> begun to feel that Time Past contained secret messages meant for me. In the midnight dark I would lie in bed and imagine I heard whispers from Time Past. It wasn't the dead people speaking; that was a dry whispery sound like Uncle Runkin's voice when he spoke so lovingly of graveyards. This voice was a murmur warm but muffled, the syllables

flowing together like drops of rain joining in streams on a windowpane. Time Past was full of story as the Junior Classics Library in its twelve colorful volumes in my brick bookcase; the persons my mother and grandmother told me of were as startling as the planet Saturn swimming in space, the way it was pictured in my Father's discarded general science textbooks. (136)

Like his father, Jess has become critical of organized religion. Though tolerant, and more influenced than he realizes by his mother's and grandmother's religion, he is still capable of reflecting on their amusing contradictions: "My grandmother enjoyed lauding the virtues, my mother delighted in excoriating the vices, and I'm convinced that neither of them ever thought that all of their palaver about religion provided only a pious excuse for flavorsome gossip" (178). But what he learns from these women is the seriousness of vocation and how poetry, passion, and love are linked. His mother tells him: "*Passion must feed on something, Jess, and a poet's passion must feed upon truth*" (106).

One of the most valuable lessons he learns, morally and technically, is from his mother. She tells him a story about her cousin—how, as a girl, Earlene learned the fine art of trout fishing from a rough-edged, rough-tongued old man named Worley, and how, when he broke his ankle in a remote trout stream, she managed to save his life. Following his mother's humorous and touching story "The Fisherwoman," Jess asks her:

"How come you know so much about it? The things she was thinking and talking to herself?"

"She told me a lot and then I put myself in her place so I could tell the story to you. That's what storytellers do. Maybe you'll remember that if you ever take a notion to tell stories. Do you think you'd like to be a storyteller?"

"Maybe. But I don't hardly know any stories."

"Don't worry," my mother said. "You'll learn some. All you have to do is listen." (100)

❋

In *Brighten the Corner Where You Are*, a-day-in-the-life novel, we see that Jess has taken his mother's advice, for, with a few interruptions to remind

us of the first-person point of view, we see everything through the eyes of
Jess's father on the day he is to appear before the school board to answer
charges that he is teaching evolution. The story takes place immediately
after World War II, a bloody event which proves to Joe Robert how terribly
unevolved humans really are. Jess is an effaced narrator, largely absent from
the story except for the chapter "Shares," which is about his being goaded
into a bloody fistfight with the son of a tenant farmer and which also serves
to underscore the latent brute nature of all human beings, even sensitive
would-be writers. No matter how much Jess sympathizes with the poor
Farnums, he nonetheless is driven to bloody the face of Burrell Farnum:

> But I knew what I knew. The thoughts were as sharp in my mind
> as pistol shots: I wish I was grown up now already and owned me a
> farm with some poor folks on it. I wish I had me some tenants on a
> farm. I'd whip their ass three times a day. (114)

But most often Jess's imagination runs to the angelic, not the demonic.
In fact, in the "Medal of Honor" chapter about the returning soldier, Jess
imagines what is going on in his father's mind when he speaks with the
boy's parents. Jess knows that his father is thinking about Johnson Gibbs,
accidentally killed in boot camp, now buried in their family plot: "The more
he tried to think about Lewis, the more he thought about Johnson and
thought about all the good times past and gone and how the world still
went on, a world that Johnson could know nothing about" (60–1). At this
point, Jess's imagination won't allow what he has just imagined his father's
thoughts to be. Jess, like the God of creation, interrupts the narrative in
italics:

> *But he knows about it, Johnson knows. He stands beside us even now as I
> tell you our story.* (61)

Such is the power of the imagination, which explains why Shelley called it
"the great instrument of moral good" and why Wallace Stevens wrote, "The
poet is the priest of the invisible."

Part of Jess's narration is an attempt to understand his father, to imagine his way into the fabric of his father's thinking. Another aspect of the
narrative endeavor is to keep his father intact from the erosive nature of
time. The death of Johnson Gibbs has shocked the whole family into a

bitter awareness of time and mortality. Jess imagines his father thinking, "Even the mountains were beginning to change" (56). Jess's own sense of shaken foundations is eloquently registered in *I Am One of You Forever:* "I had learned, maybe without really knowing, that not even the steadfast mountains themselves were safe and unmoving, that the foundations of the earth were shaken and the connections between the stars become frail as a cobweb" (92).

In *Jess*, the menace of nothingness is deeply felt, but along with it comes a way to deny our nothingness and ensure that those we love are not annihilated. The idea and the buoyant redemptive image come to him from classical literature, the *Aeneid*. A bookish boy, he has been reading a translation of Virgil on the day of his father's ordeal. Jess describes himself on that early morning his father looked in on him before leaving for school:

> I slept on, never waking ever in my life, dreaming of the man who battled the devil-possum and the false prophet and the forces of dark ignorance. I dreamed, too, of Aeneas carrying his father on his shoulders toward the shores of the future. I dreamed of ilex arid osier and of the honeybees that were the souls of the dead. (37)

❖

Carrying the father toward the shores of the future is exactly what Chappell does in *Look Back All the Green Valley*, the final installment of the Kirkman narrative, which proves the truth of *finis coronat opus*, for this novel indeed crowns and royally closes the tetralogy. The book gives us glimpses, through flashback and dialogue, of characters in the earlier novels. Along with new details and anecdotes about Joe Robert (the comic tale of his successful attempt to get preachers to invest their savings in business enterprises they know to be sinful) and the childhoods of Jess and his sister Mitzi (her aborted boxing match with Rollie Sikes), we learn that Joe Robert Kirkman has died ten years earlier; that his wife Cora is now dying of congestive heart failure in Graceful Days, an assisted-living complex; that Jess has become a professor at the University of North Carolina at Greensboro and is finishing, under the pseudonym of Fred Chappell, his final poetic volume on the four elements, *Earthsleep*; that his sister Mitzi has become successful at a working partnership with the chamber of commerce in her town. In the earlier Kirkman novels, Jess was to a large extent an un-engaged narrator, but in *Look Back All the Green Valley*, he steps from the shadows to become fully dimensional, a man who is actively in search of his father—the very project ridiculed by James Christopher's father in *It Is Time, Lord*. And unlike Chappell's earlier Kirkman books, which are novels in the way that Faulkner's *Go Down, Moses* or *The Unvanquished* are novels (i.e., collections of independent but tightly related stories), *Look Back* is linear in its development and resolution.

Preparing for her own end, Jess's mother charges him with making her funeral arrangements and cleaning out his father's workshop, which turns out to be a trove of mysterious finds (maps, a list of women's names, strange devices, sketches, and notebooks), the kind of items fit for a detective or private investigator. But Chappell has written a *roman comme recherche* and what Jess is really after is something more elusive: the nature of—and the impediments to—faith at the end of a scientifically advanced yet barbarous and blood-drenched twentieth century. His father's notebooks, "Thoughts of Fugio" *(fugio* being from the Latin *I flee)*, provide help in his search, and part of what he discovers is a new and encouraging way of looking at time itself. He is also humbled by what he discovers. The contraptions, writings, experiments with geranium breeding, especially the "Thoughts of Fugio," and other "evidence" in his father's workshop, located under a clock shop ("Times Past Antique Clocks"), make Jess realize that he didn't know his father as well as he thought he did. He says, "I was collecting my father's leavings, reading his words, tracing his routes. I was pursuing the image of his spirit, a diminishing image, through a wilderness of time-tangled shadows" (79). But why?

When he tells his mother about the strange contents of the workshop, she advises him to leave well enough alone. But she also tells him that he is trying to make it up to his father, trying to understand him when it is too late. This stings Jess, but he knows she is right when she says, "I don't think you'll be able to figure him out. I couldn't." He also knows that his father is a trickster, an elusive fox, and that the desire to understand and make everything right is not pure: "I probably have other motives, too, that I don't know about. But one of them is the sheer interest of the matter. You said it was like a puzzle—well, finding out these things is like being in a detective story. I keep learning something new" (174–5). Though his father never mentioned reading any of his poetry, detective Kirkman finds a penciled note in a copy of *Twelfth Night,* in the scene in which Sir Toby and Sir Andrew talk about the four elements, "tope and confabulate"—"See *Fred Chappell's scheme!*" (66, my emphasis). Father and son are more alike than they know.

One of the ways Jess will acknowledge a debt and ease his sense of guilt is by writing and inserting a science-fiction story into the narrative we are reading about his journey home to help his dying mother. The story bursts unexpectedly upon the reader and involves a space ship of alternating time drive. A tribute to his father's speculations about time and space, "Into The Unknown" is yet another attempt to understand him; it is also a reimagining of his father's death and the likelihood of his survival in that country from whose bourne no traveler returns. One of Fugio's thoughts is, *"The question is not* what, *but* which, *time it is."*

Jess imagines a time (July 18, 1949) when Joe Robert drives his family to the workshop in order to take the space ship he has built, the *Isambard,* for a shakedown cruise. The ship transforms itself from a blue porcelain box into a "gossamer silver starship" before the astonished eyes of his mother, his grandmother, and Mitzi. Once on the bridge of the starship, Joe Robert distributes uniforms to everyone. Before blastoff, he explains to the crew that it is both July 18, 1949, and July 18, 1969 (a day crucial to the Apollo mission to the moon). Naturally Cora thinks her husband has lost his mind, but after showing them his Floriloge, or flower clock, Joe Robert patiently reassures them and explains that time is "an organic entity":

> "I tell you, Dr. Einstein got it right—and so did Shakespeare when he observed that time travels at diverse speeds with diverse persons. This stupid mechanical way of counting time has got the human race into big trouble. *Tick tick tick, bong bong bong.* Who can believe that those puny little gizmos have anything to do with *real* time?" (231–2)

The story/chapter finishes with a potent tour de force of the imagination wherein Jess's father has to go ahead alone to test "Veilwarp," an uncertain sector of space that might crush the starship. His body stays aboard the ship but his mind disengages with the help of a "psychic observation projector." The starship's speakers broadcast the returning voice but Joe Robert's lips do not move; the voice, full of static, cuts into transmissions between Houston control and the Apollo spacecraft as it descends to the moon's surface. Finally Joe Robert's body collapses as if hit with a hammer and the last message heard is from Apollo: "*Tranquility Base here. The Eagle has landed*" (244). In its own way, the received message is as powerful as "The Lord has risen."

If Jess is able to write convincingly about the relative nature of time, it is because earlier in the novel he has had a revelation. This occurs when he goes to the cemetery to visit his father's grave. Standing over the plot, he feels himself very much a fool, the obligatory trip unnecessary. What he thinks and glimpses prefigures the novel's end:

> The dead are not silent, not even shy; they are speaking to us continually, as voluble as the October wind among the falling leaves. There was nothing I could hear at the gravesite that I did not hear always and everywhere, nightlong, daylong. A grave plot and a truculent stone would not make those voices more intelligible. (101)

Turning away, he catches a glimpse of an "old man" moving among the grave stones, "someone from a long time past," someone "unmistakably familiar." Though not identified by name at this point, a reader of the other Kirkman novels recognizes immediately the figure of Uncle Zeno, the storyteller. It is perhaps here that Jess fastens on to the idea that his father is not really dead—nor, in all likelihood, is Uncle Zeno.

The novel's final chapter beautifully stitches together the final strands of narrative design and the themes of art, religion, and everlastingness. Jess and his sister have hired a bluegrass band (mostly cousins) and organized a picnic, a final family reunion, with the purpose of drawing from a hat—so as not to give offense—one name from among a number of generous relatives who have offered space in their own farm graveyards so that Joe Robert and Cora can be buried side by side (a bureaucratic mixup has left no space for Cora in the cemetery where Joe Robert is now buried). After everyone is fed, Jess steps to the microphone and reads his father's last will and testament, a seriocomic document he has uncovered while cleaning out "Dr. Electro's Secret Laboratory." The document hilariously evens scores with Joe Robert's greatest adversaries. I'll give only a few of the final scores. To Bible-thumpers and sticky-fingered politicians, Joe Robert bequeaths his "psychic observation projector." "Clap this visionary helmet upon your heads and strain your minds forward toward your lifetimes' endings: see how it feels to meet your Maker after all your years of sham and pretense" (261). And to the Tipton School Board which was ready to release him from his teaching position for presenting the theory of evolution, he bequeaths "a signed edition of the complete works of Charles Darwin. 'Is man descended from the monkeys? . . . Not in the case of the Tipton School Board, where such descent has not yet occurred" (262). Jess finally touches upon his father's prediction that there would be a man landed on the moon and implicitly acknowledges that he was wrong about his father's lacking imagination, albeit his father's imagination was of a kind very different from his own. He reminds the audience that the nay-sayers were wrong because they lacked his father's knowledge of science and his visionary imagination, because they misconstrued the very nature of reality itself. In one impressive rhetorical flourish, Jess links the imagination and religion:

> You have mistaken the nature of reality and made penurious this fleeting existence that it is our duty to enjoy and celebrate in all its splendors and miseries, in all its triumphs and anticlimaxes. What we imagine is what we are; what we desire is what we become. As Jesus told us in a different context, If we so much as thought the deed, then we have committed it. "Everything has come true, ladies and gentlemen. Our lives are but poetry, after all." (265)

Jess ironically becomes a kind of haunted preacher while he finally rids himself of obsession and eulogizes his father before a congregation of uncomprehending relatives. Like the failed minister James Christopher in *It Is Time, Lord*, Jess Kirkman is deeply concerned with the past but not defeated by it. On the contrary, he has found a way to redeem it with language, but with language that is, like Christopher's, too figured and sophisticated to be completely followed by his hearers.

They do, however, respond to and are stirred deeply by the poetry of music, in this case the old-time favorite—sung by the New Briar Rose Ramblers—which gives the novel its title: "Look Back All the Green Valley":

> Now our days are dwindling down
> The fresh green leaves have turned all brown.

Look back look back the May time days
Look back all the green valley.

Yet oh my darling think of me
When you are in that far countree
The wonders there so strange to see.
Look back all the green valley

Look back look back the time will come
When you and I are past and gone.

The song acknowledges that "far countree" where Jess's father and all the other lost ones quite possibly survive. But the song is also a *carpe diem* and reminds listeners of the need to drink deeply of the now—something that Sir Toby Belch and Sir Andrew comically do in the passage of *Twelfth Night* marked by Jess's father. In fact, at one point in the reading of the last will and testament, where Joe Robert bequeaths to bluenoses a recipe for moonshine, the Ramblers finally hear something they like and perk up. "Hear, hear," they cry.

The central importance of poetry, story, and song in our lives is beautifully affirmed in an exchange of dialogue when the band members have packed up their instruments and are about to make their exits from the stage—a Shakespearean moment. Jess compliments the players on having a fine band. It feels good, he says, to know somebody is keeping old tunes alive. "'Well, actually,' Harley said, 'it's the other way around. It's the songs that keep us alive—or keep the life worth living, anyhow'" (269).

In the last lines of the novel proper, Jess is on the phone telling his wife Susan when to expect him home, telling her that he has not solved his father's mystery but explaining his various discoveries, especially the one about *Twelfth Night* and his father's annotation of the late-night celebrations of Sir Toby and Sir Andrew. After some warm and amusing byplay that Susan teasingly calls "sexy," she says she doubts his promises: "It's probably nothing but poetry." Jess ends the conversation with a wonderfully buoyant line: "'What else is there?' I asked, burning to know" (272).

As if this were not enough of a crowning closural gesture, Chappell carries his affirmation into the italicized nocturnal graveyard scene, which frames the novel. A graveyard affirmative? Well, yes. By now we know that Jess has paid two of his cousins to help dig up his father's grave, an impulsive act that makes him very much like his father. Jess's intention is to prove his father is not really dead. After taking turns with the other diggers, Jess unearths the skull of a fox; readers will recall that, at the beginning of the novel, he has called his father "your classic folklore trickster" (26). Jess climbs out of the grave. He shows the fox skull to his cousins and tells them to pack it in. His father is not there.

> "How do you know?"
>
> "I just know."
>
> Because I wasn't going to say, That's him; my father was the fox, even though it was the living, breathing truth, obvious as fire.
>
> "What's that?" Ned said. "There's somebody sitting over there on that gravestone."
>
> But when he struck the beam that way, there was no one. Yet we all thought that someone had been seated there and only a moment ago had stood up and walked away into the rain. (278)

I don't have any glib jargon to explain why the scene makes a believer of one, or why it works, but it does. The novel's final words, with the quote from *Twelfth Night* on the facing page, convey a sense that father and son *now* understand each other, two men who are, after all, similar restless spirits and makers, but of a different kind. And when the immortal Uncle Zeno, storyteller, ghosts by in the rainy dark, the novel receives a supernatural benediction and reminds us of the everlasting, of that "inexhaustible" voice within us.

WORK CITED

Kierkegaard, Søren. *Stages in Life's Way*. London: Oxford University Press, 1940.

ELEVEN

The Flashing Phantasmagoria of Rational Life
The Platonic Borderlands of Fred Chappell's
Forever Tetralogy

WARREN ROCHELLE

IN FRED CHAPPELL'S KIRKMAN tetralogy, readers find themselves in a fantastic world in which a man's beard, freed from restraints, fills a house to overflowing, "with trailers coming out of the downstairs kitchen windows, and from the chimney a long flame-like banner of it reach[ing] toward the stars and sway[ing] in the cold breeze" (*I Am One of You Forever* 61). In this extraordinary world, a boy is taken by his mother to see the Wind Woman, the keeper of the sounds of the hills, sounds the boy knows he must learn to "lay out" in "proper fashion," to become the tales he will tell; and in this same world, ghosts are a present and troublesome part of reality. Alongside the fantastic, there is the ordinary, the mundane, the expected. Men and women fall in love and go to great lengths to get each other's attention—to the point, in one instance, of one man's knocking himself out with a hammer. Elaborate practical jokes are played, and a young man's death brings haunting grief to the family that loved him. As Fred Chappell describes it, "the exaggerated and the mundane" coexist, they "shake hands and [are] friends" (Chappell, interview by author, 20 June 1997).

Or in other words, the rational and the irrational are not separate. There is a "blurring of boundaries" between the fantastic and the realistic; they occupy a mutual borderland between two worlds that often seem not to touch. It is to this borderland that I want to give attention here. The borderland is not his exclusively. It has a long history of some two thousand years, and Plato should be given much credit for its founding. Chappell's borderlands reflect this Platonic heritage. And, as with Plato, Chappell's use of this territory in his fictional world becomes rhetorical, an argument for how a human life can best be lived. To ground my argument, and to place Chappell's rhetoric in its Platonic context, I will first review Plato's ideas on the value of the rational and irrational, particularly as expressed in the *Phaedrus*. Second, I will examine Chappell's borderlands in the *Forever* cycle as expressions of these Platonic ideas; and finally I will conclude with a consideration of Plato's and Chappell's shared vision of the good human life.

At first glance, and in the popular imagination, it would seem that Plato does not consider the irrational, the imaginative, to be valuable in human experience as a way to truth. But as Martha Nussbaum points out in *The Fragility of Goodness: Luck and Ethics in Greek Tragedy and Philosophy*, Plato's philosophy was not static or fixed; his thinking changed, particularly in the value he assigned to the irrational as a worthwhile aspect of human experience. Nussbaum sees Plato's philosophy as a progression toward this acceptance, from the *Republic's* expulsion of the poets to the *Phaedrus*, which she reads as a recantation of "seeing erotic passion as a degrading madness" and "passions as mere urges for bodily replenishments with no role to play in our understanding of the good" (201). Plato grew, Nussbaum contends, to accept both the rational and irrational as essential to how a human life can best be lived.

There is evidence of this organic growth and change in the *Republic*. Yes, Plato does expel the poets from his ideal city in Book X of the *Republic*. Their works are "at the third remove from that which is and are easily reproduced without knowledge of the truth" (*Republic*, 598e–9a). But even as Plato sends the poets into exile, he uses the imaginative, the irrational, to teach his philosophic truth. The *Republic* is a work of interpretive fiction, after all. Even given that Plato is writing down what he remembers of Socrates' conversations, the dialogue is an interpretation of what Plato remembers. Story is also used in the *Republic's* content. Plato has Socrates using imaginative myths to teach: the Myth of the Metals, the Myth of the Cave, the Myth of Er. These allegorical stories all come at crucial moments in the dialogue when Socrates is trying to impress upon his companions an ultimate truth. To express this truth he resorts to metaphor and symbol. As Robert Scott Stewart points out in his essay, "The Epistemological Function of Platonic Myth," "myth serves as the medium through which is made possible any discussion of the first principles of philosophy" (260). Through metaphoric and symbolic language, Plato uses myth to "speak of those things which cannot be dealt with directly." And it is "through myth alone that Plato is able to write of that [about] which he is the most serious" (275–6), which in this case are the Forms of the Good and the Beautiful, Plato's first principles. Plato, according to Stewart, *only* discusses the Good in symbolic language, as in the Myth of the Cave in which the Sun is the Good. Thus, even as Plato condemns poets for their use of the imagination, he uses it to reveal rational truth.

In the *Symposium*, it is the speech of Aristophanes, the Myth of the Round People, that is of interest here. On the surface it is a comic tale, but critical interpretations of the story's meaning range from individual love and the impossibility of ever truly being with the beloved (Nehamas and Woodruff xvii) to questions about how the desires of Eros keep us from self-sufficiency (Nussbaum 176) to the Good itself (Jaeger 185). Aristophanes' comic story of the round people is, then, not just a funny tale, regardless of its interpretation. Rather, it is another illustration of the power of story—whose source is the imagination, the irrational—to express philosophic truth. Plato again uses myth in the *Phaedrus* to express a philosophic truth. And it is in the *Phaedrus* that Plato's growing acceptance of the value of both the rational and irrational in the good human life, the life in the borderlands, bears fruit. The *Phaedrus* is not only an apologia for Eros, but, also, with some qualifications, it is an apologia for poetic writing, and thus for the value of the irrational. According to Nussbaum, the *Phaedrus* "displays a new view of the role of feeling, emotion, and particularly love in the good life" (202). The "nonintellectual elements" of the soul are now seen as "necessary sources of motivational energy" (214).

This acceptance, qualified as it may be, of the irrational, is seen first in the fact that Socrates and Phaedrus have left Athens to wander in the countryside. Socrates has, as Phaedrus points out, never gone "beyond the frontiers of Attica or even, as far as I can see, outside the actual walls of the city" (*Phaedrus* 230). Socrates has left his familiar urban environment and entered a place both "of burgeoning sensuous beauty" and of danger, erotic and passionate danger. Socrates is in the place where a "pure young girl was carried off by the impassioned wind god" and where the "mad god Pan has his shrine". And Socrates has gone to this place of the senses at the "hottest hour of the day," a time when one is vulnerable to Eros, with a beautiful young man (Nussbaum 200). Here, beneath the plane tree, Socrates delivers the speech attacking "erotic passion as a form of degrading passion." But when Socrates turns to leave, he receives a "supernatural sign" from his *daimonion,*[1] forbidding him to go. Socrates has wronged Love. Socrates' second speech atones for his first and argues that "certain states of madness or possession are said to be both helpful and honorable, even necessary sources of the greatest good" (Nussbaum 213). Plato thus admits he was wrong: the irrational is of value and can lead a person to the good.

This admission is stated even more persuasively in the Myth of the Charioteer. Again story is used to express philosophic truth. The charioteer, the white horse, and the black horse are allegories of Plato's tripartite soul. Just prior to this allegorical story, Socrates has explained to Phaedrus, in straight exposition, the soul's immortality. But to describe the soul's nature that way, Socrates says, "would require a long exposition of which only a god is capable":

> Let us adopt this method, and compare the soul to a winged charioteer and his horses acting together. Now all the horses and charioteers of the gods are good and come of good stock, but in other beings there is a mixture of good and bad. First we make it plain that the ruling power in us men drives a pair of horses, and next that one of these horses is fine and good and of noble stock, and the other the opposite in every way. So in our case the task of the charioteer is necessarily a difficult and unpleasant business. (*Phaedrus* 246a)

Initially, the myth would again seem to be condemning the emotional, the irrational, as it is the black horse who is "crooked, lumbering, ill-made, stiff-necked, short-throated, snub-nosed." The charioteer, the rational element of the soul, must beat the animal into submission. But, consider: the horses, good and bad, are, with the charioteer, a unit, the complete soul. All three elements, the rational charioteer, the appetitive white horse (or feelings), and the emotional black horse (or passions) comprise "three parts of the same soul" (Grube 133). Both horses, firmly under the charioteer's control, pull him to the beloved, the object of desire. Both horses are necessary. Also, the entire myth is written in charged, emotional, poetic, and highly symbolic language—and it is through myth that Socrates expresses his philosophy to Phaedrus. A story, then, a product of the imagination, is a way to truth. As Nussbaum puts it, our emotions and appetites, the "nonintellectual elements" of the soul, "have an important role to play in our aspirations toward understanding." They are performing a cognitive function as they advance us to the Good. A "person feels no gap between thought and passion, but, instead a melting unity of the entire personality" (Nussbaum 214, 215, 216). Thus "[t]he passions, and the actions inspired by them, are intrinsically valuable components of the best human life . . . . This life involves shared intellectual activity, but it also involves continued madness and shared appetite and emotional feeling" (218–9).[2]

Or as Chappell would put it, such a life involves a blurring of boundaries: "I wanted each to fade into the other so that you would be in a kind of sphere, a sphere of perception that would be complete" (Interview). It is this sphere of perception, these Platonic borderlands, in which Chappell is working that I want to examine now. This sphere is not a big place; it is no more than a village, and indeed, Chagall's paintings of village life are in part the inspiration for the Kirkman tetralogy. As Chappell explained on "Soundings," a radio program produced by the National Humanities Center, Chagall's paintings "incorporate all kinds of fantasy elements, all kinds of color, all kinds of playfulness, and at the same time, for all their fantastic surface, strike the deepest chords for those people who are familiar with them" ("Soundings"). And as does Chagall's art, so does Chappell's art.

In *I Am One of You Forever,* there are several exemplars of the Platonic view of the irrational as valuable in the good human life. Uncle Zeno literally leads a life of fiction, creating his world (and the world of others) through the language of story. Johnson Gibbs becomes part of a storm, or a "further element the storm was trying to become, an extension of itself both human and inhuman" (*Forever* 71). He becomes, for a time, something outside of the tangible, the provable. It is, however, Jess's encounter with Uncle Gurton and his beard that is unquestionably inside the border territory.

Uncle Gurton is first presented as a man not of this reality. His beard, which has been growing untrimmed for forty years, is "fabled" and "legendary." His mode of travel is unknown: "An apparition, he simply became present." And Uncle Gurton continues to appear and reappear without warning during his visit with the Kirkmans: "No footsteps of departure, no sound of the side door, nothing." As Jess's father, Joe Robert, says, Uncle

Gurton "has got some interesting ways about him" (49, 50). But even as he is described as an "extraordinary-appearing person," with his arms "too long for his shirtsleeves" and his overalls legs too short, Uncle Gurton is also described as a man of the mundane. He wears brogans and overalls, and those too-long arms "dangled out like price tags." He has a healthy appetite and his favorite drink is ordinary buttermilk.

The fact that Uncle Gurton apparently inhabits Chappell's "sphere of perception," in which fantasy and reality fade into each other, is not troubling to Jess, his father, or the rest of the Kirkmans. When Joe Robert presses Jess's grandmother to tell him when Uncle Gurton is coming, all she says is that he will just have to wait. Uncle Gurton will appear when he is ready; this is how he is. These constant vanishings and reappearings bother no one. Rather Jess speculates that Uncle Gurton might actually be "translated into another and inevitable dimension of space." Joe Robert, a man of science and fact, suggests that to record these events "would take some kind of invention that is beyond the capacity of present-day science."

The most fantastic element is, of course, the beard. When Jess and his father drug Uncle Gurton and let the fabled beard out of the old man's overalls, it begins to move:

> Then suddenly it was upon us, billow on billow of gleaming dry wavy silver beard, spilling out over the sheet and spreading over the bed like an overturned bucket of milk. It flowed over the foot of the bed and then down the sides, noiseless, hypnotic. There was no end to it. (58)

In the beard they see and hear a singing mermaid, Moby Dick, and sharks. Thus, the world in which the Kirkmans live, of which Uncle Gurton is an integral part, is one of the rational and the irrational, the real and the fantastic. The story itself, as the Kirkmans are obviously good and happy people, becomes an argument for the value of such a way of living.

The story is, of course, a tall tale—or is it? As Chappell points out, Joe Robert and the reader aren't "entirely sure how to take that story." Joe Robert, who would normally try to find a rational explanation for Uncle Gurton, can't. Chappell insists "we absolutely could explain everything in the world rationally," but then points out that "our universe is made of a lot of different intersecting realities" (Interview). The Kirkman reality appears to be one inside such an intersection.

Brighten the Corner Where You Are, as it is Joe Robert's story, might seem to be a step out of the fantastic or an attempt, as Joe Robert does, to rationalize the irrational. Or is it? The novel opens not in a world of the tangible and the explainable, but rather in the borderlands. Jess and his father are up before dawn to milk their cows, a mundane and essential task for anyone with dairy cows. But the moon is so large and close that it scrapes Jess's head and knocks off his "blue wool cap." There is too much moon; to solve the problem, Joe Robert pulls the moon out of the sky and stuffs it in a milk can. At first there is some pleasure in all the extra newly visible stars, but the moon is missed. Its poetry and magic and mystery are gone, except for what can just barely be contained in the milk can: "The outside of the can was rimed with the grainy moon-silver that sometimes made shapes like words we could not make out; perhaps these words were in a lunar language no one knew" (*Brighten* 5). In the end, Joe Robert releases the moon and the world is restored.

This capture of the moon is, for Joe Robert, an experiment. He considers himself the "champion of modern scientific attitude . . . the local champion of reason and science" (7). "He sees it as his duty to pull this [locality] out of its benighted state and get them to read Darwin and Spencer" (Interview). But Chappell also describes Joe Robert as being "mounted backward on his noble charger" on his quest for reason and science, with "shining armor," a white knight, a quixotic figure of romance. Joe Robert can be said to be an embodiment of a Platonic soul. He is ruled by reason, but integral to his being are the emotional, the appetitive, and thus the imaginative. We need both lunar magic and the clear rational light of stars.

Joe Robert seeks, as did Socrates, the truth, which is sacred to both. And, like Socrates, Joe Robert uses fiction to reach truth. As Jess explains, "The truth was so sacred to my father that he generally refused to profane its sanctity with his worldly presence" (*Brighten* 28). As acting high school principal, Joe Robert seeks to keep his teachers engaged in an effort to reach the truth and not "too concerned with personal status among equal colleagues, too industrious at gossip, rumormongering, backbiting, social climbing, petty jealousy, pointless intrigue, and underhanded politicking." To do so, again like Socrates, Joe Robert uses myth. Using the archetype of the Bad Kid, Joe Robert invents the "Ungodly Terror, a mysterious and utterly rotten kid, a student who was a danger to them all" (51). Joe Robert, of course, brings the myth to life himself and gives full vent to his love of practical jokes and pranks.

Joe Robert's life thus belies his devotion to the rational. Yes, science and reason are important and Joe Robert does believe they should rule human life. But he cannot live his own life as a life of pure reason let alone champion it for others. Joe Robert is a "farmer, a scientist, an inventor, an explorer" and "a wizard just about ready to come into his full powers" (53). Rational life is a "flashing phantasmagoria," a "wild endearing circus of sense and circumstance" of perceived sensations and physical phenomena, so much so that, as Chappell says, if we were aware of all of it at once, we could not bear it. We are not meant to be purely rational. Joe Robert is an argument for this.

The argument that humans are meant to live lives of rationality and irrationality is continued in the third book of the quartet, *Farewell, I'm Bound to Leave You*. According to reviewer Donald Harrington, its chapters are bound together "not by arbitrary plot developments but by music: melody, counterpoint, rhythm, timbre, and tune" (6A). Or in other words, not by the rational, the tangible, but by the intangible—by sounds. And this collection of "eleven prose ballads" that tell "the tales of eleven mountain women, "are enclosed by a frame that is outside of normal reality (Betts [unpaginated]). Annie Barbara Sorrells, Jess's grandmother, lies upstairs dying, watched over by her daughter Cora. The two women talk as they wait. But do they? Can they? Or are the daughter and mother hearing each other's thoughts? The mother is dying; she is past conversation. Such a thing is impossible, irrational—but then they are speaking in the irrational language of love, of grief, of coming death. Annie Barbara Sorrells is somewhere between death and life—a place similar to Plato's Cave. In the shadows around her, "There are spirits . . . but none of them is Jesus." Jesus will not be in "shadow but in light." So she begins her journey, in shadow, toward the light, to "a country where [she has] never been. . . . It's not real to walk in, but it is a real place"—the reality that exists outside the Cave, the reality of the forms, Truth, Good, Beauty (*Farewell* 15, 18). Jess and his father, Joe Robert, wait downstairs, and "The wind had got into the clocks and blown the hours awry." All the clocks tell a different time, and time for the Kirkman family, as Joe Robert tells Jess, will stop with his grandmother's death. Her time, "a steady time that people could trust," is ending.

The family exists in an in-between zone, a waiting area, between life and death, between one time and another (3, 5).

To fill the waiting, Joe Robert and Jess will retell the stories the two women wanted Jess to hear—stories that blur the lines between the rational and the irrational, stories whose truth is metaphoric, not literal. Jess, at first, seeks the literal, as he tries to sort out the different versions of stories he has listened to, over and over, from his father, his grandmother, his mother. The versions don't agree, even when it is a story in which all three were directly involved, such as the story of Cora's and Joe Robert's courtship, "The Shooting Woman." "Specific events didn't always match; sometimes, in fact, they were totally contradictory." The truth of the stories is an elusive mystery, a puzzle, such as the ongoing family puzzle of the contents of the unlabeled jars of canned fruits and vegetables in the Kirkman storeroom. Time, which changes any story, has changed the appearance of the jars' contents so much that sight alone isn't enough to discern the truth of what is inside. Each year, the jars are "dusted and inspected," and the Kirkmans all attempt to guess the contents—and all are proven wrong. The content, the truth, of the stories is just as elusive and comes in multiple versions. Truth is a matter of perspective, of discovery. Truth is also a matter of the imagination, as Jess learns from his mother. After hearing the story of "The Fisherwoman," he asks her how can she know so much, "the things she was thinking and talking to herself?" Like any good storyteller, she tells him, she takes what she already knew and then she "put [herself] in [Cousin Earlene's] place" and thus could tell him the story. Truth is not bound by literal reality; it is, instead, metaphor (100).

And where do these true/not true, rational/not rational stories come from? Who is the Wind Woman, the keeper of the sounds of the mountains: "the wild, desolate, heartbroken voice of a woman crying away away away . . . square-dance music, joyous and copper-bright . . . houses and barns, ropes and straps, gunshot and sword slash, iron and calico"? His mother warns Jess not to eat or drink anything while he is in the house of the Wind Woman—do these sounds, the elemental parts of a story, come from the deepest recesses of human life, the dark from which there is no easy return? The story of the Wind Woman is, on the surface, fantastic, yet below the surface, it is true: Jess must learn, as the Wind Woman will teach him, how to put the sounds in their proper order, so that the stories can be told. Is she then Jess's Muse, a divine source of inspiration, as Plato speaks of her in the *Ion?* Allegory, myth, fairy tale, a mother and her son—what lines there are blur and merge, and the real and the fantastic coexist (114–5).

The story in *Farewell* that is perhaps the best exemplar of this coexistence is that of Aunt Sherlie Howes, "The Figuring Woman," a tale in which the natural and the supernatural are found side by side. Aunt Sherlie is described as "not supernatural in the least." She is a "very rational, deductive kind of woman," the "wise woman of the village," a mountain Sherlock Holmes, as it were (*Soundings*). Yet this thinking, rational woman is called upon in the story of the Shining Woman to solve a ghostly mystery. Are ghosts real? According to Jess's grandmother, the narrator of this story, "There's a lot to be said both ways. There's ghosts in the Bible, and maybe that ought to settle the whole question. But a lot of people don't believe, thinking it's all old-time superstition and rank foolishness" (*Farewell* 136). Jess's grandmother does believe, however, as do the Lucases who must deal with a ghost haunting their house. They go to Aunt Sherlie, the wise woman, for advice. Aunt Sherlie doesn't dispute the ghost's existence or the sanity of the Lucases. She deals with the problem as one that needs solving, not as an uncommon situation. She solves the problem through deductive reasoning, and the ghost is appeased and ceases to appear. Rational thought, the charioteer, has made the two horses toe the line. Yet the two horses do exist and are both a part of life.

Which horse is pulling the chariot in *Look Back All the Green Valley* is a matter of debate—or perhaps it is something of a race between the two steeds. The novel itself seems to parallel Plato's Myth of the Cave—with reality itself somewhat uncertain. In the myth, humans have been chained in the darkness since childhood, with their backs to the open cave mouth. A fire burning above and behind them provides light. A path is between them and the fire, and on the path is a wall. People are on the wall, moving artifacts. Shadows from the people and what they carry are cast on the wall in front of the chained people. The chained ones also hear echoes from the people behind them. For those chained, the truth of existence is in the shadows. One man is freed and turns around to see that what is behind him is truer than what he has known all his life. But he sees the moving artifacts—and these are still a step removed from the Real. This man is dragged out of the cave and into the sunlight, the pure sunlight of Reality, of the Forms.

What is Real for the reader in *Look Back* is uncertain. Fred Chappell is, as Jess's nursing homebound mother says, the "strange name," the "silly name," under which he writes poetry. Jess is married to a long-suffering Susan and teaches at the University of North Carolina at Greensboro, details which, as a quick glance at the back flap will verify, are also descriptive of Fred Chappell, who is actually writing *Look Back.* So Chappell is writing a first-person novel in the voice of Jess Kirkman, a poet, who is writing under the pseudonym of Chappell, a poet whose life mirrors Chappell's own. Chappell's sister still lives in Haywood, a.k.a. Hardison County, but whether the two have had to find a double plot for their parents is another story. But then Chappell has never pretended *not* to be drawing on his own western North Carolina mountain boyhood in this quartet of novels or its poetic counterparts, the first of which is named *River,* which is also the title of Jess's first book of poetry.

Is the imagined Jess an alter ego for Chappell? Yes. Is Jess's story true? No, it is fiction. But Chappell uses his own life to create that of Jess and his family. Is Jess the shadow? He is certainly Chappell's artifact—or is he? Jess carries with him his "staunch comrade, [his] date book, work book, and silent confidant . . . [his] fat and battered, worn gray at every corner" notebook. In this notebook Jess has "telephone numbers, titles of books and journal articles, partial notes for lectures," and, among these and other things, "suggestions for [his] fourth book of poetry, to be called *Earthsleep.*" This volume, the fourth, is to be "centered around the last of the Pythagorean elements, earth." *River* is, of course, water. *Earthsleep* is to be bound with the "connective tropes of gardens and graves, intimate engagements with dirt," as is *Look Back* (19–20). Jess is seeking a place where his parents can be buried side by side, a mutual grave. *Look Back*'s prologue, "The Moon Behind the Clouds," is of an intimate engagement with dirt, as Jess and other men are digging, exhuming Jess's father. *Earthsleep* is, of course, the name of another book of Chappell's poetry.

This correspondence with the four mythic elements holds true for all the works in the Kirkman tetralogy (Chappell, E-mail to the author, 22 March 2000). *I Am One of You Forever* opens with water. In the prologue, aptly entitled "The Overspill," the Kirkman house is located by water, "a small creek ran through [the] the sideyard, out of the eastern hills" (5). It is over this creek that Jess and his father build an ornamental bridge to "please" Cora—and it is the destruction of this bridge, caused by an overspill from Challenger Paper, which motivates Joe Robert to a protracted and elaborate scheme for revenge in *Look Back.* Water—tears—of sorrow, regret, of vexation, engulfs the entire family:

> The tear on my mother's cheek got larger and larger. It detached from her face and became a shiny globe, widening outward like an inflating balloon. At first the tear floated in air between them, but as it expanded it took my mother and father into itself. I saw them suspended, separate but beginning to drift slowly to another.
>
> Then my mother looked past my father's shoulder, looked through the bright skin of the tear, at me. The tear enlarged until at last it took me in, too. It was warm and salt. As soon as I got used to the strange light inside the tear, I began to swim clumsily toward my parents. (6)

And so Jess swims toward his parents throughout the novel, throughout the quartet. The title of *Brighten the Corner Where You Are* suggests as its element the bright light of fire. When Joe Robert steals the moon, only the cold fire of starlight is left in the night sky. The fire of reason, of intellect— Joe Robert's—burns throughout the novel. Air—the wind that blows the clocks awry, the wind of Wind Woman on Wind Mountain—pervades *Farewell.* The stories themselves are of, on, and in the air, told in speech, carried from the teller to the listener on this wind. Chappell has, in effect, with this mythic structure, with tales of the fantastic and the mundane, created his own mythos, a personal mythology. This mythology of his own life, his family history, and of the Appalachian mountain culture, is both phantasmagoric and rational, in the Cave and yet far outside it.

In what reality is this Cave? How much of these stories is objectively true? Does Chappell, for example, carry such a notebook as Jess does? I don't know, but chances are good that he does—a notebook of pieces and jottings of creation, of the mythos. That the reader cannot separate what is real from what is imagined is not, however, the point. Rather, as does Plato, Chappell, in this quartet, and particularly in *Look Back,* creates a truth that is fiction that is the truth.

Jess's quest for a mutual gravesite, the continuing action of the novel, exemplifies this interweaving of the rational and the irrational, the real and the unreal. He discovers one of his father's secret laboratories, which parallels Plato's cave. Jess descends into the lab on "sagging but sturdy stairs," and outside is a lush meadow, "folded and unfolded in the gentle breeze," washed in gleaming sunlight. He walks down into darkness and dust and the "musty smell of desertion" and, when he turns on the light, he is surrounded by artifacts, devices, and clutter, which include a strange Goldbergian device and a fat notebook of his father's, "The Thoughts of Fugio. Here was a collection of maxims, epigrams, mottoes, and proverbs." After first thinking that his father had garnered these sayings from other sources, Jess realizes they are original, "genuine specimens of [his father's] creative impulse . . . his private ideas and feelings" (61, 63, 64). This laboratory holds the artifacts that represent Joe Robert in all his quixotic quirkiness. Besides the Goldbergian machine, Jess finds the expected clutter of "ash trays . . . scattered around, heaped with pipe dottle . . . red cans of Prince Albert. . . . Balls of string and twine, tape measures, a Mickey Mouse alarm clock, a tangle of fish hooks, a Boker pocketknife . . . the ordinary gimcrackery of a restless masculine imagination." He also finds Cherokee artifacts, photographs of rockets, scores of "ordinary spiral-bound notebooks." One notebook in particular, labeled *Fugio,* a collection of original maxims and aphorisms, is for Jess a "treasure trove," "a genuine specimen of [his father's] creative impulse." A flyer for "Satanic Enterprises Amalgamated"—evidence of Joe Robert the prankster. And a map of western Hardison County, hand drawn, and curiously marked with women's names—perhaps the names of secret lovers (61, 62–3, 65, 69). This last surmise, Jess decides, must be investigated, the truth must be determined; so he goes out into the sunlight to find the truth—thus adding another object to his quest.

Jess finds himself constantly sifting through truth that is fiction that is truth. His is a Platonic quest, "pursuing the image of [his father's] spirit, a diminishing image, through a wilderness of time-tangled shadows" (79). And, of course, Jess's discovery of the mysteries left by his father, the mystery of his father himself, begins in story, the memories of his father left behind with those who knew him. He learns of his father's dream to make Hardison County a great garden, a "showplace for flowers." And the "more of Hardison County [he] saw, the more stories [he] learned . . . the more

[he] knew, or felt [he] knew about [his] father." Through the irrational, the subjectivity of memory, Jess learns more of the man his father was.

What, then, does Jess learn? The names on his father's treasure map are not the names of women but the "intimate yet official names of different breeds of roses," planted in thirteen specially selected places throughout Hardison County. The roses are, Jess also learns, part of what his father calls a Floriloge, a huge time-telling device that will relink humankind with the "living and breathing cosmos" and reestablish "an essential harmony of human spirit with the regular processes of the cosmos." The "fictitious little units" of nanoseconds, milliseconds, seconds, and hours "will be wiped out" and the "hearts and minds [of humanity] will be serene" and free of the "tyranny of mechanical time" (160, 232–5). Joe Robert Kirkman, the apostle of science and reason, who had lost his teaching job for expounding the "tenets of Darwin," was, it seems, something of a mystic; "instead of per-forming miraculous deeds, he had turned to symbolic rituals" (162, 163). Jess also learned, as he uncovered the multiple and overlaying trails of his father, that Joe Robert Kirkman had left too many trails—that he was like a fox, wily and elusive—and that one trail led to the elaborate scheme of revenge against Challenger Paper for washing away the bridge Joe Robert had built for Cora years ago. Jess learns that his father was man and myth—that in-stead of a chariot with a white horse and a black horse, Joe Robert flew a starship, the *Isambard*,[3] a spaceship that was both a dream and an echo of the reality of space exploration, an echo-dream that existed in multiple time streams, alternate existences, mythical and otherwise. The day his father's heart finally gave out, the day men first landed on the moon, July 20, 1969, was the day when man and myth were finally equal, "when the treachery of his heart closed the gates of his body and exiled his spirit to the infinity it had always yearned after" (244).

Joe Robert described the universe into and out of which the *Isambard* dips as stochastic—and therefore as an existence of chance and probability, involving random variables. Such an existence seems contrary to a Platonic universe of light and order and succeeding levels of awareness leading to the ultimate truth of the Forms. But are these existences contrary? If Plato gives equal weight to the irrational as a way to the truth as the rational—if myth and the imaginative are ways of knowing, doesn't then myth, story, inherently include the stochastic? Each time a story is retold there is the addition of a random variable: the storyteller. Each new storyteller will interpret and reimagine the myth as it relates to his or her theory of the world. Joe Robert is such a storyteller, as are, it seems, all the Kirkmans, including Jess, a.k.a. Fred Chappell; and the *Forever* quartet is, as it is based in Chappell's own life, in stories real and imagined, told and retold, both autobiography and myth, fantastic and mundane.

Look Back has two successive climaxes—the picnic at which Jess announces whose place has been chosen for the grave plot of his parents and the late night exhumation of his father, to take the remains to the new grave, avoiding the morass of public-health rules and regulations. The first, the picnic, is the mundane—yet it isn't completely that. As Jess prepares his "semiformal address," friends and relatives—the characters whose stories are within the greater story of the quartet—arrive, and with them, story, his and theirs: "this was the story of [his] youth unfolding and a larger tale, too, than that very small one: the chronicle of a period of mountain culture of rare and striking flavor," Chappell's mythos (251). The stories are told again at this picnic. The only fair way to choose which family to host Joe Robert and Cora Kirkman forever, Jess has decided, is a lottery, a name drawn from a hat. Before drawing the name, he reads his father's will—not of property and valuables, but of jokes and curses and remembrance. Or, in other words, stories. The two last tasks, Jess tells them, after reading his father's mock will, are the huge pie-in-the-face revenge on Wesson, the Challenger Paper executive who was responsible for the washing of Joe Robert's bridge, and a longed-for trip to the moon. These last two events never happened yet they did: dream is reality, myths are true: "What we imagine is what we are; what we desire is what we become. As Jesus told us in a different context, if we have so much as thought of the deed, then we have committed. Everything has come true . . . [and] our lives are but poetry" (265). Look back all the green valley, "Things have come round at last; all things will come round again" (267).

And as these stories begin in myth, are myth, so they end—in the second climax, at the graveside, in this last tale, that of the earth. Jess finds not human remains, but rather the skull of a fox. He knows this is his father: Joe Robert, the fox, the trickster, the boy whom Jess found in his pursuit of his father's mysteries, Joe Robert, the storyteller, who has become story. Yet, as these stories begin in reality—the building of an ornamental bridge—they end in the very mundane and muddy reality of an open grave. Jess finds myth—Jess finds his father in the borderland between the rational and the irrational. The myth is true.

This borderland, this region of blurred lines between fantasy and reality, is clearly where a human life can best be lived. As Plato argued in the *Phaedrus,* and as Chappell is arguing in his mythic *Forever* quartet, humans need both fantasy and reality to live full and valuable lives. Both are essential to the good human life and indeed are interconnected. As Chappell argues in his essay, "Fantasia on the Theme of Theme and Fantasy," fantasy shines a light on the "normal order of things"—because of it, we can see more clearly the world as it is (183). That our reality is, in addition to perceived phenomena, one of metaphor, is essential to our understanding of ourselves. The women in the Kirkman tetralogy are mothers, grandmothers, sisters, aunts, and at the same time, they are archetypes (Harkins): the wise old crone, the virgin, the maternal spirit. The ordinary is extraordinary (Chappell, *Naked* 147). Humans, both Chappell and Plato argue, cannot live rational lives alone. As T. S. Eliot says, "Human nature is able to endure only a very little reality" (quoted in Dodds 215). As Nussbaum says, there are two universal tendencies or propensities in human life, the Dionysian and the Apollonian. The former is the "tendency to move and act in accordance with irrational focuses," and the latter, "to approach the world with cool reason, carving it up and making clear distinctions. . . . [A] full human life needs fluidity between the Dionysian and Apollonian" (Introduction, *Bacchae* xxv, xxv–xxvi, xlii).

We would like to believe and live as if we are wholly rational beings. We want to quantify and measure life, approach it scientifically, objectively, and logically. The irrational, the imaginative, and the subjective are seen as less: less reliable, less trustworthy. Our culture, according to Thomas Moore in *The Re-Enchantment of Everyday Life,* is a "magic-starved society, trying to create an effective and humane culture on the limited basis of scientific method, machinery, and materialistic philosophies" (374). The Kirkman tetralogy, like Plato's *Phaedrus,* argues that this is *not* how we should live. Moore agrees, and he asserts that we need to recognize "our need to live in a world of both fact and imagination" (x). Rather than seeing fact and imagination in opposition, Moore sees "enchanted living and practical, productive activity" as serving one another: "one delighting the spirit of ambition, the other comforting the heart" (xi). After all, "we all wax and wane and have a moonlit consciousness that is hazy, mysterious, changing, and not completely rational" (320).

Or as Chappell puts it, "One part would not reject the other part, or make another part obsolete or ridiculous." Fantasy and reality, "the exaggerated and the mundane [should hold] hands and be friends" (Interview). And how else should we live? We are not wholly rational beings, nor are we creatures of fantasy. Humans live, as Plato argues in the *Phaedrus* and Chappell in his *Forever* quartet, in a borderland between the two, a region where we can be fully and truly human.

NOTES

1. According to Nussbaum, the *daimonion* is Socrates' "divine sign," a "serious individual who intercedes infrequently to hold back Socrates when he is about to undertake something wrong" (202). The term is further defined as the attendant power or spirit, or genius, of a place or a man.
2. Much of the previous discussion of the *Phaedrus* is taken from an earlier essay of mine, "Story, Plato, and Ursula K. Le Guin," *Extrapolation* 37, no. 4 (winter 1996), 316–29. I have also used this material in a forthcoming book, *Communities of the Heart: The Rhetoric of Myth in the Fiction of Ursula K. Le Guin*, to be published by Liverpool University Press.
3. Isambard Kingdom Brunel (1806–1859), born in Portsmouth, England, "designed many bridges, tunnels, and viaducts and was one of the first to use compressed-air caissons to sink bridge foundations into deep riverbeds. He was also a railway builder and the designer of London's Paddington Station. His greatest work was the design and construction of three oceangoing steamships, each the first of its type" (*Grolier Multimedia Encyclopedia*, 1995. *Your Dictionary*. Online. 22 March 2000). Obviously such a man would be a hero for Joe Robert Kirkman and a likely namesake for Joe Robert's starship.

WORKS CITED

Chappell, Fred. "Fantasia on the Theme of Theme and Fantasy." *Studies in Short Fiction* 27, no. 2 (spring 1990): 179–90.

———. E-mail to the author, 22 March 2000.

———. Personal interview, 20 June 1997.

Farewell: Fred Chappell. "Soundings." Narrated by Wayne Pons. National Humanities Center. WUNC 91.5 FM, Chapel Hill, N.C. April 1997.

Dodds, E. R. *The Greeks and the Irrational*. Boston: Beacon, 1951.

Grube, G. M. A. *Plato's Thought*. Indianapolis: Hackett, 1980.

Harkins, Susan Lynne. "Mountain Moonshine Intoxicates." Review of *Farewell, I'm Bound to Leave You*, by Fred Chappell. *Orlando Sentinel*, 5 January 1997 (page number not available).

"Isambard Kingdom Brunel." *Grolier Multimedia Encyclopedia*, 1995. *Your Dictionary*. Online research, 22 March 2000.

Jaeger, Werner. *Paideia: The Ideals of Greek Culture*. 2 vols. New York: Oxford University Press, 1939–44.

Moore, Thomas. *The Re-Enchantment of Everyday Life*. New York: Harper-Collins, 1996.

Nehamas, Alexander, and Paul Woodruff. Introduction. *Plato's Symposium*. Trans. Alexander Nehamas and Paul Woodruff. Indianapolis: Hackett, 1989.

Nussbaum, Martha. *The Fragility of Goodness: Luck and Ethics in Greek Tragedy and Philosophy*. Cambridge: Cambridge University Press, 1986.

———. Introduction. *The Bacchae*. By Euripides. Trans. C. K. Williams. New York: Farrar, Straus, Giroux, 1990.

Plato. *Phaedrus and Letters VII and VIII*. Trans. Walter Hamilton. London: Penguin, 1973.

———. *Republic*. Ed. C. D. C. Reeve. Trans. G. M. A. Grube. Rev. ed. Indianapolis: Hackett, 1992.

Stewart, Robert Scott. "The Epistemological Function of Platonic Myth." *Philosophy and Rhetoric* 22.4 (1989): 260–80.

TWELVE

Windies and Rusties
Fred Chappell As Humorist

JOHN LANG

WITH THE PUBLICATION of *The Gaudy Place* in 1973, Fred Chappell's writing began to draw regularly on the humor that has become a prominent feature of his fiction and poetry during the past three decades. The four books of poems that compose *Midquest* are notable for their extensive use of humor, as are many of the epigrams of *C* and the poems of *Family Gathering*. Chappell's two collections of short fiction—*Moments of Light* and *More Shapes Than One*—also contain humorous stories, especially the former's "Mrs. Franklin Ascends" and the latter's "Mankind Journeys through Forests of Symbols" and "The Adder." But it is in the Kirkman tetralogy of novels, which themselves grew out of material generated during the writing of *Midquest,* that Chappell has established himself as one of the premier humorous writers of late twentieth-century America.

The four Kirkman novels, Chappell has said, are meant to parallel the four volumes of verse that compose *Midquest,* "surrounding that poem with a solid fictional universe" ("Fred Chappell" 124). In enlarging the world he had portrayed in *Midquest,* Chappell continued to seek inspiration in two major sources of that book's comedy: the oral storytelling tradition of his native Appalachia and the literary tradition of Old Southwest humor that achieved its finest artistic expression in the writing of Mark Twain. Viewed from the perspective of nineteenth-century American literary history, these two influences are themselves interconnected, for much of the writing of southwestern, or frontier, humorists builds upon the oral tradition of the tall tale. That humor derives much of its power from what M. Thomas Inge calls "the hyperbole and comic exaggeration that have characterized American humor from William Byrd to John Barth" (3). Although the frontier designated by the term "Old Southwest" is usually associated with Alabama, Georgia, Tennessee, Mississippi, Louisiana, Arkansas, and Missouri, the western North Carolina of Chappell's birth would certainly have been considered part of that frontier in the nineteenth century.

Walter Blair lists among the major features of Old Southwest humor its use of vernacular narratives derived from oral storytelling; its focus on such masculine activities as hunting, fishing, gambling, drinking, and fighting; its wild exaggeration, including tall tales and frontier boasts; its reliance on humor originating in "physical discomfort" (often resulting from practical jokes); its episodic structure; and its effective use of framed narratives to heighten comic or ironic incongruity (62–101). Many of these traits are readily apparent in both the Kirkman tetralogy and *Midquest,* though Chappell typically softens the humor of physical discomfort and enlarges, especially in *Farewell, I'm Bound to Leave You,* the roles played by women. Blair says of the authors of Old Southwest humor, "Alike in making their writings local, authentic, and detailed, these humorists were also alike in imparting to their stories a zest, a gusto, a sheer exuberance" (69). That exuberance is equally evident in Chappell's work. What has become increasingly clear with the publication of each new volume in the Kirkman tetralogy is Chappell's stature as the rightful heir, perhaps the fullest twentieth-century embodiment, of the tradition of Old Southwest humor and of Twain's and Faulkner's transformation of that tradition. The spirit of such humor is ubiquitous in Chappell's tetralogy, with its frontier boasts (Johnson Gibbs's bragging in the opening chapter of *I Am One of You Forever*), its tall tales, its many practical jokes, its hunting and fishing episodes, its vernacular speech, its colorful characters, and its vividly concrete figurative language.

Chappell's use of this comic tradition began with *Midquest,* whose first volume appeared a decade before *I Am One of You Forever* was published. David Paul Ragan was the first critic to point out the influence of Old Southwest humor on Chappell's poetry. In an essay entitled "At the Grave of Sut Lovingood: Virgil Campbell in the Work of Fred Chappell," Ragan emphasized the importance of George Washington Harris's *Sut Lovingood's Yarns* (1867) to Chappell's conception of his own rustic storyteller. According to Ragan, "the similarities between Virgil and Sut Lovingood are perhaps the most striking because both Virgil and Sut poke fun at sham and pretension" (24). For Ragan, the two characters are also linked by the whiskey that is their constant companion, by their skillful storytelling, and by their independent spirits (30). Ragan considers "Three Sheets in the Wind: Virgil Campbell Confesses" as the poem in which Chappell "draws most directly upon the style and subject matter of Sut Lovingood's yarns" (27).

Ragan is certainly correct to detect Harris's influence in this poem, for there Virgil resembles Sut not only in his storytelling skills but in his reliance on his feet to rescue him from his pursuers. Sut repeatedly refers to his legs as his best feature, declaring, "All my yeathly [earthly] 'pendence is in these yere laigs" (83). Similarly, Virgil, caught in adultery by his wife and a Baptist preacher, leaps out of bed thinking, *"Feet don't fail me now"* (*Midquest* 126; Chappell's italics). What Ragan fails to note is that Harris's influence extends beyond the Campbell poems, as when Ole Fred (in "The Autumn Bleat of the Weathervane Trombone") addresses Uncle Body as "old hoss," Sut's frequent epithet for Harris as interlocutor (*Midquest* 114). But Harris's direct influence on Chappell's work is minimal, and there are far more differences than similarities between Virgil Campbell and Sut. About *Sut Lovingood's Yarns* Chappell has said, "I've only read a couple of sketches in textbooks or somewhere and was not attracted strongly enough to read on" (letter to author).

Mark Twain is a far stronger influence on Chappell's fiction and poetry. Yet Ragan does not comment on the impact Twain has on a poem like "My Father's Hurricane," which appears two poems before "Three Sheets in the Wind" and which Ragan simply identifies as a further example of the influence of Southwestern humor, one that helps to reinforce the comic tone of Virgil's confession. In fact, the wind described in "My Father's Hurricane" appears to derive directly from Twain's account of the Washoe Zephyr in chapter 21 of *Roughing It*. Twain depicts a daily windstorm that creates a multilayered "soaring dust drift" containing an exotic conglomeration of objects:

> [H]ats, chickens, and parasols sailing in the remote heavens; blankets, tin signs, sagebrush and shingles a shade lower; door-mats and buffalo robes lower still; shovels and coal scuttles on the next grade; glass doors, cats and little children on the next; disrupted lumberyards, light buggies and wheelbarrows on the next; and down only thirty or forty feet above ground was a scurrying storm of emigrating roofs and vacant lots. (156)

The hurricane Fred's father describes, Bad Egg, also has multiple layers, five in all, including a layer of roofs (though in *Midquest* that layer is on the top rather than the bottom). Among the twists that Chappell adds to Twain's tall tale is having Fred's father transported upward through the layers on a "corkscrew" counterwind (118).

Chappell actually surpasses Twain in his comic catalog of the hurricane's contents. Among them are

> Water pumps, tobacco setters, cookstoves,
> Girdles shucked off squealing ladies, statues
> Of Confederate heroes, shotguns, big bunches
> Of local politicians still talking of raising
> Taxes. (117)

Whereas Twain portrays the Washoe Zephyr in his first-person narrator's semiautobiographical voice, Chappell puts this tale in the mouth of someone other than his first-person protagonist—and then has that storyteller flirt with the comic bragging of frontier humor:

> "Before I could holler I zipped up to Layer Two,
> Bobbing about with Chevrolets and Fords
> And Holsteins . . . I'm not bragging, but I'll bet you
> I'm the only man who ever rode
> An upside-down Buick a hundred miles,
> If you call holding on and praying 'riding.'" (118)

Twain devotes four paragraphs to the Zephyr; Chappell, more than four pages of loose blank verse. But both authors employ the tall-tale techniques prominent in Old Southwest humor, with its "stretchers" (Huck Finn's term for Twain's exaggerations), its comic juxtaposition of terms, and its understated improbabilities. Moreover, Chappell makes the hurricane's layering part of *Midquest*'s larger symbolic structure by having J. T. initially identify four layers (as *Midquest* is built around the four natural elements of earth, air, fire, and water) before J. T. discovers a fifth layer, a discovery seemingly meant to allude to the presumed fifth element, quintessence, beyond the earthly sphere.

Twain's influence is also apparent in "Three Sheets in the Wind" itself. Virgil's punishment by his wife and the preacher has supposedly made him

"a sobered feller" (127). Yet when J. T. responds to Virgil's tale by remark-
ing, "Too bad I can't drink with a man on Reform," Virgil immediately
replies, "A drink, you say? . . . Well, where's the harm?" (127). Such an
exchange is reminiscent of Twain's satire on reform in chapters 32 and 33
of *Roughing It* and in chapter 5 of *Adventures of Huckleberry Finn.*

Both "Three Sheets in the Wind" and "My Father's Hurricane" appear
in the *Wind Mountain* volume of *Midquest.* Their placement there may be
meant to remind readers that the Appalachian term for a tall tale is a
"windy." Yet in *Midquest* Chappell draws on the oral tradition for serious
as well as humorous purposes, and he utilizes a range of narrators, not just
Virgil and J. T., to present that humor, as Twain uses a variety of storytellers (e.g., Bemis and Jim Blaine and Dick Baker) in *Roughing It.* Thus,
when Laura Niesen de Abruna contends that "[Virgil] Campbell provides
the major source of amusement" in *Midquest* (77), she does not consider in
this judgment "My Father's Hurricane," "Birthday 35: Diary Entry," "My
Grandfather Gets Doused," "My Mother Shoots the Breeze," and "The
Autumn Bleat of the Weathervane Trombone." Despite the serious intent
of *Midquest*'s overarching thematic structure, with its Dantean motif of
spiritual rebirth, the book's humor is pervasive. That humor is often a matter of tone, of Chappell's characteristic refusal to take himself too seriously.
But one of its distinctive elements is the tall-tale humor of Harris, Twain,
and other nineteenth-century American writers.

The influence of Twain is likewise evident in the Kirkman novels; Fred
Hobson, writing about *I Am One of You Forever,* was among the first critics
to observe this. Hobson focuses on Twain's impact on the tetralogy's opening novel, pointing out that "Johnson Gibbs exaggerates his pitching prowess in the manner of one of Twain's keelboatmen in *Life on the Mississippi*"
and noting that "Uncle Zeno is a first-rate yarn spinner, telling stories with
the deadpan earnestness of Mark Twain's Simon Wheeler" (86). For Hobson, in fact, the novel's narrator, Jess, is "still another version of Huck Finn,
playing Huck, that is, to his father's Tom Sawyer, going along with his
father's pranks but rarely initiating them" (84). Yet Twain's influence in this
novel is far more extensive than Hobson's comments indicate. It is apparent
not only in Chappell's creation of incident and character but also in the
book's style and episodic structure.

In an interview with Resa Crane and James Kirkland, Chappell speaks of Twain as one of his early and continuing influences (12–3). This acknowledgment is supported not only by *Midquest* and the Kirkman novels but also by poems LXVI and LXVII in *C.* These paired single-line statements—"The only animal that dares to play the bagpipes. Or wants to" (32)—echo Twain's famous epigram in *Following the Equator*, "Man is the only animal that blushes. Or needs to" (256). Chappell has also affirmed the importance of Twain's work for him by telling another interviewer that *Adventures of Huckleberry Finn* is the only novel he has read more often than Thomas Mann's *Doctor Faustus* (Broughton 111).

Twain's decision to use a vernacular narrator in *Huckleberry Finn* was heavily influenced, as many critics have demonstrated, by his reading of the Old Southwest humorists. Twain's novel, in turn, decisively shaped subsequent writers' use of the colloquial style, as Richard Bridgman, among others, has shown. Given Chappell's desire to celebrate the Appalachian region in the Kirkman tetralogy, Twain's example undoubtedly proved significant in Chappell's creation of his own characters' colloquial style. At times, in fact, readers can hear echoes of Huck's diction in Jess's vocabulary, as when Jess says of his grandmother, "a tear had *leaked* around the edge of her glasses" (*Forever* 36, italics added), the same term Huck uses to describe the king's and duke's pretense of grief over Peter Wilks's death. Jess's grandmother also uses the words "trashy" and "trashing" (67, 174) in ways that parallel Jim's rebuke of Huck in chapter 15 of Twain's novel, and Jess's phrase "such truck as that" is likewise reminiscent of Huck's diction. In addition, Chappell employs the rare term "sockdolager" in *Look Back* (48), the same term with which Huck describes a thunderbolt in chapter 20 of *Huckleberry Finn.*

In more general ways, too, Chappell builds on Twain's legacy by endowing his narrator with a vocabulary, like Huck's, filled with the vividness, concreteness, and metaphorical richness of folk speech. Bridgman cites such examples as the following from Twain's novel: "Huck 'smouches' a spoon, he has 'clayey' clothes, and he notices 'shackly' houses; he speaks of an undertaker's 'softy soothering ways'" (117). Of that same undertaker, Huck says, "He was the softest, gliddingest, stealthiest man I ever see; and there warn't no more smile to him than there is to a ham" (*Huckleberry Finn* 801). Chappell often provides a similar range of diction and seeming spontaneity of figurative language. Jess depicts his Uncle Luden, for instance, as having "squirreled through" a window. With his face "mashed flat against the glass," Uncle Luden "looked like a drugged catfish," Jess adds (45). Elsewhere Chappell has Jess use "riproar" as a verb (62), "meanousness" as a noun (129, 142), "yellower" as a comparative (160), and "ghostally" as an adverb in the phrase "ghostally moans" (142). Of Aunt Sam, Jess remarks, "She dredged up another clutch of Kleenex and scoured her broad face" (168), a sentence whose forceful nouns and verbs have all the vigor of Huck's. Nor is such vivid diction limited to Jess. His grandmother, for example, speaks of the antics of Joe Robert and Johnson Gibbs as "a lavish of tomfool" (27).

In character and incident Chappell also draws directly on Twain in *I Am One of You Forever*, not only in the ways Hobson identifies but in additional ways as well. Uncle Runkin of the chapter entitled "The Maker of One Coffin" is a case in point. Among the novel's gallery of eccentric visiting relatives, Uncle Runkin is easily the most bizarre—and one of the most thematically significant. At the center of this predominantly comic novel, Chappell has placed the italicized section "The Telegram," which reports the death of Johnson Gibbs in a training accident at Fort Bragg. Death is a pervasive presence in Chappell's fiction and poetry, an inevitable dimension of human experience. Thus, for Chappell, humor must remain conscious of human finitude, must confront sorrow, not ignore it. But Uncle Runkin, like Twain's Emmeline Grangerford, whose outlook he shares, is enamored of death.

Arriving at Jess's home with his coffin, his "treasure" (133), and sleeping in that coffin every evening, Uncle Runkin is a grotesque artist-figure. He has already devoted twenty-five years to carpentering the coffin—"the sole lick of work the old man ever struck," says Jess's father (123)—and yet the lid remains unfinished. Much of this chapter turns on Uncle Runkin's quest for a suitable inscription for the coffin. *Come lovely Angel, Sweet death comes to soothe,* and *In Life's full Prime Is Death's own Time* are among his favorite candidates. Emmeline Grangerford's melancholy sketches and her scrapbook of "obituaries and accidents and cases of patient suffering" (*Huckleberry Finn* 725) create a mood similar to that induced by the radio program "Meditations" to which Uncle Runkin listens. During that program the announcer reads from what Jess describes as "a book of dejected thoughts" (130). Both Twain and Chappell satirize the excesses of these two characters' obsessions with death and instead commend a hearty embracing of life in the face of sure mortality.

As the budding-artist figure of the Kirkman tetralogy, Jess has little of a positive nature to learn from Uncle Runkin. Rather, Chappell implies, Jess must orient himself to Uncle Zeno, whose chapter, "The Storytellers," precedes "The Maker of One Coffin" and directly follows "The Telegram." Chappell's juxtaposition of these three sections of the novel invites the reader to see Uncle Zeno and Uncle Runkin as contrasting responses to the fact of human finitude. As storyteller, Uncle Zeno represents one traditional means of confronting death: that is, through the species of immortality that art—and storytelling's collective memory—bestows. Significantly, Chappell places Uncle Zeno in the context of the tall-tale humor of Twain and the Old Southwest, thereby intensifying the novel's comedy immediately after "The Telegram" has plumbed the depths of death and loss.

Not only does Uncle Zeno's manner of storytelling resemble that of Simon Wheeler, as Hobson indicates (86), but it follows the principles laid out in Twain's essay "How to Tell a Story." "The humorous story is told gravely," Twain comments; "the teller does his best to conceal the fact that he even dimly suspects that there is anything funny about it" (*Literary Essays* 8). "To string incongruities and absurdities together in a wandering and sometimes purposeless way, and seem innocently unaware that they are absurdities, is the basis of the American art," he adds (11). Jess thinks of Uncle Zeno in precisely such terms. Jess considers Zeno more a voice than a man and says of that "unremarkable" voice, "Dry, flat, almost without inflection, it delivered those stories with the mechanical precision of an ant toting a bit of leaf mold to its burrow. . . . And he [Zeno] took no interest in our reactions. If the story was funny our laughter made no more impression upon him than a distant butterfly" (97–8).

In "The Storytellers" Uncle Zeno narrates several disconnected stories, each of which involves elements of Old Southwest humor. For example, he portrays Lacey Joe Blackman, a well-known hunter, as just as enthusiastic about hunting as Twain's Jim Smiley in "The Notorious Jumping Frog" is about betting. Whereas Jim will bet on anything ("if there was two birds sitting on a fence, he would bet you which one would fly first"), Lacey Joe will hunt anything: "Go a-hunting pissants . . . if they was in season" (99). Uncle Zeno describes Lacey Joe's role in a bear hunt, one of the staples of

Old Southwest humor, and also tells of Buford Rhodes and his coon-hounds, one of which is called "a cross between a bloodhound and a Shetland pony," a dog the children ride all day long, "he was that good-natured" (105). Such comic hyperbole is archetypally American.

But Buford is "most proudest of" his dog Elmer (105). Elmer's role in this chapter is anticipated in *Earthsleep*, the final volume of *Midquest*, when Ole Fred refers to "the coonhound that could measure lumber" as the subject of one of Virgil Campbell's tales (167). In "The Storytellers" Chappell has Uncle Zeno remark, "That dog Elmer was so smart that if Buford showed him a piece of oak board or a joint of pine siding, he'd take off and tree a coon which when the hide was skinned off and stretched would exactly fill out that length of wood" (106). In typical tall-tale fashion, Uncle Zeno heightens the absurdity of this claim by recounting Elmer's racing into the woods after the dog sees Buford's wife's ironing board, though Buford remains uncertain "whether Elmer already had a coon that big somewhere he knew about or it just sparked his ambitions" (106). When Buford himself disappears for two years while searching for Elmer, the dog returns home and supports Buford's family by teaching arithmetic and natural science at the local high school. The absurdities of such narratives are integral to the tall-tale tradition that Chappell inherits from Twain and Harris.

The same can be said for the practical jokes that help to structure *I Am One of You Forever* and that resurface in other novels in the tetralogy. Such practical jokes ("rusties," as they are called in southern Appalachia) are central to *Sut Lovingood's Yarns*. But hoaxes of various kinds are also a staple in the humor of Twain's newspaper sketches (e.g., "Petrified Man" and "A Bloody Massacre Near Carson") as well as of the trick played on General Buncombe in the landslide suit brought to trial in chapter 34 of *Roughing It*. In fact, such practical jokes appear to have been a common source of amusement on the frontier, as the life and writing of George Horatio Derby (John Phoenix) also demonstrate (Stewart passim). Like Twain, Chappell tends to eliminate the extreme physical discomfort and outright cruelty that such pranks regularly exhibit in *Sut Lovingood's Yarns*. Chappell's humor is far more genial than Harris's. Uncle Luden, Uncle Gurton, Uncle Runkin, Jess's grandmother, Johnson Gibbs, even Jess himself in "Satan Says"—all have practical jokes played on them, with varying degrees of success. None of those jokes, however, is as malicious as the ones Sut routinely initiates in such stories as "The Widow McCloud's Mare," "Old Skissum's Middle Boy," or "Old Burns's Bull-Ride." Similarly, Joe Robert's elaborate plans for revenge against the Challenger Paper Mill's official responsible for the flood in "The Overspill" (schemes described at length in *Look Back All the Green Valley*) owe more to Rube Goldberg than to Sut. Also physically harmless is Joe Robert's stratagem, in the same novel, involving the sale of stock in Satanic Enterprises Amalgamated to several of his community's fundamentalist preachers.

In building on Harris and Twain, Chappell diverges from their work in other important ways as well. First of all, he makes his own writing style more accessible by reducing the unconventional dialectal spelling that is so pronounced a feature of *Sut Lovingood's Yarns*. Twain had already distanced himself from the mangled orthography of Harris and of such a literary comedian as Josh Billings, but Jim's dialect in *Huckleberry Finn* continues to perplex many modern readers. Chappell, in contrast, almost never uses dialectal misspellings, and he employs nonstandard English sparingly, heightening its presence in the speech of a vernacular narrator like Uncle Zeno but limiting its use elsewhere to those occasions when he wants to invoke regional Appalachian dialect. At such times Jess or his grandmother or his father will resort not only to regional terms like "play-pretty" (113) or "si-gogglin" (*Farewell* 66) but also to nonstandard grammar such as "Just look what them crazy boys done" (9) and "I seen me a chance to pitch" (21). Chappell avoids extensive reliance on such locutions in part, I suspect, to subvert stereotypes of the illiterate mountaineer.

Chappell also diverges from the child's point of view that Twain maintains in *Huckleberry Finn* by having Jess retrospectively narrate *I Am One of You Forever* and the other novels in the Kirkman tetralogy. As a result, Chappell is able to alternate whenever he wishes between the re-creation of Jess's childhood perspective and the insights Jess achieves as an adult. The latter viewpoint affords Chappell a greater range of vocabulary and a more sophisticated array of figurative language and allusion than Twain is able to use with Huck. Yet Chappell regularly invokes the vernacular voice that Twain employs so effectively.

Indeed, the influence of Twain is nowhere more evident than in the profusion of figurative language in Chappell's tetralogy. It is, in fact, style or voice that ultimately unifies the often episodic plots and disparate characters of these novels. Although Jess narrates retrospectively, Chappell imbues his voice with a child's freshness of vision and a country storyteller's vividness of diction. Nor does Chappell strain for literary effect. With few exceptions, the many similes and metaphors that Jess and other speakers employ arise naturally from their daily observations and experiences. Such figurative language pervades these novels, often (as in Twain's fiction) to startlingly humorous effect. In *Brighten the Corner Where You Are,* for instance, Jess's father sports a black eye "as lumpy and purple as a blackberry cobbler" (46). In *Farewell,* the reader is told that Jess's grandmother "hated waste worse than a hard-shell deacon hates sin" (25). The same novel says of a young man pressed into a duel with the sharp-shooting Ginger Summerell that "Orlow looked as uncomfortable and puzzled and gloomy as a tattooed sailor at a church social" (171), while another character is said to be "as closemouthed as a miser's purse snap" (119). Such figurative language not only calls attention to the details of daily experience but also posits a continuum between folk speech and literary discourse that reveals Chappell's profoundly democratic commitment to the dignity and worth of every individual, a commitment manifest in *Huckleberry Finn* as well.

In addition to drawing on Appalachian folktales and on the tall-tale traditions of Old Southwest humor, Chappell uses fantasy, allegory, and dreams as major literary devices in the tetralogy. These devices often figure significantly in each novel's italicized sections, as they do in "The Overspill" "The Telegram," and "Helen" of *I Am One.* But fantasy, allegory, dream, and elements of the supernatural occur at other points as well—for example in "The Beard" (*Forever*), "Bacchus" (*Brighten*), "The Shining Woman" (*Farewell*), and "Into the Unknown" (*Look Back*). The presence of these devices produces an atmosphere distinct from that of Old Southwest humor and from the humor of Twain and Faulkner. Several reviewers and critics have applied the term "magic realism" to this dimension of Chappell's writing, but he rejects that label. In an interview conducted after the publication of *Brighten,* Chappell remarked, "I don't see magic realism as an influence on my most recent fiction. I was trying to get away from it, as a matter of fact. . . . I decided to go more directly to folklore, to use the tall tale" (Palmer 408). Similarly, in an interview given at the time *Farewell* was published, Chappell reiterated that he has "no interest in magic realism per se. I'm interested in blurring the demarcations between what's generally thought of as realism and what's thought of as fantasy" (Howard 56).

As this latter remark makes clear, Chappell intends to create a sense of fluidity, of the potential for liberating transformations, both in literature and in life. Just as Uncle Zeno's stories make Jess and his family "doubt [their] own outlines" (97), so Chappell's fiction dissolves the customary distinction between the real and the imagined. But Chappell effects this dissolution of boundaries not on behalf of the radical skepticism of much postmodernist thought, with its despair of ever attaining truth, but on behalf of life's myriad possibilities. Underlying both *Midquest* and the Kirkman tetralogy is a sense of life's plenitude and mystery, a view that the comic spirit reinforces. As George Core has written, Chappell's work creates "a comedy that sustains and elevates" (xlii).

In emphasizing the influence of Old Southwest humorists and Twain on Chappell's comic techniques in *Midquest* and the Kirkman novels, I do not mean to suggest, it should now be clear, that Chappell's work is merely derivative or that these authors are the only important literary antecedents for Chappell's use of humor. He is noted for his wide reading and for his willingness to embrace and acknowledge his precursors. For Chappell the literary tradition is a crucial cultural resource, and he avails himself of it repeatedly. His comic vision, like his moral and religious vision, arises from varied sources. Chaucer's *Canterbury Tales,* Shakespeare's comedies (both *Midquest* and *Look Back* conclude with the same passage from *Twelfth Night*), Cervantes's *Don Quixote,* which Chappell has called "the greatest novel ever" (Patterson and Lindsey 74), Byron's comic epics—all have been cited by Chappell as significant influences on his work. Not surprisingly, however, given the fact that *Midquest* took as its initial structural model "that elder American art form, the sampler" (*Midquest* ix), nineteenth-century American humor—and the tall-tale tradition out of which it grew—also plays a prominent role in Chappell's poetry and fiction. Readers need only recall the opening chapter of *Brighten,* "The Devil-Possum," to recognize Chappell's indebtedness to Old Southwest humor. For a more subtle example of that influence, readers should consider the use Chappell makes of one of the frontier humorists' favorite devices, the frame tale, in his structuring of *Farewell.* In that book, however, the opening and closing sections deal not with comic materials but with Jess's grandmother's impending death. As in Twain and Faulkner, so in Chappell humor combines with other literary modes to articulate the author's full artistic vision.

Chappell's incorporation of comic elements throughout *Midquest* and the Kirkman tetralogy contributes substantially to these works' celebratory quality. Though Chappell never fails to acknowledge the centrality of death in human experience, his poetry and fiction also affirm the possibility of rebirth, of resurrection. According to Northrop Frye's taxonomy in *The Anatomy of Criticism,* comedy is "the mythos of spring" (163), the season of rebirth. As Chappell moved away from the bleak vision of his first three novels, his sense of life's possibilities expanded. "Something I discovered in writing *Midquest,*" he once told an interviewer, "is that comedy/humor is much more serious than tragedy. . . . It says more about . . . the way people live day to day" (Ruffin 133). To another interviewer Chappell remarked, "I've come to believe that the comic vision is a truer vision of life, of our condition" (Stephenson 11).

Now that the Kirkman tetralogy is complete, much more research needs to be done on Chappell's use of humor and comedy. Carolyn Brown's 1987 study, *The Tall Tale in American Folklore and Literature,* for instance, makes no reference to Chappell. The 1988 entry on Chappell in the *Encyclopedia of American Humorists* appeared when only *I Am One of You Forever* had been published. Thus, de Abruna's conclusions in that entry—"Chappell's greatest contribution to the history of American humor is the Southwestern character Virgil Campbell" and "Chappell's reputation as humorous writer and comic artist will ultimately rest on *Midquest*" (79)—are no longer tenable. More insightful, however, are de Abruna's comments that Chappell's work as a humorist is underrated and that "his finest contribution to American humor is his mastery of the vernacular language and values of the mountain folk of western North Carolina" (79).

Here, once again, readers encounter a vital way in which Chappell diverges from his precursors. Unlike many of the Old Southwest humorists, who were not natives of the regions they described and who often used humor to distance themselves from the native populace, Chappell shows none of the "need to belittle" that Pascal Covici identifies as a central impulse in Old Southwest humor (4). According to Covici, "The effect of their [southwestern humorists'] stories upon a reader is to insulate him from any emotional involvement or identification with events, characters, or region" (6). Chappell's intention is precisely the opposite. Just as Twain encourages his reader to identify with Huck's moral and emotional perspective, so Chappell asks the reader to recognize, as Jess's grandmother puts it in *Farewell*, "that we [Appalachians] were people like other people, wise and foolish, brave and frightened, saintly and unholy and ordinary" (197). Chappell's humor both delights and instructs as it affirms the region of his birth, the importance of laughter, and our shared humanity.

WORKS CITED

Blair, Walter. "Humor of the Old Southwest (1830–1867)." In *Native American Humor*. New York: Chandler, 1960.

Bridgman, Richard. *The Colloquial Style in America*. New York: Oxford University Press, 1966.

Broughton, Irv. "Fred Chappell." In *The Writer's Mind: Interviews with American Authors*. Vol. III. Fayetteville: University of Arkansas Press, 1990.

Chappell, Fred. *Brighten the Corner Where You Are*. New York: St. Martin's Press, 1989.

———. *C*. Baton Rouge: Louisiana State University Press, 1993.

———. *Farewell, I'm Bound to Leave You*. New York: St. Martin's Press, 1996.

———. "Fred Chappell." *Contemporary Authors Autobiography Series*. Vol. 4. Ed. Adele Sarkissian. Detroit: Gale, 1986.

———. *I Am One of You Forever*. Baton Rouge: Louisiana State University Press, 1985.

———. Letter to the author, 27 May 2000.

———. *Look Back All the Green Valley*. New York: St. Martin's Press, 1999.

———. *Midquest*. Baton Rouge: Louisiana State University Press, 1981.

Core, George. "Procrustes' Bed." *Sewanee Review* 93 (spring 1985): xxxix–xlii.

Covici, Pascal. *Mark Twain's Humor: The Image of a World*. Dallas: Southern Methodist University Press, 1962.

Crane, Resa, and James Kirkland. "First and Last Words: A Conversation with Fred Chappell." *Dream Garden: The Poetic Vision of Fred Chappell*.

Ed. Patrick Bizzaro. Baton Rouge: Louisiana State University Press, 1997.

De Abruna, Laura Niesen. "Fred Chappell." *Encyclopedia of American Humorists.* Ed. Steven H. Gale. New York: Garland, 1988.

Frye, Northrop. *Anatomy of Criticism.* New York: Atheneum, 1967.

Harris, George Washington. *Sut Lovingood's Yarns.* Ed. M. Thomas Inge. New Haven: College and University Press, 1966.

Hobson, Fred. *The Southern Writer in the Postmodern World.* Athens: University of Georgia Press, 1991.

Howard, Jennifer. "Fred Chappell: From the Mountains to the Mainstream." *Publishers Weekly* (30 September 1996): 55–6.

Inge, M. Thomas. *Faulkner, Sut, and Other Southerners.* West Cornwall, Conn.: Locust Hill, 1992.

Palmer, Tersh. "Fred Chappell." *Appalachian Journal* 19.4 (1992): 402–10.

Patterson, Sarah, and Dan Lindsey. "Interview with Fred Chappell." *Davidson Miscellany* 19 (spring 1984): 62–76.

Ragan, David Paul. "At the Grave of Sut Lovingood: Virgil Campbell in the Work of Fred Chappell." *Mississippi Quarterly* 37 (winter 1983–84): 21–30.

Ruffin, Paul. "Interview with Fred Chappell." *Pembroke Magazine* 17 (1985): 131–5.

Stephenson, Shelby. "'The Way It Is': An Interview with Fred Chappell." *Iron Mountain Review* 2 (spring 1985): 7–11.

Stewart, George R. *John Phoenix, Esq., The Veritable Squibob: A Life of Captain George Horatio Derby.* New York: Henry Holt, 1937.

Twain, Mark. *Adventures of Huckleberry Finn.* In *Mississippi Writings.* New York: Library of America, 1982.

———. *Following the Equator.* Hartford: American Publishing Company, 1897.

———. *Literary Essays.* New York: Harper & Brothers, 1899.

———. *Roughing It.* In *The Works of Mark Twain.* Vol. 2. Berkeley: University of California Press, 1972.

THIRTEEN

Tracing the Hawk's Shadow
Fred Chappell As Storyteller

KAREN JANET MCKINNEY

IN HIS ESSAY "The Storyteller," Walter Benjamin eulogizes the art of storytelling. His regret is palpable:

> [T]he art of storytelling is coming to an end. Less and less frequently do we encounter people with the ability to tell a story properly. More and more often there is an embarrassment all round when the wish to hear a story is expressed. It is as if something that seemed inalienable to us, the securest among our possessions, were taken from us. (83)

This strange alteration of human nature is caused, Benjamin believes, by the fact that "experience has fallen in value"; as with the visual arts, mechanization has affected everyday lives powerfully and pervasively. Few writers of criticism or creative prose have responded directly to the view Benjamin expresses in the passage above. But Fred Chappell's novels, particularly *I Am One of You Forever* and *Farewell, I'm Bound to Leave You* from his semi-autobiographical series, do provide us with a response.

I

Storytellers, as Benjamin points out in another essay, "The Work of Art in the Age of Mechanical Reproduction," function in a close-knit community, a community that, in past times, was sustained by its connection to the eternal, a connection which "has ever its strongest source in death" (93). In *I Am One of You Forever,* the first novel in the Kirkman tetralogy, Chappell embodies this complexity in the character of the orphan farm boy Johnson Gibbs. Johnson himself has become a storyteller to win acceptance in the family into which he has been adopted. Jess is Johnson's only audience at first, although later the rest of the family comes to hear about his stories. Johnson and Jess share sleeping quarters, and Jess begs Johnson to tell one of Jess's current favorites, a ghost or jungle-adventure story. But Johnson proves inadequate as a teller of this type of tale because, as Jess explains, Johnson leaves out too many details. Johnson is more successful at tales of his own prowess at sporting activities. He mesmerizes Jess with a story of his incredible skill at pitching baseballs and, this time, he overwhelms with details, particularly the evocative names of his pitches: "the Submarine Surprise, the Blue Flash, the Blitzkrieg, the Snaky Shaker . . . Sissie's Powderpuff, Slow Boat to China, the Rare-Back-&-Letter-Rip, and of course . . . Old Reliable" (17). Johnson's specialized terminology is impressive, too. His opponents are not just intimidated and confused; they're "hornswoggled and hooligated" by Johnson's mighty steel and rubber arm. But when Jess sees an actual performance of Johnson's less than stellar pitching in a local game, he is confused by the contradiction. Johnson, who appears to be totally unscathed by his embarrassing experience, explains that he had never actually pitched in a baseball game before because the orphanage he grew up in couldn't afford to supply the children with any equipment. "'Now I don't hold with lying,'" Johnson admonished. "'But I was bound to pitch me a game'"(21). Johnson repeats his tall-tale performance on the subject of trout fishing. When he receives an expensive rod as a gift from Jess's parents, Jess again witnesses Johnson's ridiculously inept performance. Yet Johnson's stories achieve their goal. His place within Jess's family is confirmed and, as Jess puts it, these were "bright, happy days" (21) which all too soon come to an end as Johnson leaves to fight in a distant overseas war.

Once Johnson has gone into the army and is lost to death, his stories become part of the family's memory of him. Benjamin asserts that the storyteller "has borrowed his authority from death" (94). Johnson, transmigrated into eternity, remains throughout the novel as the thread that binds all together; it is he who utters the closing words of the novel that initiate Jess into full membership in the community.

Then when Uncle Runkin and his coffin appear, Jess, and the reader, are able to explore humanity's fascination with death even more deeply. When Jess sneaks a nap in Uncle Runkin's unusual bed, daring himself to be terrified, he is surprised by the fact that he is not frightened by the visions of blood and skeletons created by his fertile imagination. Jess reflects, "I began to know that death was the Meadow of Vision, where dream was wrested from the marrow of stars" (131–2). Through his experiences, both tragic and titillating, with Johnson and Uncle Runkin, Jess comes to understand death as life's great transformation, "the authority [which] is at the very source of the story" (Benjamin 94).

Another quality that storytellers have and novelists do not, according to Benjamin, is usefulness; they impart advice, even wisdom. But in *I Am One of You Forever*, some people tell very useful stories, stories to right wrongs and mete out justice. Both Jess's mother and his father, although in different circumstances and manners, tell stories to this end. Jess's mother Cora becomes a storyteller impelled by moral necessity; it is her duty as a mother to explain difficult truths to her son. Her words have a powerful effect on Jess; she causes his imagination to "blow all its fuses" (171) as she recounts her mother's (Jess's grandmother's) youthful dream and how it was crushed by the custom of a father's omnipotent power.

During a visit from Jess's grandmother's cousin, Aunt Samantha Barefoot, a noted performer on the Grand Ole Opry, Jess learns that his grandmother—who has always appeared to him to have a god-like dignity and infallibility only slightly tempered with mercy—was also once a musical performer. When his grandmother stubbornly refuses to give any details, his mother relates the story of his grandmother's show-business aspirations and how she was one of the best square-dance fiddlers in the mountains. Cora tells the story with evocative detail:

> The dancers were invited to a festival in Scotland and they were to dance before the queen and then be presented to her. It meant a lot to Mama. It meant a lot to everybody, taking our music and dance across the ocean for the queen to enjoy. Her heart was just set on it. I've heard Aunt Minnie Lou tell about your grandmother practicing her curtsy in front of a mirror. For hours and hours. (171)

But, Jess's mother explains, grandmother's father says no, fearing that "music and celebrity" would be bad for his daughter. The moral of the story, as Jess's mother is quick to point out, is that his grandmother suppressed her feelings and prepared Aunt Samantha to go in her place, all without any feelings of jealousy or bitterness between the young women.

Jess's mother tells this story to reinforce a basic tenet of their community: women set the standards of courage and right behavior. This picture of his grandmother as Shining Woman is in stark contrast to the behavior of Jess's father and of Johnson, who generally act like overgrown schoolboys.

Yet Jess's father Joe Robert is also a powerful storyteller on at least one occasion. And he needs to be, for he is combating another powerful storyteller, Canary, the lay preacher, who never tires of regaling certain "sinners," particularly Joe Robert's friend Virgil Campbell, with tales of their sure destination in hell unless they mend their ways. Canary regularly visits Virgil's store in order to corner his audience of one with a tale made vivid by analogy, metaphor, spit-flecked lips, and flapping arms. He begins his tale with this horror:

> You might have burned your hand on the stove one time and thought that hurt you some. . . . But Brother Campbell, that wasn't nothing to what you're going to feel. . . .You'll be praying for water and the devil will bring you brimstone. (65)

Canary even paints an evocative picture of the divine one, sorrowing over his lost child: "Jesus will done've turned his back on you then . . . there'll be tears in his precious eyes but it'll be too late" (65). After verbally pinning his victim, he cagily offers relief: "but they's a way out, Brother Campbell. . . . If you'll just turn to him right now, this very minute and hour, and accept the lord as your own personal savior, then you won't never see the insides of hell, not even the sorry gates of it" (65). Canary presents himself as telling a sacred story in order to restore moral standards to his community. Yet his stories fail; they have no effect on their audience except irritation because there exists no shared truth between storyteller and audience. Canary mouths words he has heard and read but which have no grounding in the experience and knowledge of the people he lives among.

Joe Robert makes this phoniness clear when he confronts Canary with a "sacred" story of his own. He poses as having had a "vision" in which the Lord spoke to him. The Lord told Joe Robert:

> [T]his man Canary is using my name in vain . . . to poke his snout where it's got no business . . . he has got an ungrateful heart, yes an ungrateful heart, the Lord told me, because he ought to be on his knees

all he can, thanking Me that somebody hasn't busted his nose for him, thankful that some godly and modest man hasn't grabbed a meat cleaver and chopped off his runty little old pecker. (66)

Joe Robert's story successfully rebuts Canary because his words evoke a pleasurable response with earthy humor and the cleverness of turning a man's own style against him. His story also reveals truth by pointing out how Canary's actions violate an important community imperative to mind one's own business. Joe Robert's "true" story achieves its purpose of defending a friend against the evil intention of Canary's false one.

Yet Benjamin also asserts that the storyteller "has council not just for a few situations, as the proverb does, but for many, like the sage" (108). As Chappell demonstrates with Jess's account of Uncle Zeno's visit, wisdom is not simplistic advice or cut-and-dried answers but meditations on life's complexities, as is the act of storytelling itself. Unlike the other storytellers in the novel, Uncle Zeno tells without impetus from his environment; he has no purpose of moral instruction, self-aggrandizement, entertainment, or any audience response at all. With his eyes staring blankly into the distance, he begins, breaks off, and resumes his tales with total disregard for the demands or reactions of his audience. He, in fact, seems to have no control over his stories; Jess and Joe Robert see Uncle Zeno in the Platonic "mad poet" model as simply "repeating words whispered to him by another voice issuing from behind the high, fleecy clouds he loved to stare at" (98). When Uncle Zeno finishes a complicated narration about the killing of a nuisance bear with the comment that the bear's body, which by a complicated turn of events had fallen out of a tree and was suspended by the chain of a bear trap attached to its leg, was "'swinging just . . . a mite . . . slow'" (102), Joe Robert demands to know the point or at least the joke. When no explanation is forthcoming, the father falls back on his "booklearning" involving storytelling. He tells his son about Homer, comparing Uncle Zeno's ability to tell the stories of the community without personal involvement to Homer's blindness. Homer, Joe Robert explains, could tell about a soldier's life so vividly, as he did in the *Iliad*, because he could never have actually been a soldier, and therefore he could understand objectively. "'If Uncle Zeno ever struck a lick of work,'" he says, "'if he ever had dealings with people at all, maybe he couldn't tell his stories'" (103).

Peculiar as his mode of telling is, Uncle Zeno's stories do seem to arise from everyday working people and the events of their lives. He tells of Lacy Joe Blackman's silver watch, of which he was so proud because it came from his father; of Turkey George Palmer, who had killed more bears than another hunter in the country; of Setback Hunter, who had retired to a little place right up next to the Smoky Mountains National Forest with his wife Mary Sue. While Jess's mother and grandmother serenely abide or ignore the prating of someone they consider an old harmless man, Joe Robert is goaded by the seemingly pointless nature of the stories. Both Jess and Joe Robert have an uneasy feeling that there is some connection between Uncle Zeno's stories and a world beyond the mortal realm. The climax comes when Uncle Zeno begins a story about Buford Rhodes and the loss of his amazing coon dog.

As usual, Uncle Zeno breaks off the story in midstride: "'But then the houses got scarcer and not many people to ask, and Buford was getting worried—'"(106). But this time Jess's father sees a way to put his uncomfortable speculations to rest; he is sure that he knows Buford—that Buford, in fact, did a bit of house painting for him a while back—so he sets out to track down Buford and get the "real" story from him.

But Jess has other things to worry about. While his father is off chasing the notorious Buford, Jess accidentally comes upon Uncle Zeno sitting alone in the lowest limb of a tree in a deserted part of the family's mountain pasture land. Uncle Zeno's body is slumped and lifeless; only his mouth is moving as the words pour out, and Jess hears him pick up the thread of the tale about Buford. Uncle Zeno informs the uncaring trees that Buford has gone in search of this favorite coon dog, has become lost, has been saved by a Cherokee woman and then entranced and imprisoned by her. Buford finally becomes fed up with his imprisonment and contemplates his fate: "'but just right then when he was thinking his darkest thoughts, he heard a rustling over in the bushes'" (110).

Uncle Zeno breaks off the story—or rather, as it seems to Jess, "the story impulse died in him, or maybe this story flew from this roosting place across the world to another storyteller, Chinese or Tibetan, who sat waiting for inspiration" (110). Late in the afternoon, Joe Robert returns home after spending the day in a fruitless search. Buford's supposed house was deserted; people thought maybe they remembered him but on reflection they did not; a check Jess's father was sure he had written to him was listed with no name attached.

It is then that Jess is struck with an idea, the basis for a theory of storytelling that would take into account both Uncle Zeno's seemingly involuntary tales and his father's Homeric stories of the ancient Greek wars. What if a really gifted storyteller's words absorbed his characters so completely that they disappeared from the temporal world? He proposed this theory to his defeated and demoralized father, adding weight to his evidence by reminding his father that the gold mask belonging to Agamemnon has never been clearly identified as belonging to the ancient hero. Real storytellers, Jess exclaims excitedly, use up the worlds they tell about and send such worlds into a separate realm from everyday existence. Joe Robert doesn't contradict him; perhaps he is simply too tired for Jess's "metaphysical speculations in the philosophy of narrative" (113), or perhaps he has never heard of postmodern theory.

But Chappell has, of course, and Jess's explanation of the mystery of Homer and Uncle Zeno and all the storytellers in between is reminiscent of contemporary theorists who picture meaning as dependent on difference, on gaps. In *The Practice of Everyday Life,* Michel de Certeau proposes that an unbridgeable gap exists between the act of writing and the act of reading: "Writing accumulates, stocks up, resists time by the establishment of a place," while "reading has no place." While writing engraves stories in granite, fixing them against the vicissitudes of time, the reader moves through time, keeping nothing because she is neither inside nor outside the story (174). So, as Jess proposes, reality only exists within stories and, between them, as Uncle Zeno understands, is only the "vast inane" (Chappell 115). Of course, to Jess's great relief, his theory doesn't play out as he expects it to. Even though Uncle Zeno finally tells a story about the Kirkmans, they continue to go about their ordinary lives after Uncle Zeno's monotonous voice has ceased to reverberate.

And they exist for us, the novel's readers, sitting alone in our chairs, who feel connected to Jess and his family in ways that are hard to verbalize. While Benjamin believed that novel readers were totally isolated in their silent absorption, in *I Am One of You Forever* Chappell painstakingly creates the impression that this is Jess's story and the readers are the listeners, and he thus creates a community where none existed before. He inscribes sections of the novel with the peculiar tag lines or oral narrative. Jess uses such phrases as "There came a time" (135) and "To the best of my knowledge" (166) along with sections of carefully intimate wording that bring us into the fire's circle. In beginning the tale of Uncle Gurton's beard, Jess explains that he will refrain from relating the "long and complex history" of that facial phenomenon with the aside, "I will try not to bore us with much of that " (48). Later he opens the chapter detailing his father's confrontation with Canary by saying, "I have some difficulty describing my father's attitude toward religion. Let us say that he was tolerant" (62). The "us" in both of the phrases and elsewhere in the novel makes the readers part of the conspiracy to believe that which is about to be related.

But the opening lines of both the beginning and ending sections are the clearest examples. The first line of the novel, contained in the dreamlike section titled "Overspill," is "Then there was one brief time when we didn't live in the big brick house with my grandmother . . ." (1). The opening word "then" implies that something has come before, something with which the audience is familiar. We are treated as intimates, as members of a community, as the listeners in a traditional setting of oral storytelling would be.

This impression of intimacy is gently completed with the ending section of the novel, also a dreamlike recreation, which begins, "It seemed that there were four of us in a hunting cabin high on a mountain on the Tennessee border" (180). We have come so far with Jess that we now will be entrusted with hearing about something of which he is unsure; this is a remembered dream, a tale in which members of the hunting party, while asleep, call out "Helen," the name of that bewitching central figure in Homer's tale. In this dream, Jess also thinks he sees Helen in the darkness of the cabin, but he isn't sure. In the broad light of morning, no one but he remembers the experience. And in the final scene of the novel, in which Johnson Gibbs—transformed from a raw, country teenager into a mysterious and powerful being, a figure black as velvet, "blackly burning"—asks the question that is answered only by the novel's title, " 'Are you one of us or not?' " (184).

This question is asked of Jess, but it is asked of the reader, too. Is it, as Hilbert Campbell argues, a question that implies the "really big" questions about humanity and morality that good literature used to be supposed to ask? (109). Are we isolated readers or part of a community that shares loves, passions, and sorrows? Are we inside or outside the story, or somehow both at once, as de Certeau supposes? Can novelists be storytellers who provide continuity, cohesiveness, and wisdom for their community?

Answers to such questions are elusive, but perhaps a hint is to be found in Benjamin's description of the storyteller whom he believed to have vanished from human society: "He is the man who could let the wick of his life be consumed completely by the gentle flame of his story. . . . The storyteller is the figure in which the righteous man encounters himself" (109). Or, to adapt from Jess's description of Uncle Zeno, Chappell's stories leave nothing more behind them than "a hawk's shadow" (113) passing overhead—gone in a moment but endlessly remaining in the memory of powerful talons and the beauty of beating wings.

2

"Do you think you'd like to be a storyteller?" This is the question that Jess's mother asks him out of the blue, just as she concludes a story about Cousin Earlene Lewis, "The Fisherwoman." When Jess protests that he "don't hardly know any stories," his mother replies reassuringly, "'Don't worry. . . . You'll learn some. All you have to do is listen'" (100). And the novel at the midpoint of which this exchange is found, *I Am One of You Forever,* is about listening, a kind of listening that offers insight and consolation amid the irritations and tragedies of human life.

"The wind had got into the clocks and blown the hour away" (3). As we read this opening line of *Farewell, I'm Bound to Leave You,* the third novel in Chappell's autobiographical series, we are caught up with Jess in the nightmare of waiting for the death of the grandmother. Through the stories of the previous two novels, Jess has made us love her, too, and in the face of such an enormous loss, the lessons of the past seem trite and meaningless. In the opening section "The Clocks," it seems that the fabric of the universe is threatened; Jess and his father feel that they can no longer depend on anything in the temporal universe; even time itself has betrayed them. All the clocks in the house display different, inaccurate times, and Jess's father explains to him as they sit alone in the front room, forbidden to approach the grandmother's bedside, that time is indeed stopping for their family. To prevent their own destruction, Jess's father continues, "'We will listen to the wind whisper and weep and tell again those stories of women that your mother and grandmother needed for you to hear'" (5). And so Jess listens with the ear of memory, listening to the same "voice" that we do as we read the text; we listen to stories, both "novelistic" and traditional, and we try to learn the lessons they contain.

But the first story, "The Traveling Woman," has no teller in the traditional sense, although here, too, Jess is the seeming narrator. It opens with the prayer of his grandmother and mother, bound together in the grandmother's bedroom, now become the death room: "Jesus Jesus O now Jesus, they said or thought, now show Your sweet face" (6). He repeats what his grandmother and his mother "said or thought," emphasizing his uncertainty and heightening ours. In an unabashedly novelistic passage, the thoughts/words of the dying mother and the grieving daughter interweave and separate, sometimes aware of each other as in a dialogue and sometimes locked in their own separate reflections. Yet, even in this disjointed, surreal representation, the sustaining thread is stories that the two participants tell sometimes to each other and sometimes only to themselves.

Jess's grandmother tries to explain to her daughter the loneliness of the death experience by reminding her of the time long ago when that daughter stayed in the big poplar tree all day long and thought that she had passed into another world where no one knew she existed. But what the daughter remembers is the comforting familiarity of the contents of her mother's apron pockets when she returned home—one event but two very different remembered stories. Throughout this chapter, the tension between the unifying force of story and memory and the isolation of death is almost unbearably taut. Fragments of remembered disappointments, frustrations, joys and hilarious "rusties" from both women's consciousness mix and then separate. For Cora can only go with her mother a little way; she must "turn back to the world," as must the readers, at least until our own time comes (21).

Benjamin contends that the novel is distinguished from the story in two related ways: it depends on the "technology" of the book and the resulting isolation of the writer and reader from each other as well as from all other humans, whereas the storyteller takes experience, his own or that of others, and makes it the experience of "those who are listening to his tale" (87). Chappell is keenly aware of this isolation and emphasizes it in the structure of the body chapters of *Farewell* in which the novelistic portrayals of Jess's storytelling sessions with his mother and grandmother are further distanced because they are only Jess's memories, with which he comforts himself while his grandmother lies on her deathbed. Yet this novelistic creation is so compelling that we disregard the distancing mechanisms and find ourselves caught up in the story, becoming listeners alongside Jess.

In *Farewell*, the women tell stories to educate the boy in their charge about the nature of women and the conflict that sometimes arises between this nature and the social roles they are obliged to fill. The catalyst that seems to set this series of tales in motion is Jess's own awakening interest in the opposite sex and his adolescent confusion regarding this new aspect of his life. In "The Shooting Woman," Jess's grandmother comments on his obvious interest in one of his classmates, Sarah Robinson, while they are closeted together in the canning storeroom. To open his eyes to some of the secrets of courtship, she reveals the secret of how she brought his own mother and father together through the use of a scarlet slip and a shotgun. The culmination of the story (which Jess is not entirely able to process) is her explanation of how the revelation of her daughter's badly bruised shoulder on the wedding night was "the beginning of a love as deep as she desired" (39). The following story, "The Figuring Woman," gives Jess a hint of the complicated turns a love affair can take as well as the implication that only a woman, and a "smart" one at that, can sort such things out. The most powerful of the love-and-marriage stories is the story of Selena and Lexie, the gentle woman mysterious with silence and the rude, boisterous woman who becomes her companion. In "The Silent Woman," gentle implication rather than dramatic revelation enthralls Jess, so much so that he speculates, "[T]he nature of it sometimes makes me think that she never told it at all, that she communicated the whole of it without speaking a word" (61). A story that celebrates a relationship that evolves beyond the need for words (that perhaps may not have been told with words, even to Jess) becomes not contradictory, or even confusing, but simply a Mystery, like the workings of Nature, like "the wind raw behind the snow" (78).

Another important aspect of Jess's education in the nature of women is the manner in which the strongest of them depart from the accepted paths carved out for them by society. Jess's mother delights in telling "The Fisherwoman" story because she so admires Cousin Earlene—a woman of her own generation who, as a young girl, defied tradition to become a champion in the arcane art of fly-fishing under the tutelage of a crusty veteran, Old Man Worley. By emphasizing Earlene's daring rescue of Mr. Worley, Jess's mother turns the tale into a rite of passage in which Earlene, on the same day she catches the biggest fish of her life, risks injury and death to drive down the mountain for help, overcoming not only the physical obstacles but also her fear of becoming a woman.

But, Jess wants to know, how does his mother know so much about Cousin Earlene story if she wasn't actually there herself? In Jess's mother's reply, Chappell speaks as directly as he ever has on the nature of the storytelling craft, speaking both of the oral tradition and the novelistic manifestation of that tradition:

> She told me a lot and then I put myself in her place so I could tell the story to you. This is what storytellers do. Maybe you'll remember that if you ever take a notion to tell stories. (100)

And all you need to do to learn stories, Jess's mother continues, is listen. Perhaps Jess suspects that such a simple-sounding formula contains difficult depths yet to be plumbed.

Chappell, the novelist, wastes no time in confirming such suspicions in the next chapter, a dreamlike memory forming, as a similar chapter does in *I Am,* the center of the novel. Jess narrates the tale tentatively, beginning sentences with "It seemed" and "It was like," searching for a memory that seems too fantastical to be true but tense with concrete detail and secrets spoken aloud. As he and his mother set out to pay a visit to "The Wind Woman," the allegorical nature of this memory quickly becomes obvious. First, they must pay a visit to the River Woman, the Cloud Woman, the Fire Woman, the Moon Woman, the Deer Woman, the Happiest Woman, and, oddly, Aunt Priddy. Jess's mother is distracted, not watching the road but "peering into something, a dim corner or a deep well" (103). Jess's mother confesses to him her own attempts at poetry writing and how she gave it up and destroyed her work. She wants Jess to be spared her own intense regret, which is why she is taking him to see the Wind Woman on this day. Their journey is strewn with forbidding details. Aunt Priddy, in appearance "like a hummingbird," reminds his mother that her "'Dying Swan' sunflowers" sing only once, just before they are torn apart by crows

(106). The Happiest Woman reminds his mother that she is "'welcome here any time,'" although she hasn't paid a visit for much too long. When they finally reach Wind Mountain, the abode of the Wind Woman, Jess's mother cannot reach the top; Jess must continue alone against a heavy wind. When he reaches the cabin at the top, he finds it empty, but as he sits and listens, the sound of the wind gradually resolves itself into the music and sounds, not only of Jess's own experience, but of the experiences of his people for many years back:

> I heard in the wind in that room houses and barns, ropes and straps, gunshot and sword slash, iron and calico, jubilation and lamentation, country and city, old age and childhood, birth and death, the whole of the world below the mountain, and in the midst of it all, like a pallid queen in a silver throne raised above a clamoring multitude, the great round silence of the moon that looked down pitiless on Hardison County and all the surrounding counties out to the horizon. (115)

This visit was for me, Jess understands. This is what it means to be a teller of stories, telling the good and the bad, recalling the kind and the cruel. This understanding comes to Jess not on the printed page or even in spoken words but in sounds that only the Wind Woman can teach him how to "lay out . . . in proper fashion." As he does in *I Am*, Chappell recalls ancient Greek concepts as he conceptualizes this skill in "laying out," or arrangement, what is usually referred to as creativity or inspiration, as being in the hands of a muselike being who is capricious in her attentions; she cannot be summoned. The storyteller, the artist must "come and beg the favor of her aid" (115).

In portraying only women as the storytellers in *Farewell*, Chappell underscores the concept that women are the most powerful, the truest, storytellers in society. They see the whole story and understand that it is sometimes necessary to tell the secret stories, the stories from the dark side of human society and human nature. "The Madwoman," with its details of illicit love, murder, and possibly sexual mutilation, is not a story to tell lightly. But Jess's mother believes that Jess must begin to understand that nothing in life is unmixed, that passion can bring destruction as well as pleasure, and that even music can sometimes bring not balm to the soul but unbearable suffering.

She tells Jess of Aunt Sam's girlhood sojourn with Aunt Chancy and her attempts to soothe the old woman during violent fits with the music Sam was learning to play and sing so beautifully. She thought at first that she had been successful; Aunt Chancy would eventually begin to listen to the songs; "she would grow quiet and her face would gentle and her hands would stop their sawing motions and she would look at Sam with a smile of pleasure" (122). But when Aunt Chancy heard the strains of "Oh, Shenandoah," a song that Sam was just learning, Aunt Chancy had a nearly murderous fit and revealed the secret she had kept so long, the name of her long-lost lover whom her abusive husband had probably killed. "'That's a scary story,'" Jess comments at its conclusion, and his mother is dismayed that he hasn't grasped the essential truths of the story when he goes on to express a desire to hear Aunt Sam sing that song sometime: "'If you don't have some good sense to go with all those brains you're supposed to have, you might as well open up your head and feed them to the barn cats'" (134).

As Jess thinks on this vivid suggestion, he realizes how much he still needs to learn to be a grownup person, much less a storyteller in his own right. Early in the following chapter, "The Shining Woman," Jess, in his role as adult narrator, remembers that by age fifteen he had awakened from adolescent self-absorption and "had a hunger to listen almost as urgent as my hunger to read. I had begun to feel that Time Past contained secret messages for me" (135). In an echo of Benjamin, he realizes that books alone are not enough to sustain a person. Chappell has led us to this contradictory, "postmodern" moment in which we absorb this truth, which is, of course, communicated by means of a book. Is what we're reading a mere facsimile of storytelling, a pale substitute for the "real thing"? But before we have time to ponder this question deeply, Jess has more stories to hear that emphasize the difference between men and women. In the story of "The Shining Woman," Jess's grandmother recounts the story of how a gruff old mountain man and his second wife react very differently to an apparition, a "haint," that has begun appearing in their bedroom. As they recount their problem to the wise woman, Aunt Sherlie, the wife, Sarah, seems to find the ghost more appealing than frightening while her husband, Talbot, just wants "'to be shut of it for good and all'" (146). His wife smells apple blossoms when the ghost appears and isn't bothered by the fact that the beautiful figure doesn't mind that they can see she is a "natural woman" (147). Ultimately, the spirit of Talbot's first wife leaves the couple in peace after Talbot goes against his no-nonsense nature by buying Sarah an "unnecessary" treasure like a locket on her birthday.

In "The Feistiest Woman," Jess's mother tells how Ginger Summerell rejects an abusive male-dominated community and wins her beloved by offering to best him in a duel. Ginger's story is brought up in the kitchen where Jess and his mother and father are having breakfast, but Joe Robert, who calls Ginger "the friend of women and the scourge of men," is unable to tell the story; he knows the basic facts but lacks understanding. Jess's mother agrees to tell the story because it's "'[b]etter for Jess to get it from me than listen to some wild tale you'd dream up'" (157). The story, with its dramatic last scene in which the two lovers lie unconscious with their bodies forming a cross, may be wild indeed, but it wasn't dreamed up; in Chappell's universe, the women are the truth-tellers, passing along stories of their experience and the experience of others whom they know. This is part of Benjamin's definition of the vanishing storyteller; he is one who has the gift of telling not only his own life but the lives of others that he has learned of by listening: "[W]hat the storyteller knows from hearsay is added to his own" because the person with the gift of storytelling also has the gift of true listening, listening with empathy, so that the truth of the experiences of others becomes his own (108).

"Hearsay" also forms the basis of the following story, a story in which the teller, Jess's grandmother, has no firsthand experience at all; but, assisted by his mother with encouragement and reminders, she reconstructs her narrative from what she has heard others tell (what the uninitiated might call gossip). "The Helpinest Woman," Angela Newcome's story, is a community fable, knitting the contradictory truths about the nature of charity and the possibility of miracles into the web that holds their universe together. Angela, Jess's mother explains, was an irritant because everyone was always "beholden" to her; her good deeds were too numerous to ever be paid back; they became a "ponderous burden" (181). However, this is a gossipy story with the usual spice to it; Jess's mother recounts with relish how Angela took over one too many of a sick wife's duties and wonders how her own Joe Robert would react if she were caught in such an act of neighborliness. This is one of the charms of listening to, and recounting, gossip, Chappell seems to remind us—partaking vicariously in the more excessive foibles of humanity without any personal harm.

But then the grandmother, conscious of her role as moral guardian, takes up the story of Angela's miraculous end. After a crippled farmer is driven to the edge of madness and violence by Angela's three-year stint of overwhelming helpfulness, Preacher Hardy finds a way to restore harmony by giving Angela the challenge of her life, caring for an elderly widow who lives so far up in the hills and in such primitive conditions that no one else could bear it. But this is the job Angela was born for, someone who needs her completely, someone beyond caring about "paying back." Jess's grandmother warns Jess that no one really knows the end of the story but "'[m]any another woman has puzzled at it just as close as I have, and, as far as I know, we all reached the same conclusion'" (191). But Jess is learning the lesson that the wisdom of the community's women is more valuable that any amount of eyewitness testimony. Thus, when Preacher Hardy finds the two women dead but their bodies uncorrupted, "'fresh and untainted as sleeping children,'" Jess is willing to believe the cause of this miracle is Angela's desire to do the ultimate kindness for her elderly friend, to die in her place. But, in a signal that the circle of story in this story/novel is about to be completed, Grandmother reminds her audience, particularly her daughter, that "'nobody can go that journey for another. Somebody might try to go with you; it would have to be somebody real special. But they can't go far'" (193).

In the final story, "The Remembering Woman," Chappell celebrates the strength of novelistic storytelling, but the celebration is tinged with a warning about the limits of the novel. "This is a story with four tellers," Jess begins. Jess, the boy, heard the story of the visit of the famous folklorist Holme Barcroft from both his grandmother and his mother, but he recalls it from the perspective of the famous man himself and knows that his own telling places an imprint on the story, too.

Of all the stories in the novel, this one demands the most of its audience. We are asked to be the most careful of readers while straining to be listeners as well—to hear the music of the fiddlers at the Lafferty's party while also considering the impact of the writing of outsiders on the mountain people, however well meaning they might be. Chappell's Dr. Barcroft is presented as the ideal outsider, writing truthful books in which Jess's people are presented as "people like any other people, wise and foolish, brave and frightened, saintly and unholy and ordinary" (197). That few ethnologists have been so enlightened remains quietly in the subtext; the point is that Jess sees Dr. Barcroft in this light because he identifies with him more than with any other storyteller he has known. He sees Dr. Barcroft as a sympathetic listener but one armed with knowledge that only the outside world can provide. And Dr. Barcroft has another necessary quality for a writer (as opposed to a storyteller), the distancing perspective of the scholar—which Jess knows he too must gain if he is to become a writer. Jess portrays the purely scholarly perspective in one speech that the good doctor is remembered to have made, even though his audience consists only of an uneducated mountain woman and her young daughter. Indeed, he seems to be imagining an audience of scholars like himself as he speaks while watching the Lafferty family and friends swing through the traditional square-dance formations at the party given in his honor:

> He felt that he was standing near the origins of a strength that helped to animate the world, a power that joined all things together in a pattern that lay just barely beyond the edge of comprehension. He felt that an individual personality would feel itself conformably and joyfully a part of this pattern simply by giving in to the current of the dance, this small current being but a small streamlet of the larger current that poured through the world and everything that was in the world and beyond it. (215)

But Dr. Barcroft refuses an offer to join in the dance; he sees the connectedness of life only in the abstract through his role as an observer. Jess's grandmother acknowledges the value the world places on such observations and how little value is placed on the kind of wisdom she possesses: "'I don't know what he was talking about . . . He was a highly learned man.'" She feels ashamed of her lack of understanding and the fact that she has never read any of his books, having been too busy raising her family.

But Jess, narrating from his perspective as a grownup writer, understands the situation in a way that neither Dr. Barcroft nor his grandmother does; he knows that it is merely the high-flown words that get in the way of his grandmother's understanding. Memory and wisdom are not truly capturable in words, although the best storytellers and novelists can achieve brilliant failures. As Dr. Barcroft continues to attempt to put his experience into words, the jargon of academia dissolves into the language of simile and poetry, of dreams in which the bounds of reality are loosened. As the house seems to heave into circular movement along with the dancers, he sees the moonrise:

> The moon: the moon rose all at once, as if it had escaped the mountains, as if there had been a force in those hilltops that held it back, restrained it until it bounded away from them and rose like a hot-air balloon, as silent and as awing, and it was the hugest moon this doctor of music had ever seen or imagined, so huge and close, it seemed to spread a perfume in the air, the scent of frost on new-mown grass, the smell of the cold, rough linen sheets you crawled into on a deep winter night with the moonlight pouring onto the bed, a smell almost odorless, like the smell of porcelain plates taken from the dark cupboard shelf. (219)

As he tried to put his vision of the dance into words, "'He got excited in talking . . . and almost drove us off the road,'" Jess's grandmother remembers.

But for her and her daughter, the magic of that night is expressed in far fewer and simpler words. Jess's mother remembers that she had thought, in her childlike way, that the dead had come out of their graves to take part in the dance. But her mother had explained that it was only people who liked to dress in old-fashioned clothes. Still, for those listeners who understand the full implication of her words, the departed generations did indeed appear: "'Maybe they honored their departed that way, I don't know. Dullards, that's who they were'" (220). Despite her modest disclaimer, Jess's grandmother does know. She possesses the knowledge, not just of her own life, but of a people who remember to honor their ancestors and can call all their neighbors by name. Dr. Barcroft works to explain his insights to an alienated audience, a bookish audience that has nothing to draw upon but his words. Jess's grandmother and mother need fewer words to talk of the most complex and sacred things because their audience is part of the same cultural web as they. Jess, and Chappell, know they are somewhere in between, educated in the traditions of the outside world yet having the story web of their culture to sustain them.

And here lies the limitation, in Chappell's view, of a writer's ability to create a novel while genuinely fulfilling the storyteller's role: both traditions are necessary. In the brief epilogue, "The Voices," Chappell, through Jess, reveals his own uncertainty. Jess and his father know with the first light of morning that the grandmother has at last seen Jesus and gone to be with him, leaving her daughter alone and desolate. We are reminded of the comment Jess remembers his mother making in the previous story, that "[s]ometimes it seems that all the really good people are gone" (207). Jess fears that this may be true, that while the clocks in the house have restarted, "it would be a different kind of time we live in now; it would not be steady in the least and the winds would be cold in our faces against us all the way"(228). The only way that his family can survive is to go down that dark hallway and together come "back into the light."

Jess writes down the stories he has heard, and Chappell bundles these stories into novels; Jess and he are hybrids, shaped by the storytelling culture they were born into as well as by their "booklearning." The question then becomes, how many more hybrids like these can our postindustrial, cyberdependent world produce?

3

The stakes involved in the loss or retention of the practice of storytelling may be very high indeed. De Certeau suggests that a child's ability to learn to read is based on her mastery of oral communication:

> [C]ultural memory (acquired through listening, through oral tradition alone) makes possible and gradually enriches the strategies of semantic questioning whose expectations the deciphering of a written text refines, clarifies, or corrects. From the child to the scientist, reading is preceded and made possible by oral communication, which constitutes the "multifarious" authority that texts almost never cite. (168)

Thus, according to de Certeau, the most basic oral communication is dependent on a tradition that has an authority that mere symbols on paper or screen lack. I would posit further that parents communicate the most basic aspects of life to their children in story form; humans are "hard wired" for stories.

It may be that orality per se is possible without the ritual of storytelling as practiced in the dwindling communities of village and work that Benjamin envisions, as practiced by Chappell through Jess and the other voices in his novels; but without it, our culture becomes an increasingly isolating, ultimately chaotic and frightening place. Storytelling binds the web of community together; without this web, neither the scientist nor the kindergartner sounding his first words can reach the greatness they are capable of.

But as Chappell and many other writers and tellers remind us, while the web of community is threatened, it has not yet been entirely destroyed. In high-rise apartment buildings, mountain hollers, and even chat rooms in cyberspace, individuals feel the need to answer, with Jess, the question, "Are you one of us or not?" And as long as there are even a few of those peculiar hybrid souls to help us find the way, the answer will be yes.

WORKS CITED

Arendt, Hannah. Introduction to *Illuminations,* by Walter Benjamin. New York: Schocken Books, 1969.

Benjamin, Walter. "The Storyteller." In *Illuminations.* Translated by Harry Zohn. New York: Schocken Books, 1969.

———. "The Work of Art in the Age of Mechanical Reproduction." In *Illuminations.* Trans. Harry Zohn. New York: Schocken Books, 1969.

Campbell, Hilbert. "Fred Chappell's Urn of Memory: *I Am One of You Forever.*" *Southern Literary Journal* 25 (1993): 103–11.

De Certeau, Michel. *The Practice of Everyday Life.* Trans. Steven Rendell. Berkeley: University of California Press, 1984.

Chappell, Fred. *Farewell, I'm Bound to Leave You.* New York: Picador, 1996.

———. *I Am One of You Forever.* Baton Rouge: Louisiana State University Press, 1985.

FOURTEEN

Tales Tall and True
Fred Chappell's *Look Back All the Green Valley*
and the Continuity of Narrative Tradition

JAMES W. KIRKLAND

WITH THE PUBLICATION of *Look Back All the Green Valley,* the Kirkman tetralogy comes to an end, bringing the adult Jess back, after a long absence, to the place of his birth and the scene of the three previous novels. Yet the closure that the novel seems to promise is more apparent than real, and the mysteries Jess seeks to unravel prove to be as elusive as the meanings of Uncle Zeno's stories. Stories are, in fact, the essence of the novel, appearing early and late in varied forms and contexts, ranging from isolated, single-motif anecdotes to extended storytelling events. While some of these stories come from the pages of the *Metamorphosis* or the *Divine Comedy,* and others are modeled on juvenile science-fiction and adventure books, most are rooted in folk tradition. Thus any meaningful study of their role in the novel must necessarily take into account not only the lore and the literature, in equal measure, but also the "ways in which the disciplines of oral narrative and literary history and criticism interact" (Rosenberg 1).

Such an approach raises a number of questions crucial to an understanding of Chappell's transformations and recontextualizations of folkloric phenomena in *Look Back All the Green Valley.* First, what is his conception of folklore and its relationship to literature? Second, what specific folk-narrative genres and processes are evident in the novel, and how closely do they correspond to established folkloristic models? Third, in what fictional contexts do they occur, and with what frequency? Finally, what is their meaning and function for audiences within and outside the story? In particular, what bearing do they have on Jess's search for the father and his efforts to reestablish his connections with the community he left many years earlier?

Chappell's fascination with the cultural traditions of the southern Appalachians and his personal acquaintance with such renowned storytellers as Homer Campbell, the inspiration for the fictional Virgil Campbell, have long been a matter of public record, but a recent *Carolina Quarterly* interview, conducted just after the publication of *Look Back All the Green Valley*, sheds new light on the nature and extent of his folkloric knowledge and its impact on his life and art. "You would be hard put to find any novel of real literary worth that did not have a folk literature basis at bottom," Chappell observes in response to George Hovis's question about Chappell's Appalachian heritage. "Probably folk art and high art, if you want to call it that, have more in common than they do with popular art, simply because they try the harder thing. They have the more individual stamp upon them. They are more deeply rooted than pop culture, which is, after all, designed to disappear" (77).

Although Chappell does not elaborate on what constitutes "folk literature" or "folk art" at this point in the interview, his concept of folklore as a powerful form of human communication with closer affinities to "high art" than "popular culture" clearly aligns him with contemporary folklorists like Dan Ben-Amos, who defines folklore as "artistic communication in small groups" (quoted in Brunvand 16); Jan Brunvand, who conceives of folklore as "a diversified and complex subject" revealing the "whole intricate mosaic of human culture" (22); and Roger Abrahams, who argues that both folklore and literature are artistic performances designed "to set up rhythms and expectancies which will permit—indeed insist upon—a synchronized audience reaction" (78).

As noted at the outset, the folk art that matters most to both Chappell and his characters is the folk narrative, especially one of the two "ethnic (or native) categories" (Brunvand 10) that Aunt Ora Ireland describes in response to Jess's announcement that he thinks he has just seen Uncle Zeno near the site of his father's grave: "He [Uncle Zeno] was a storyteller, you know. I don't mean a liar kind of storyteller. He just told stories about people, mostly true as I've heard" (208).

When a story is told as a fictional account "in the form of personal narrative or anecdote, which challenges the listener's credulity with comic outlandishness, and which performs different social functions depending on whether it is heard as true or as fictional" (Brown 11), it is what Aunt Ora would call a "liar kind" of tale—that is, a tall tale—a genre of the folktale known by various names, including "windies," "whoppers," "lies" (in the sense Vance Randolph uses the term in his collection of Ozark tales entitled *We Always Lie to Strangers*), and "tales of lying" (the title of one of the major headings in Stith Thompson's *Motif-Index of Folk-Literature*). When a story is repeatedly told and received as a true account of what "allegedly happened to ordinary people in everyday situations" (Brunvand 196), it is a legend, which Timothy Tangherlini defines more specifically as "a mono-episodic, localized, and historicized traditional narrative told as believable in a conversational mode" (437) and reflecting what he calls "the collective experiences and values of the group to whose tradition it belongs" (437).

Although Aunt Ora mentions no specific "liar kind of storyteller" comparable to the legend-teller Uncle Zeno, Cary Owen—Jess's guide through Hardison County—is certainly worthy of that title. In fact, Cary and Jess both help to keep the tall-tale tradition alive through their active participation in an extended folk "lying contest"—a traditional storytelling event in which two or more people, almost always males, attempt to top one another's tales. Within the framework of this traditional communication event, Chappell freely adapts the tall-tale genre to suit the fictional context, sometimes building stories around traditional plot motifs or tale types and sometimes inventing stories similar in form and content to those documented by ethnographers.

Jess inadvertently initiates this storytelling event with a brief anecdote about Bailey Ridge, "a place name in a story my mother had told me," which evokes a comic rejoinder from Cary, who claims it was originally named "Horney's Ridge because 'the horniest people in the world' live here" (114).

Having grown up listening to the stories of Virgil Campbell, who "had explored the tall tale and the whiskey jug with intrepid thoroughness" (81), and his father, a man noted for playing rusties (which many folklorists consider to be nonverbal tall tales), Jess knows when he is being "gulled" or "skylarked" and how to respond. First he interrupts the narration, an action that parallels the folkloric model in which "a liar with an absurdity in his presentation provokes his listener into making an objection" (Henningsen 196). Then he counters with "a story of my own, a tale about my sexually gluttonous friend, Jim Dickey"—but this invented "whopper" is no match for the tall-tale extravagance of Cary, who "topped my story about Jim and the Black Leather Stewardess Coven with a story about a jackleg Hardison County preacher named Gaddon" (135).

Although we never actually hear the stories about the poet or the preacher, we do learn about other local characters through the sequence of tales inspired by Jess's and Cary's arrival in Glutton field—narratives built around traditional tall tale motifs involving extraordinarily large or strong people.

Cary tells a story about "Lane Gentry, who let himself grow so mountainously fat that he broke the back of his favorite horse" (136). Jess counters with "the story of Big Mama Stamey, the moonshining woman who became so wide in girth that she was made a prisoner in her own house [see Ernest W. Baughman's *A Type and Motif Index of the Folktales of England and North America*, X 923. Lie: "great girt of large person"], the doors no longer accommodating such a breadth of avoirdupois" (136). The story sounds like a personal legend up to this point, the genre to which Jess had assigned it years earlier in *Midquest*, but by crediting it to his father, who heard it from Virgil Campbell, both noted for their tall tales and practical jokes, Jess undermines the credibility of his own narrative: "I'd got the story of Big Mama from my father, who passed it to me from Virgil Campbell; it was the sequel to a tale about a Founder's Day parade out in Hayesville, in which Big Mama was a proud exhibit, being at that earlier time not yet housebound" (136).

In the very next sentence, Cary tops Jess's story again by recounting a traditional tall tale with numerous oral analogues (see especially Baughman X 940. Lie: "person of remarkable strength"). "In Proudvale, he regaled me with the chronicle of Broadus Waner, who was so vain and boastful of his prowess as a catch-as-catch-can wrestler that, having bested all the competition in Hardison or out of it, undertook to wrestle a standing barn and succeeded so thoroughly that he pulled the structure down upon himself and was crushed nigh to death" (136).

Just as firmly rooted in oral narrative tradition is Cary's story about Darl Simpson, who is reputed to be the laziest man in Hardison County. Ostensibly an etiological or etymological legend intended to explain how the town of Lazybones got its name, the story is actually a windy, narrated in the first person by Cary himself and built around Motif No. "W iii. Laziness" in Baughman:

> "You hear that expression of speaking about lazy people being too trifling to strike a lick at a snake. Well, it was the true fact about Darl Simpson. Had him a little old flimsy shack up in the holler yonder and it was all growed up about with weeds and brush, and sure enough, he was too lazy to keep them out and the copperhead snakes moved in on him, must've been dozens. Bob Jackson told him, 'Darl,' he says, 'you better take care of them copperheads or they'll likely take care of you.' And Darl, he says, 'Well, Bob, these here copperheads will make many a good meal for the blacksnakes that will show up as soon as word gets to 'em.' He didn't worry about no copperheads biting on him; Darl Simpson never moved fast enough to alarm a snake." (137)

Like the skilled yarn-spinners of folk tradition, Cary first insists on the truth of his tale and supports that claim through realistic details about the "flimsy shack" and overabundance of "weeds and brush," which make it seem plausible that snakes might find Darl's house an attractive nesting place. But subsequent details about the copperheads moving in by the dozens, like unwanted tenants, and the blacksnakes just waiting for "word" of the copperheads' arrival, clearly reflect the kind of escalating comic exaggerations that folktale scholars associate with the central-plot phase of the tall tale of oral tradition. The conclusion of the tale is also formulaic, representing a variation of the basic tall-tale pattern in which "instead of building to a climax the tale may wind down to a humorous understatement" (Brown 21).

While tall tales are in one sense a form of esoteric lore that, in cultural context, requires skilled raconteurs and an audience with firsthand experiential knowledge of the genre and its performance conventions, readers need not be active participants in the tradition in order to understand and appreciate the humor of Chappell's fictional simulations and recreations. For the tall tale has been closely associated with American comic tradition since the nineteenth century when, according to Henningsen, "America became for one reason or another a liar's paradise"—a phenomenon that "holds true to the same degree in the twentieth century where states and districts compete to see which have the finest tall tale traditions, and where there are found liars' clubs whose primary purpose is to elect the year's greatest liar" (181).

Even more widely known and told are stories belonging to the second of Aunt Ora's two categories, the folk legend. The appeal of such narratives for both teller and audience is that they are a medium of every-day communication, unconstrained by rigid genre or performance conventions and adaptable to almost any subject or circumstance. Of the five major forms of legend recognized by most folklorists—local, supernatural, religious, personal, and urban—all but the last appear in the novel, sometimes in the context of a storytelling event such as the lying contest in chapter 6 but more typically during the course of informal conversations or in direct addresses or asides to the reader.

Local legends—one of the most common of the legend genres—are concentrated in Jess's account of his travels in Hardison County, the section of the novel that focuses on his efforts to discover the meanings of the women's names associated with each of the place names marked on the map he discovers in his father's workshop. These stories range from Jess's brief anecdote about the origin of the name Truelove, which he believes to be "a corruption of the name Treloft, a nickname given out of fondness" (155) to the family who had originally settled there, to Cary's more elaborate narrative about the origins of the name Irongant. "The name Irongant was a mistake," Jess reports his guide's saying as they approach the area:

> Back around 1915, the U.S. Postal Service was trying to establish names for all these scattered mosquito-bite hamlets. The postal man took one look at the muddy road before him and lost all enthusiasm for following it farther. He accosted a bearded mountain man with a rifle held in the crook of his arm and said, "Scuse me, feller, but what's up that way?" He wrote down what he heard, but the laconic hunter had said, "Aaron Gant," referring to an industrious but luckless farmer who lived near the head of the holler. So Irongant it became. (144)

The story conforms not only to the legend pattern, as Tangherlini defines it, but also to the specific subgenre that Brunvand calls "local place-name etymologies" (220), which are themselves "local legends"—stories "closely associated with specific places, either with their names, their geographic features, or their histories" (Brunvand 219). And while the name

Irongant is unlikely to appear in any published collection of local legends, the story is similar to frequently collected folk etymologies that trace the origin of a particular place name to a mistake by postal workers who "either misread the handwritten name that townspeople submitted or made an error while taking it down" (Brunvand 220).

Another familiar legend type that Chappell adapts to his fictional purposes is the supernatural legend, a primary example being the story of Aunt Sophie Medlin, which Cary tells Jess as they approach Treloft, the last place marked on Joe Robert's secret map. Like other stories of this genre, Cary's legend is grounded in the events of every-day life. Beginning with a realistic description of a traditional quilt pattern—with "the circles inside and outside of each other, locked together like that" (151–2)—Cary proceeds to describe the loving relationship between Sophie and her husband Booker, her excitement about completing the quilt to commemorate their marriage, and the circumstances surrounding his untimely death. Only when this realistic context has been established does Cary move on to the more overtly supernatural implications of the story, which he further validates by telling Sophie's dream narrative in her own words: "While I was sleeping there in that armchair, it came into my sleep a picture of him [her husband Booker] in a place as bright as a rainbow. He was wearing my quilt, but now it was his robe for always and it just fit him perfect" (154). Although the wedding-band quilt is itself a detail unique to this story, the narrative nonetheless contains several well-known motifs cited in the Baughman *Index:* E574: "Appearance of ghost serves as death omen"; E363.4 (a): "Return from the dead to reassure person of life after death"; and D1812.4.3.3: "Death knowledge learned through presentiment."

First-person accounts of the supernatural are so widely disseminated in cultural tradition that folklorists have coined a special term, "memorate," to distinguish them from full-scale legends, but other types of first-person narrative often raise more complex questions of traditionality: "How many repetitions are needed," Brunvand asks, "or how widely must a personal narrative be spread for it to qualify as folklore? How can we distinguish between unstructured musings, polished retellings of events, memorates, personal narratives, and personal legends?" (Brunvand 214). Chappell resolves this problem fictionally by combining what Brunvand calls "first-person reminiscences and family stories" (214) with traditional personal legends and anecdotes to create cycles of stories that revolve around the exploits of particular individuals, notably Joe Robert and Uncle Zeno.

Although Joe Robert has been dead for ten years when the novel opens, he lives on in the stories of the people who knew him. Several of these narratives—including Mr. Hillyer's story about the rusty Joe Robert pulled on a group of local preachers and the Irelands' reminiscences about the equally outrageous prank he was planning to play on Challenger Papermill foreman T. J. Wesson—are told for the first time in this novel, enlarging Joe Robert's already substantial reputation as a practical joker and at the same time filling in gaps in the Kirkman family history. Others, notably Uncle Gray's brief reminiscence about Joe Robert's and Johnson Gibbs's chicken-eggs-for-chocolate swap when Jess was a young boy, are so well known, both to the novel's characters and to readers familiar with earlier works about the Kirkman family, that even a fragmented version of the story like Uncle Gray's is sufficient to evoke what folklorist Linda Degh refers to in another context as the "components" that "are traditionally known in a given community" (74). Still other stories—particularly those concerned with Joe Robert's and Uncle Zeno's reputations as storytellers—pose a more difficult challenge, offering multiple and sometimes conflicting versions of the same "truth."

When Aunt Ora, for example, tells Jess that his father "wasn't expert at telling stories" (208), she is voicing an opinion shared by most of the community, including her husband, who responds, "'That's the truth! . . . When he tried to tell a windy, he'd get so tangled up, it was like he had wandered into a laurel hell. He couldn't even tell the stories of his own pranks and antics" (208). There are other stories, however, such as the one Cora tells Jess when he first visits her at the nursing home, that give a totally different picture of Joe Robert's storytelling abilities:

> She launched into a story about a European tour they had enjoyed. In the town of Roussilon in Provence, they were provided with a bus driver, but the tour guide didn't show. My father decided to serve as cicerone and devised colorful chronicles to match points of interest in the landscape that rolled past the bus windows. His conception of history rested on perfidious princes, bloody revenges, daggers and crossbows and mutual poisonings, and he was warmly partial to accounts of

naked ladies on horseback a la Godiva. The peaceful fields of lavender, he made out to be corpse-strewn battlefields; the gray castles surmounting the brushy hills still contained dungeons, and the dungeons still contained the children of the children of figures like Duc Philippe of the Ugly Ankles and the unlucky queen, Matilde Who Had No Butt. These tales, my mother averred, had kept the tour bus teary-eyed with laughter. (16)

Although Jess immediately questions the authenticity of the story, stating unequivocally, "I didn't believe her" (16), his further comment that whenever his father "tried to construct a story he unfailingly banged his thumb with the punch line" (16) is itself contradicted elsewhere in the novel, most obviously in Jess's account of Joe Robert's windy about a fierce 1930s storm known throughout the community by the comic epithet "Bad Egg." Following the basic outline of a story told many years earlier in *Midquest*, Jess characterizes the narrative as one of his father's "best, and most elaborate, tall tales"—a story that

my father had described . . . at great length, recounting the awe-inspiring incidents that had happened to him and detailing meticulously the embarrassments of several well-known citizens of Hardison. That tall tale, that "windy," was the Kirkman fifth canto, for he had alluded to Paolo and Francesca in his story, tucking in a little jest that Mitzi and I were too young to understand. Whether my mother had noticed it, I couldn't know. (86)

Just as stories told about different events in a person's life may represent that person in different ways, so might a single event inspire multiple stories, each different from the others. An especially revealing example of this traditional folkloric process can be found in the diverse body of narratives known to Jess and almost everyone else in the community as the "kite story." Told originally in *Midquest* by Cora and elaborated by Annie Barbara Sorrells in *Farewell, I'm Bound to Leave You*, the story surfaces again in the third chapter of *Look Back All the Green Valley* in the form of a personal legend told by Dilly Elden but ascribed to Joe Robert:

He [Joe Robert] told me a story about when they taught school together up at Tipton. She [Cora] taught Spanish and English and he taught science and geography and math. He had in mind to show his science class about Benjamin Franklin's kite, how it discovered electricity. He didn't have any cloth to make a kite with, so she offered to make one for him out of an old petticoat that had gone to rags. But she sewed firecrackers into the sides of it and braided a long fuse into the tail. Then when she was holding the kite for him to get a running start to make it fly, she lit that tail fuse, and when the kite was in the air, it blew all to ruin. Four or five times he told Royal and me that story and laughed himself red in the face every time. He said he wished he could dream up a sweet prank like that and he thought maybe he would make that his life's ambition. . . . Those were his very words, "sweet prank." (55)

The story, Jess explains for the benefit of anyone unacquainted with the earlier versions, had "passed from the realm of family reminiscence into folklore and looked now as if it were on its way to epic status," expanding and changing as it is passed from person to person over an extended period of time. As he goes on to say,

I'd heard it from my mother and father and grandmother, from aunts and uncles, from friends, acquaintances, and rank strangers. There were many versions of the tale, sometimes similar, sometimes exotically different. Any one of them had proved an adequate hour-killer down at the old community gossip post, Virgil Campbell's Bound for Hell Gro. and Dry Goods. Now Mr. Campbell had passed away and his establishment had turned into a consignment clothing shop, but the story of the kite still lived on and bade fair to survive us all. (56)

The same processes are at work in the formation of the novel's second major legend cycle, which focuses on Uncle Zeno, one of the most enigmatic of all Jess's relatives. For most members of the community, he is simply an ordinary person with a gift for telling stories and a history of outwitting Joe Robert in the same kind of verbal contests that Jess and Cary engage in. Thus, when Jess announces to the Irelands that he has seen Uncle Zeno in the graveyard, several members of the family express skepticism, noting that if Jess's story were true, Uncle Z would have to be well over a hundred years old. Uncle Gray, however, is more receptive to the idea, which he validates—in the typical manner of legend performance—by telling a story of his own about Joe Robert's conviction that Uncle Zeno was immortal: "'Maybe he won't never die.' That's what Joe Robert said about him one time. 'Uncle Zeno is immortal because he doesn't belong to this world. He lives in another world and only visits this one every once in a while to drive people insane.' That was his idea of Uncle Zeno" (208).

It is also Jess's idea, as evidenced by this account of what he claims is eyewitness testimony verifying Uncle Zeno's physical presence in the graveyard scenes that begin and end the novel. "'I saw him. Plain as day'"(275), Jess says. When Bud replies that it couldn't be because Uncle Z would be too old, Jess responds, "Maybe he really is immortal. . . . That's what my father thought. Maybe that's how he knew the story" (275)—the "story of the world. . . . The story of you and me. All the stories that ever were or will be" (275).

The immediate audience here is Bud Ireland, but the language evokes an earlier story that Jess tells directly to the reader in a chapter appropriately titled "On the Foggy Mountaintop." The chapter begins realistically, with little hint of anything out of the ordinary. "It seemed I was standing on a foggy mountaintop and the mist was so thick, I couldn't see who was speaking. It was a familiar voice as it sounded close by my ear, just behind me on my left side" (129). The third sentence continues in the same manner, though the voice now becomes less familiar, more enigmatic: "Dry, flat, almost without inflection, it seemed to have been going on for a long time" (129).

By the beginning of the next paragraph—in the very next sentence, in fact—the tone and situation change dramatically, as the thus far disembodied voice tells us, "So there she was, standing before the Pearly Gates, with no idy what would happen next." Who, we might legitimately ask at this point, is "she"? How did we get from the misty mountains of western North Carolina to the Pearly Gates? And how do we reconcile this as yet unnamed speaker's vernacular language ("idy" and "reckon") with the lyric style of the remainder of the paragraph? Rather than answering these questions, the second narrator simply continues the story with a kind of deadpan logic, typical of the tall-tale raconteur, introducing a new character (St. Peter), who despite the celestial trappings speaks in the same colloquial dialect ("What are ye a-waitin for," "They's a place set for you," "What are ye dawdlin along out here for?").

So realistic is the language, so conversational the tone, that we momentarily forget that the two individuals engaged in this dialogue are Jess's deceased grandmother and St. Peter, a dislocation that becomes even more pronounced as the subject shifts from the fate of Annie Barbara Sorrells and her son-in-law Joe Robert to the "problem" of "Joe Robert's rowdy friend Virgil Campbell." Prompted by Annie Barbara's remark that Virgil would profit from "a little hard work," St. Peter begins to indulge in the same kind of comic extravagance as Cary Owen. "'We got endless acres of the finest vineyards you could picture,' he said. 'And an ace distillery that runs a whiskey beyond mankind's neediest hankering. It seems in good order for Virgil to be our wine and liquor sampler and do all the tasting for us. We set a handsome table up here and we don't allow any slouch vintages'" (131).

With that comment, the voice fades, indicating that the story of Annie Barbara at the Pearly Gates is over, but then resumes with an expression familiar to anyone who has encountered Uncle Zeno in any of the previous three novels: "'You are my eerie and mysterious uncle Zeno who will never stop telling stories. I remember you from long ago, from when I was only a youngun'" (131).

Jess's confusion and surprise are perfectly understandable, because the dream story he is attempting to tell us continually alters the terms of its own reality as well as the ways in which we and Jess respond to it. As noted earlier, Uncle Zeno is both a legend in his own right and a legend-teller, but here he seems indistinguishable from tall-tale performers like Virgil and Joe Robert, and in the role of St. Peter he assumes the mantle of one of the most widely recognized figures in American jokelore.

This blurring of boundaries between one type of story or storyteller and another is just one further indication of Chappell's knowledge of folklore and its potential as a medium of fictional expression. And the novel as a whole reveals his intuitive understanding of a premise that has long been central to folklore/literature scholarship: that "the deliberate shift, or the accidental transference of any folklore text to a different literary, historical, or cultural context grants it a new meaning" (Ben-Amos 158).

In the fictional world of *Look Back All the Green Valley*, meaning is neither stable nor absolute; rather, it is constantly being constructed by the reader in collaboration with the author and the narrator, who by an ironic twist of narratological logic are one and the same. Like Chappell, whose name Jess claims to have adopted as a pseudonym, the narrator is both a participant in and an interpreter of tradition—a cultural insider with an ethnographer's knowledge of "the folklore the anthropologists recognize, the myth the mythographers recognize" (Hovis 74) and the role of both in "our ordinary lives, too" (Hovis 74).

Whether telling us his own stories, as he does in "On the Foggy Mountain Top," or passing along the stories of others, as he does when he ascribes a windy to Cary Owen or a personal legend to Uncle Gray, Jess invites us to participate, vicariously, in what he refers to as the "rituals of remembrance" that satisfy the basic human need to revisit and relive the past. If we accept the invitation, we cannot help but empathize with people like Dilly, who says to Jess near the end of his visit to his father's workshop, "It's been good to remember Joe Robert and the old times" (79), or Mr. Hillyer, for whom even a brief conversation with Jess about Joe Robert and Cora is enough to make him reminisce about "the old times, when life showed a more favorable countenance" (184). Jess, too, is drawn back into the past, for reasons that he shares with us near the end of a long conversation with the Irelands, as people begin arriving for the picnic he has arranged: "If only I could recall the faces and the episodes they belonged to, this was the story of my youth unfolding and a larger tale, too, than that very small one: the chronicle of a period of mountain culture of rare and striking flavor" (251).

Although Jess dwells here on the incompleteness of his quest for self-knowledge and communal identity, the tales he has already told—both large and small—have by this point filled in many of the gaps in our knowledge of Jess's personal history and the ways in which it has become intertwined with the community chronicle. And the more familiar we are with the earlier books in the series, the more complete this picture becomes.

With this knowledge we can see, perhaps even more clearly than Jess, the connections between the story of his life and that of his father, the chief object of his quest.

Together, the larger tales and the smaller ones offer strong indirect support for Joe Robert's theory of "sympathetic resonance" (78), which Dilly struggles to explain to Jess just before he leaves Joe Robert's workshop. "He said that people, all of us, lived more than one life at a time. We lived on many different time tracks at the same time but only knew one at a time. But each life affected all the others a little bit. He said it was like plucking one guitar string. The others would vibrate slightly if you did that" (78). This is exactly what happens in the novel, where Joe Robert and Uncle Zeno and countless other characters from the earlier books continually re-appear in the current residents' narratives, reminding us of what we already know intuitively: that when we tell a story about people from a different place or time, we temporarily bring them back into our lives, just as we return imaginatively to the past whenever we attempt to recreate it through our legends and tales.

Stories are also a means of affirming one of the most crucial lessons Jess comes to learn during the course of his journey: that truth is relative and meaning ultimately indeterminate, for the very nature of orality is that whatever circulates primarily by word of mouth varies in transmission, creating a different representation of reality each time the story is told and heard. As he tells Mitzi, their father's stories were not always what they seemed. "'Lots of times when you thought he was kidding, he was actually serious. Things I thought were teases turned out to be true. Stories I took for gospel turned out to be fairy tales he made up on the spot'" (26). And even the most familiar of narratives, such the "kite story," often raise more questions than they answer, as Jess acknowledges when he contemplates what to say when Dilly asks him whether the story is true: "When I tried to answer the question it was no longer a simple one; she was requiring me to measure the amount of historical truth in a myth. So I ducked the issue. 'I think it's true enough for its purpose,' I said" (56).

Ironically Jess sees his remark as an evasion, but it is, from a folkloristic point of view, the only meaningful way in which he can respond, because oral narratives are by definition fluid in form and content, their meanings changing unpredictably as they are told and retold over time. Thus Dilly's "kite story" is neither more nor less "true" in any absolute sense than Cora's or Annie Barbara's or anyone else's. It is simply different—different in its basic motif structure; different in its emphasis on Joe Robert's repeated per-formance of the story in the Elden household; and different, too, in its representation of his wife as the "sly Cora," a kindred spirit and a trickster in her own right.

These differences prompt Jess's choice of the word "myth"—a term folklorists typically associate with sacred narratives set in a remote time and place, with gods or demigods as the central characters—to characterize a story that seems always to be told and heard as a legend—a narrative about a believable event in the lives of ordinary people. As the context makes clear, however, the word *myth*, in Jess's lexicon, refers not to a particular kind of story but to the process through which the telling and retelling of stories can transform an ordinary person into a larger than life figure who transcends the limits of a particular time and place. In this respect, Jess's views seem virtually indistinguishable from Chappell's, who had this to say to Hovis's question, in the *Carolina Quarterly* interview, about the inspiration for Joe Robert's character: "Yes. He [Joe Robert Kirkman] has a basis in reality—in my own father, and in some other teachers and people I knew. But highly romanticized, highly exaggerated. The idea was to show him slightly exaggerated in the first novel, and as time went on to show him more and more mythic, until finally he recedes into the past like all the great heroes . . . " (74).

The mythic process Chappell alludes to in the interview is actively at work throughout the novel, particularly in the two legend cycles centering on Joe Robert and Uncle Zeno. As Joe Robert is transformed, in story, from flesh-and-blood human being to myth hero, he becomes, in Jess's mind, "your classic folklore trickster" (26)—a role that he shares not only with human tricksters/liars such as Virgil Campbell and Cary Owen but also with mythic tricksters of Native American and African American folk tradition, such as Coyote and Anansi. "My father," Jess tells us as he rummages through his father's workshop early in the novel, "was too many for me, the elusive fox I had pursued all my life with no real hope of bringing to earth" (72). Later, as he and Cary near the end of their journey through Hardison County in search of clues to the identities of the women whose names appear on the map Jess discovers in his father's secret workshop, Jess returns to this theme, using much the same image as before: "The problem with tracking down my father was not that he had failed to leave a trail but that he had left too many. He was a fox of many stratagems" (164). And by the end of the novel, when Jess discovers a fox's skull in his father's grave,

Joe Robert's transformation from practical joker to cosmic trickster is complete, at least in Jess's eyes: "That's him; my father was the fox" (278).

In like manner, Uncle Zeno is transformed from a flesh-and-blood storyteller into a modern-day Methuselah—a "real" person enveloped in the surreal atmosphere of Jess's dream narratives and gravesite memorates. Whether the shadowy figure that Jess and his helpers believe they have seen is really Uncle Zeno or a product of their own imaginations is a question Chappell ultimately leaves for Jess and the reader to determine because, as he has said elsewhere, "What you imagine is real. There's no hard and fast dividing line between what you imagine and what you observe" (Hovis 69).

Nor are there any limits, in Chappell's fictional universe, on the power of stories and their tellers, as he explains in his reply to an interviewer's question about the inspiration for Uncle Zeno's character:

> Well, Uncle Zeno is partly modeled on an old gentleman I used to know and work with. He was part of the family for a while and he had an inexhaustible store of tales in which he was always the hero. He always got the last word, and he always got the better of the other fellow, he always caused things to come out all right in the end. And my father and I listened to him for six months or so at the dinner table, very impressed. And then one day I noticed my father surreptitiously scribbling down a number on a little scrap of paper he put back in his pocket. Later on, I asked him about it and he showed me this long list of numbers he had. By his account, which I thought was pretty accurate, our honorary uncle was about three hundred years old. And I thought, what if he was. What if he just be immortal. I drew him a little bit after the way Homer drew Demodocus, his epic poet, in *The Odyssey*. I thought it would be a lot of fun just to have that figure there. And I needed him in the last book, because I wanted to put forward my hope and belief that the art of fiction and poetry is inexhaustible and outlives us all. (Hovis 78)

While many of Chappell's critics will likely continue to undervalue the role of folklore in *Look Back All the Green Valley* by praising the book for the "perfection" of its "hillbilly dialect" or criticizing it for its alleged "tall tale silliness," readers familiar with the folklore of the anthropologists, the myth of the mythographers, the tales and legends of a fictional community that spans four novels and another four volumes of poetry, will undoubtedly respond in a different way. For such readers, this last novel in the Kirkman saga is not only a story of stories but a story about stories: a ritual of remembrance and a celebration of both the continuity of narrative tradition and the power of stories, both tall and true, to dissolve the boundaries between imagination and experience, reunite the individual and the community, and connect in a multiplicity of ways the past with the present, the living with the dead.

WORKS CITED

Abrahams, Roger. "Folklore and Literature As Performance." *Journal of the Folklore Institute* 9 (1972): 75–94.

Baughman, Ernest W. *A Type and Motif Index of the Folktales of England and North America.* The Hague: Indiana University Folklore Series No. 20, 1966.

Ben-Amos, Dan. "Contextual Approach." In *American Folklore: An Encyclopedia,* ed. Jan Harold Brunvand. New York: Garland, 1996.

Brown, Carolyn S. *The Tall Tale in American Folklore and Literature.* Knoxville: University of Tennessee Press, 1987.

Brunvand, Jan Harold. *The Study of American Folklore: An Introduction.* 4th ed. New York: Norton, 1998.

Degh, Linda. "Folk Narrative." In *Folklore and Folklife,* ed. Richard Dorson. Chicago: University of Chicago Press, 1972.

Henningsen, Gustav. "The Art of Perpendicular Lying." Translated by Warren E. Roberts. *Journal of the Folklore Institute* 2 (1965): 180–219.

Hovis, George. "An Interview with Fred Chappell." *Carolina Quarterly* 52 (1999): 67–79.

Randolph, Vance. *We Always Lie to Strangers.* New York: Columbia University Press, 1951.

Rosenberg, Bruce. *Folklore and Literature: Rival Siblings.* Knoxville: University of Tennessee Press, 1991.

Tangherlini, Timothy R. "Legend." In *American Folklore: An Encyclopedia,* edited by Jan Harold Brunvand. New York: Garland, 1996.

Thompson, Stith. *Motif-Index of Folk-Literature.* 6 vols. Bloomington: Indiana University Press, 1955–58.

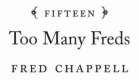

FIFTEEN

Too Many Freds

FRED CHAPPELL

I

SOME OF MY FRIENDS, cognizant of the goal I'd set myself in composing an octave of books—the poem *Midquest* in four volumes and the ensuing Kirkman quartet—have asked me how it feels to have completed the task. I can only mumble in reply that I'm glad to have done with it, but this answer is not entirely veracious. The truth is that I hardly know how I feel or even how I am supposed to feel. There has come a vague sense of completion, right enough, but also a feeling of being partially unwrapped, unprotected in an unlocatable part of my body—like the coolth of a draft on my backside, perhaps.

I had not been able to realize until I stepped out of it just how thoroughly I had been immersed in the very small universe my chosen materials had built up around me. Once composition was complete, I arrived in an outside world different from the one that surrounded me when I began. Presidents had come and gone, national boundaries had shifted, political agendas and allegiances had tilted, the literary landscape had drifted toward compass points fuzzier than before, entertainments had become noisier and more garish, fads and fancies had flashed by at dizzying rates of speed—all this happening while the enclosed sphere of my writing remained largely untouched by contemporary events. I knew what was going on, of course; the newspapers, the radio, and television, the ordinary chat and gossip of everyday life, kept me informed about the Gulf War and Monica Lewinsky, about Mark McGwire and the Hubbell telescope, about a thousand startling and inevitable events, but these could not impinge upon the Kirkmans or the other natives of western North Carolina with whom my lines engaged. When a lady, amused by my long concentration upon these humble and obscure matters, asked my opinion of Kinky Friedman, I had to answer that I didn't know what or who that was. "You live in an ivory tower," she informed me, with a crispness of intonation that indicated she would find such quarters severely cramped. I, who had inhabited this so-called tower for twenty-eight years, had found the space almost too open; time and again I had lost my way.

The purpose of this preamble is to suggest that the octave, much as it sometimes relies upon personal observation and experience, is not really an autobiographical work. Autobiography is changed by events and impressions contemporaneous with its composition. The events that autobiography recounts are continually being reinterpreted by what the author experiences during the process of writing. But my words in the poetry and fiction of the octave would be unchanged if what happened in Somalia, Haiti, Ireland, and Iraq had not happened, unchanged even if Newt Gingrich had never lived or the Whitewater investigation had never taken place.

This is because the world those books portray or imply does not absorb the light of contemporary event; it only emits the light of imaginary event, a light that the author hopes, and tries to believe, is a refreshing, informative, searching, and reflective glow. Whatever happens in 2002 is not going to affect that Appalachian exemplar, Virgil Campbell, or any of his friends and kinfolk. The newest advances in DNA research come too late to be of use to Joe Robert Kirkman in his struggle with the anti-Darwinians. The latest poems, novels, and histories can teach the Fred Chappell of the octave nothing, because in his universe they have not come into existence. In fact, there is no possibility of their existence because no premises are laid for them. Whatever I write now in 2001 could not be written by the Fred of *Midquest* and *Look Back All the Green Valley* because his limits have been so securely defined by the imagination that imagined his imagination.

Fiction and poetry are made by establishing limitations, that is, by imposing form upon imaginary experiences. But autobiography is created by accepting the inevitable limitations of self-blindness, the inability to see and know with completeness or even wise judiciousness. For autobiography, form is but an unavoidable debility.

Let us try this thought experiment: Suppose that you decided to write the story of your life as honestly, directly, and completely as possible for a seven-day period, setting down everything that you saw, heard, said, and did. No need to record psychological events like memories and dreams—the experiment will be valid without such subjective markers. Now suppose that another person, kin or stranger, impartial scientist or passionate poet, stayed with you for that same week, observing closely and recording faithfully all that you saw, heard, said, and did.

Between these two narratives there would be some similarities, but they would be so occasional as to seem almost accidental. You could barely recognize yourself in the other's memoir. You would regard the portrait with numb amazement and deny resemblance as much as you decently could. The other's account of your week might be accurate but it could not be autobiographical; its very accuracy would prevent that. So let me say once more that the Fred who inhabits the octave is not me. I have declared this fact many times before and have explained at some length why the identification is invalid. Yet explanation does little good. The oftener I insist upon the differences, the oftener many of my readers insist upon the similarities. When I become exasperated with them, so do they with me. One friend finally asserted that each and every creation of an author is no more than a self-portrait. "All writing comes from the self," he averred.

Yes, I answered, it is from the self but it is not *of* the self, and not always—maybe never—*about* the self. If I pick up a pencil from my desk with which to scribble a sonnet, I leave my fingerprints upon it. But the pencil, though it now bears my trace, is not me. The pencil has left its traces, too; here are the slants and squiggles and curlicues that make up the handwriting that makes up the poem. Yet the sonnet, unless it is a very odd one indeed, is not an autobiography of the pencil. The self may furnish methods and materials for a work of art, but the work is not autobiography unless it is deliberately intended as such. If it is so intended, it is immediately untrustworthy.

I want to ask those who so persistently address that question to me, Why do you wish my pages to be autobiographical? What is it about me that you so ardently desire to know? If you are interested in my thoughts and feelings, if you would like to have a portrait of my spirit, then it is to my poems and stories that you must turn, for these bear the lineaments of my thought and the impress of my soul. If it is the outer circumstances of my life that interest you—the names of my ancestors, the dates of my schooling, my bibliography—these are easily supplied and blandly uninformative. If you are in pursuit of my dirty secrets, I shall be glad to air them in public if I can remember what they are. I have done lots of shameful things and am willing to 'fess up if that is required, but you will find that story ditchwater compared with the trove of flaming scandal you can learn about almost any celebrity or may be able to recall from your own personal life.

From the 1950s through the 1970s there was a steady strain of personal revelation in American writing. The poets who followed this fashion came to be called "confessional poets." W. D. Snodgrass was probably the first of these with his brilliant *Heart's Needle,* a series of poems which strongly influenced Robert Lowell. Following Lowell came such uncoy self-revealers as Sylvia Plath, Anne Sexton, Allen Ginsburg, and a naked cohort of others. The frankness and candor of their poems struck a refreshing note in our literature and helped to clear away some of the prim and prissy pretenses of contemporary life. But the revelations that at first seemed shocking soon served their purpose and began to wear thin. By the 1980s there was nothing left to confess that could surprise, much less shock, anyone. The personal tone introduced in the 1950s still has not disappeared, but few poets nowadays strive for shock and unless they can come up with gaudier sins than heretofore—cannibalism, perhaps, or necrophilia—they will still fall short of surprise. Around 1985 I wrote an epigram that I designed as an epitaph for this poetic subgenre; it was called "Upon a Confessional Poet":

You've shown us all in stark undress
The sins you needed to confess.
If my peccadilloes were so small
I never would undress at all.

Autobiography presented as fiction has something shady about it, as if it were too timid to be either the one thing or the other. Even Thomas Wolfe, for all the fiery organ music of his prose style, seems to lack authenticity, especially when we compare him to his less autobiographical contemporaries—Hemingway, Fitzgerald, O'Hara, Caldwell, Steinbeck, and (most particularly) Faulkner. I think that our present dissatisfaction with his work stems from his lack of interest in discovering a suitable fictional *form* for the materials that so obsessed him. Like Rabelais, like Lady Mura-saki, like James T. Farrell and even Balzac, Wolfe was a grand novelist without being a fine practitioner of the novel form.

But *Look Homeward, Angel* is a novel and not an autobiography, no matter how sharply it veers toward the latter genre. If it were autobiography it would have to omit those grand lyrical passages that tell us who and what the novelist was when he drew his protagonist:

> He was devoured by a vast strange hunger for life. At night, he lis-tened to the million-noted ululation of little night things, the great brooding symphony of the dark, the ringing of remote churchbells across the country. And his vision widened out in circles over moon-drenched meadows, dreaming woods, mighty rivers going along in darkness, and ten thousand sleeping towns. He believed in the infinite rich variety of all the towns and faces: behind any of a million shabby houses he believed there was strange buried life, subtle and shattered romance, something dark and unknown. At the moment of passing any house, he thought, someone therein might be at the gate of death, lov-ers might lie twisted in hot embrace, murder might be doing.

Such a passage is clearly autobiographical, but it is not only that; it is character portrayal too. His protagonist is a character, not merely a Wolfe in Gant's clothing. To show the difference, we have only to cast it into first person. "I was devoured by a vast strange hunger for life." With that change in pronoun the pomposity increases, the authenticity decreases. If Gant disappears, Wolfe himself begins to bloat, reality withering in the glare of his ego.

I can go on in this vein for many pages, demonstrating that the work of art that employs autobiographical materials for theme or even for structure is not just autobiography, is not mere self-portraiture, but aims at a more gen-eral likeness, a wider application. Yet no matter how long I go on or how genuine my protestations, those who wish to see my fiction and poetry as autobiography will persist in doing so. I began to despair of making the difference clear.

Then one day it occurred to me that the reason certain readers insisted upon this special interpretation was because they read the works as their own biographies, and since they had not actually written the volumes themselves—canceling lopsided similes and furnishing semicolons—they imputed autobiographical motive to me. In short, they were confusing generality with particularity, discovering the personal trait in the broad outline. Just as Hamlet predicted, I had held a mirror up to nature and when these readers looked into it they descried their own images, thinking, "Well, since this is me, it must be Fred, too. We're very much alike, he and I."

This is surprising, considering how widely my biography differs from those of most readers. My early background is rural, my later career academic and literary. Since we live in a time when writers outnumber farmers, there is opportunity for a number of readers to identify with the older Ole Fred of *Midquest* and *Look Back All the Green Valley,* but most will be unfamiliar with such terms as "clevis," "singletree," and the verb "sucker," as in "to sucker tobacco." The life of the farm, especially that of the old-time mountain farm, is alien to them.

The explanation I might offer is that, if the general outlines of character and story are true, readers will accept unfamiliar details as important, but not absolutely essential, parts of a narrative and will attend more closely to those parts that do match their own lives and careers. The unfamiliar works along with the familiar to achieve a recognizable broad picture. If the homely details of Appalachian rural life have no counterparts in their personal experiences, the breadth of theme and the attractive force of narrative line can lure them into reading about modes of experience new to them.

I suppose I am saying no more than that, if a writer has something to say, there will be some people willing to listen. And those matters that writers expend so much agonized sweat over may be viewed as ancillary by many readers or even overlooked entirely. We are told that Flaubert made a rare faux pas during the composition of *Madame Bovary* and changed the color of the lady's eyes. That is a dire criminal offense, to be sure, but how many readers notice it without being told? The suspense of story, the force of character, the exotic elegance of tone and atmosphere, the nobility of theme, and the philosophy of his imagination draw me onward through E. R. Eddison's very strange novel, *Mistress of Mistresses,* so that I do not pause and scurry to the dictionary when I read a paragraph containing terms unfamiliar to me: "angelica water," "Brentheian unguent," "Hyperborean flowers," and "chamblet." Maybe when I read the final sentence of the book I shall come back and decode these phrases, but for the moment they have already performed their necessary task of giving the scene color, music, scent, and aura. I don't know exactly what the words mean, but I understand and approve their functions and so sweep on to the velvet-and-steel dialogue between Lord Lessingham and the ominous Prince Derxis.

But to what part of my autobiography can such a novel as *Mistress of Mistresses* appeal? What are the convincing allurements of *Alice in Wonderland* or *Mistress Masham's Repose* or *The Iliad* or, come to that, *Studs Lonigan* or *Sister Carrie*? All these books, exotic and realistic alike, fit to that part of my life that I have lived in imagination, picturing myself in the opulent gardens of a dream planet or sauntering the tough streets of Chicago.

What I will say at last is, I put as much autobiography into my poems and stories when I write them as readers do when they read them. If my experiences did not contribute to the composition of the works, I could not write them; if my readers' experiences did not contribute to their reading, they could not comprehend these products of shared imagination.

2

What I have so far described we take for granted—usually without realizing it—in the ordinary two-way relationship between writer and reader. When the relationship becomes more complicated, as in the case of what we call "metafiction," we do not take it for granted. With metafiction what had been tacit now becomes overt. Usually, a writer writes a story and the reader reads it. The writer can make her story into metafiction simply by acknowledging (or boasting, or denying) in the work itself that she is writing it. When she does so, the story is no longer a story; it has become "only a story." At that point, the reader is no longer reading; he is merely perusing. With fiction, the relationship between reader and writer is a bond; with metafiction, it becomes an arrangement. It is still the same basic relationship, but now it is a self-conscious and guarded one. When the writer confesses to authoring the story she is no longer trustworthy. She has a professional bag of tricks to pull on us. And if her story is "only a story," it is a patent falsehood and loses the importance and interest that a *real story* would have.

Consequently, the reader is no longer a reader; he becomes a mark, someone the writer must try to manipulate to her advantage, whether artistic or political. Now he must keep a sharp eye out; there is no telling what underhanded maneuver she might perform to persuade him to her cause, whatever that might be.

The result is that the style our author has labored so diligently to achieve, tipping her rhythms a-lilt or slowing them to dirge tempo, choosing her words as with a jeweler's loupe and setting them into phrases as cunningly shaped as a tiara, sharpening her characters with klieg lights or softening them with perfumed candles—all this style is now seen as "rhetoric," a term that coarsens the effects desired and cheapens the benevolent intentions of the author, she who, after all, has labored only to please.

Easy to see that metafiction makes things more difficult. That chumminess between writer and reader is changed; it is never quite destroyed, but it is significantly distorted. The illusion of verisimilitude, so difficult to achieve and maintain, is recognized as an illusion, and the reader who assents to it may be charged with being a gullible dupe or a hypocritical collaborator. An air of distrust pervades the whole enterprise.

These are disadvantages easy to remark. But metafiction has its advantages, too. The relationship of tacit accommodation now becomes one of negotiation. The reader says, "All right, Author, I know your twists and turns, your gorgeous blandishments and your powerful shock tactics. I've got my eye on you and you needn't think you're going to get away with anything." To which Author replies, "I am glad of your rapt attention, reader. I want you to keep your gaze very steadily upon me because I don't really want to get away with anything. But if I do happen to slip something by you, if somehow I do engage your sympathies and call forth your imagination and entertain your vicarious senses—well, you have been warned and if any deception takes place, then you are to blame more than I."

Thus the rules are set; thus the game begins. In his essay in this volume, the perspicuous Spencer Edmunds has spoken of this "game of the novel," though he has not offered an explanation of why either party, writer or reader, might care to play the game. If it amounts on both sides only to a sort of dilettantish competition in the exercise of complementary ingenuities, then it is an idle pastime indeed.

Metafiction can offer, however, more than that, even though there are penalties to be exacted. If we may allow a premise I believe to be valid, that every seriously intended work of art takes as one of its themes the search for reality, then this is a theme that metafictional method will emphasize and make capable of extensive exploration. Metafiction makes explicit such problems as authorial responsibility, the relative importance or unimportance of the artist's materials, the concept of the willing suspension of disbelief, the notion of truth in art, and a number of others.

In the final novel of the Kirkman quartet I deliberately turned things inside out, made the true and only begetter of the fiction and poetry the fictional narrator Jess Kirkman, turning "Fred Chappell" into an entity whose name had to be festooned with quotation marks, reduced to a pallid nom de plume. I knew what I was doing, but I sorely dreaded doing it. This kind of ploy is all too common to metafiction and is one of the reasons I like to deny writing the stuff. The novel received remarkably favorable notice, considering how closely it is related to the earlier volumes, especially to the poetry, but finally one reviewer uttered the sentence I had been dreading to hear: "Is this supposed to be cute?"

I know you will believe me when I say it was not my ambition to be cute. The real-person/nom de plume reversal was a strategy born of desperation. My technical cul de sac resulted from the fact that I did not conceive of the eight books as making up a unit until I was well into *Bloodfire,* the second of the poetry volumes. But as soon as I conceived of the work as an octave, I foresaw the problems I would have in making a closure. It was imperative to find some way, at the end, of drawing it all together and I wondered what device I might discover to solve—or to evade—the problem.

I kept on wondering during the composition of two more books of poetry and three novels, just scribbling along, sometimes blithely, sometimes doggedly, until it came time to write *Look Back All the Green Valley.* There I halted, staring fixedly at the blank walls that angled together to form the corner I'd painted myself into. It was then I decided, clutching at a feeble straw indeed, that I would declare Jess Kirkman the responsible party and make myself only the ghost of a name in his past-obsessed mind.

"Oh no," I groaned. "This idea is just too, too cute."

But after rejecting it some dozen or more times, I finally gave in because I could think of no other feasible way out. I did think of a few other means

of egress, but they were even more complicated, more elaborately metafictional, than the one I had first lit upon. So I went ahead and did the dirty
deed, understanding that I must live with the consequences.

What happened next was unexpected. Having decided what to do, I
felt an immediate relief, a curious lightening of spirit and a new freshet of
determination. I don't think I could have put it into these terms at that
time, but I had removed myself as the implied author. Now, for the seven
volumes past as well as for the one forthcoming, Jess Kirkman was both
ostensible narrator and implied author. Fred and that other odd entity, Ole
Fred, had dwindled to motivic status: monikers, figments, and nothing
more.

My removal gave Jess more freedom of narration. Now he alone was
responsible for problems of logic, chronology, plausibility, and verisimilitude. If events were out of order (as indeed they were), if distinctions between fantasy and reality were blurred (as in accordance with theme), if
utter impossibilities were reported as witnessed events (in spades!), then
these anomalies must be laid at the doorstep of Jess Kirkman—perfervid
poet, clumsy would-be novelist, ambiguously dutiful son, addled quester
after truth. I had transferred the burden of storytelling to one of the most
unreliable narrators since Baron Munchausen.

How far should this masquerade be taken? I thought of having Jess
Kirkman listed on the title page and dust jacket as author of the novel. But
this would confuse those who were trying to follow the progress of the
quartet (few people besides myself yet saw it as an octave). I queried my
highly tolerant editor, Mr. George Witte, about putting my name in quotation marks: *Look Back All the Green Valley* by "Fred Chappell." He per-
suaded me that such a move would be silly and confusing. So that now, as
it stands, we have a novel attributed to an entity the reader knows does not
exist, even though there is a picture of someone (probably a model) who
resembles Fred Chappell on the back flap of the dust jacket. If we followed
this thread of logic to its fraying end, the actual author would have to be
the Ole Fred who appears as a character in some of the poems of *Midquest*—which means that Jess Kirkman could not be the implied author of
the novel quartet.

Several of the essays that precede my own here deal with the subject of
the reduplicated narrator, and our doughty essayists have been both in-

sightful and ingenious in disentangling some of the confusions and sorting out the different roles of the different "authors." But now I recomplicate the whole matter again by writing the very sentences you are at this moment reading, because the Fred who analyzes the octave after the fact must be separate from Jess and from the earlier Freds. The Fred of present time inhabits a universe in which those books are only artifacts, neither biography nor autobiography and only putatively fictional.

Talk about your games: we now begin to get into a world constructed mathematically, like the studies in symmetry of the Dutch artist M. C. Escher, or like the harmonic permutations of twelve-tone music. We have the Fred who wrote *Midquest* mirrored by the Fred who appears as a fictional character in those poems. This fictional Fred has a slightly dissimilar alter ego, Ole Fred, who appears as a companionable figure of fun: figure, reflection, reflected reflection. Then we have an inversion, or reversal of field, in which Jess Kirkman seems to take the place of the original; Fred, only in another plane. But since the format of the book makes Jess a character issued from the imagination of Fred One, Jess must be relegated to the status of reflection, the same as Fred Chappell (Two) and Ole Fred. Yet we are told that Fred One is really the creation of Jess Kirkman—which means that he has to be a separate entity from the one who thought up Jess. This would be (unless I have lost count) Fred Four. And now at this moment we have a fifth Fred writing a commentary upon the former Freds.

But he is not alone in this book, for there are fifteen other Freds by fifteen other commentators, all Freds fairly similar but dissimilar enough, I dare say, to be counted as separate entities. It is geometry: By means of reflection, inversion, translation, rotation, and that mathematical process known as screwing, we can produce as few as seventeen Freds and as many as two hundred and thirty—all in the literary, metaphorical sense, of course.

Now we are getting all too cute, and I must think that any reader who would pursue the eluctable Fred through so many combinations and permutations must be in dire need of recreation. When I try to trace out the chain of metafictional Freds I become befuddled and weary, dizzy and bored. Here is no search for reality but an extrapolation of some of the methods of literature into the abstractions of distant abstractions. John Donne spoke of gold to airy thinness beat, but there has to be some point where the foil crumbles to grains, the grains to powder, the powder to motes, and the motes disappear in the infinite inane. We have traveled so far from the sunlight of *story* that to rediscover it is like trying to find a remote glint in a star field.

3

So when I voice my disapproval of metafiction and deny my indulgence in the vice, it is because of my distaste for, and fear of, the kind of dry, geometrical abstractions that may result from its composition. For all my desultory intellectualizing, it is blood and bone, face and feature, the living and the vivid that claim my first allegiance. I recognize that Don Quixote is a metafictional figure, the philosophical obverse of the heroes of the old romances. But he is lifelike, too; you would recognize him anywhere.

In fact, we do recognize him everywhere—as abstraction, certainly, but also as a courageous, dim-witted old coot, much troubled in his bowels and in his romantic affections. No one is more vigorous, no one frailer; no one is wiser, no one more deluded. He is a scarecrow, towering but tottering, with his crazed eyes and scraggly beard, his skinny shanks and trembling arms. He is wonderfully physical, as much a corpus as are his companion Sancho and his dilapidated steed Rosinante. It is a tenet of my credo that characters in modern literature must be real physically before they can stand for, embody, any abstract concept.

In order of primacy, then: character first, story second, theme third. This is not the order in which things are conceived because that will change with almost every story one sets out to write. But that is the order of importance for me; my experience is that story will meander like bog currents in the Dismal Swamp unless it is directed by force of the characters who enact it. Theme will look pompous or trivial or irrelevant or even become invisible unless there is a compelling story to illumine it.

The foregoing is not a description of the genesis of the octave or of any part of it. It is common among writers to confuse the inception of a work with the purposes given to it in process of composition. Often, the confusion comes about because the writer really cannot remember how or why or when the project first presented itself, cannot recall the moment when it became this particular project and not one of the other dozen or so that might have resulted from the early stages of conception or composition. For me a story or poem is in a state of dreamlike fluidity until the last comma of the last phrase has wriggled onto the page. Sometimes not even the last draft is final, for I have seen myself try to improve diction even in books published decades ago. These are private corrections; I would not irritate my readers beyond all capacity. But I can't always stop myself from making one more change in the lonesome hope that it might bring the work a micrometer further toward the ideal that inspired its completion.

This latter ideal is different from the one that inspired its germination. The ideal that inspires inception is an alluring and deceptive one, for often my first glimpse of a proposed work is of a finished product, appearing in mind-sight with glorious spontaneity, issuing formed in splendor directly from the brain, like the birth of Aphrodite from the forehead of Zeus. When work begins in earnest, the ideal changes, becoming less transcendent, threatening to resist every method of utterance except dogged labor, the effulgent golden rays dimming from its figure until at last it wears only the all-too-human and often homely guise of a creation attributable to Fred.

(Alas.)

At one time I had thought it might be fun to observe and chronicle this metamorphosis of the envisioned ideals of a work. I thought I might keep a journal of a book's composition, something along the lines of the journal André Gide kept while writing his novel *The Counterfeiters*. This, I thought, might have some value in showing the progress of an idea from the impalpable to the palpable state, from ideal purity to grubby actuality; it would be of particular interest to note the number of compromises that had to be made and of what sort they were.

But a day or two of this experiment convinced me of its futility—and of its dangers. I could not easily locate and describe the compromises (if that's what they were) that I was making. And I was beginning to spend more time writing up the journal about it than actually writing the poem *Earthsleep* itself. I recalled the famous little verse by X. J. Kennedy and desisted:

The goose that laid the golden egg
Died looking up its crotch
To find out how its sphincter worked.
Would you lay well? Don't watch.

But even these foredoomed efforts were not wasted. Some of the material from that aborted journal showed up in *Look Back All the Green Valley* as Jess Kirkman's musings as he plowed away at a poem called *Earthsleep*. Another advantage of metafiction is that it sometimes makes possible the employment of leftovers, the inchoate detritus of composition. Recycling pieces of that old journal made me feel I was recovering wasted hours.

4

Such fortuitous reclamation is not usually possible, and I was able to do it only because of the peculiar nature of the octave as metafiction and of the final novel in particular. Robert Gingher published in the periodical *The World & I* a piece that I found highly gratifying. There he compared the method of composition of the Kirkman quartet to the composition of twelve-tone music and averred that all the themes would be present in the story anywhere one cut into it.

He gave the books too much credit, of course, but he did accurately describe one of the ideals I set out to fulfill. John Lang in his essay here has spotted my penchant for the music of Schonberg and, though my enthusiasm for serial music has somewhat diminished in recent years, I still admire the goals that the serial method tries to achieve, principally among them the passion for unity. In my usual amateurish way, I studied the music and writings of Schönberg, Webern, and especially Alban Berg. It was in the lectures of the latter composer that I came across the magic square whose dog-Latin phrase, "the sower Arepo keeps the work circling," can be read backward and forward, vertically and horizontally:

SATOR
AREPO
TENET
OPERA
ROTAS

For me, as for Berg, this square became a talisman, a reminder to keep my themes interwoven, not to allow the patchwork surface appearance of the octave to submerge or obliterate the organizing themes and motifs that were to hold it together. This was a disaster that might easily result from having so broad an assortment of episodes, many of which introduced new characters, eccentric and exemplifying figures who might never be heard from again.

My themes are obvious enough: the strength and resilience of family, the disappearance or diminishment of a former way of Appalachian life, the sense of community, the grandeur of place, the coming of age of young people and grownups alike, the responsibility of the individual toward communal history, and so forth. The motifs, too, are easy to discern: music, the memory of Johnson Gibbs, Benjamin Franklin's kite, Darwin, various characterizations of the sage, industrialism, and the unifying images of the elements of water, fire, air, and earth.

But to make the work a whole, to weave the themes and interweave them with motifs, to give unity of tone as well as design to eight books, to fill out the details of structure—these were tasks necessary to maintain the daily life of the writer, the flesh-and-blood Fred who must type up the manuscript, pay his taxes, and brush his teeth. This latter Fred held a full-time teaching position at the University of North Carolina–Greensboro and he had other duties, personal and professional, to attend to besides his precious eight little books.

So there are lapses. In my humble opinion, the episode that lays the groundwork for Mitzi's strength of character, "The Tipton Tornado" in *Look Back*, is not comfortably integrated into the whole, and the longish picnic scene at the end of that novel is overly didactic. The characters change speech patterns, too. Joe Robert and Annie Barbara speak less colloquially and more formally as the pages turn; their future roles were not sufficiently conceived in the first novel. I wish, too, that I could have got the chronology in better order. But this would have required researching and reoutlining scores, even hundreds, of pages before I could begin composing anew in dawn hours that were quarantined from my hours of academic work.

I see that I should halt here, for I am beginning once again to construct a metafiction. In describing the work as I wish I had been able to perfect it, I am creating a companion octave, a Shadow Cousin, to the one that actually exists. That is the octave I was trying to read, to copy from, as I wrote, but I could not always get it focused in my mind's eye. If I don't write about it here, if I stop describing it, it will disappear from the world except as a wistful, dimly glowing regret in a far blue prospect of my fancy. We will be left with the octave as it is, worthy or unworthy, enduring or transitory, ardent or ashen.

So if you will please allow me, at this cool-headed removal, to absolve Jess Kirkman of the responsibility for the hard-won eight and to place the burden on my own drooping shoulders, I shall be heartily obliged. I have written the opus enough times; I promise not to write it again.

You have my word on that.

PATRICK BIZZARO is editor of *Dream Garden: The Poetic Vision of Fred Chappell* (Louisiana State University Press, 1997). His books of poetry include *Fear of the Coming Drought* (Mount Olive College Press, 2001), the forthcoming *Every Insomniac Has a Story to Tell,* and six chapbooks. His pedagogical work includes *Responding to Student Poems: Applications of Critical Theory* (NCTE, 1993). A professor of English at East Carolina University, he teaches creative writing and literature and currently serves as director of University Writing Programs. He is a University of North Carolina Board of Governors' Distinguished Professor for Teaching and for his poetry has won *NYQ*'s Madeline Sadin Award and *Four Quarters*' Poetry Prize.

KELLY CHERRY is the author of over twenty books of poetry, fiction, and nonfiction. Her latest novel, *We Can Still Be Friends,* was published by Soho Press in spring 2003. Her most recent book of poetry is *Rising Venus,* published by Louisiana State University Press in 2002. Her book of poetry criticism will be published by the University of Tampa Press in 2004. Cherry's awards include the Hanes Poetry Prize and the *Dictionary of Literary Biography* award for a distinguished volume of short stories. She is Eudora Welty Professor Emerita of English and Evjue-Bascom Professor Emerita in the Humanities at the University of Wisconsin–Madison and in 2004 will return to the Humanities Center of the University of Alabama–Huntsville as Visiting Eminent Scholar.

ROSEMARY COX is professor of English at Perimeter College and a faculty editor for the *Chattahoochee Review.* Her publications include poetry, book reviews, and scholarly essays on antebellum southern humor and writers of the modern South.

R. H. W. DILLARD, professor of English and head of the creative writing program at Hollins College, is the author of two novels, a collection of short fiction, two books of criticism, and five collections of poetry.

J. SPENCER EDMUNDS grew up in Roanoke, Virginia, where he earned degrees from the University of Virginia and Hollins College. After completing a doctoral degree at the University of Georgia in American Literature, he was assistant professor of English at Elon College for five years before joining the faculty at Canterbury School in Greensboro in 1998. In 2001, Edmunds assumed the position of middle school director at Canterbury, where he currently oversees the faculty and curriculum for grades 6–8, teaches creative writing, and continues to talk about metanarrative, even if in simpler terms.

GEORGE HOVIS is assistant professor of English and director of creative writing at Murray State University. His articles on southern writers have appeared in the *Mississippi Quarterly,* the *Southern Literary Journal, Southern Cultures,* the *Tennessee Williams Journal,* and elsewhere.

JAMES W. KIRKLAND is professor of English at East Carolina University, where he has taught since 1969. A specialist in composition pedagogy, American literature, and folklore, he has coauthored or coedited two literature anthologies (*Fiction the Narrative Art* and *Poetry: Sight and Insight*); three college composition texts (*Writing with Confidence, Essential English Handbook,* and *Concise English Handbook*); and a collection of scholarly essays on folk medicine (*Herbal and Magical Medicine: Traditional Healing Today*). His articles, reviews, and chapters have appeared in such publications as *English Language Notes, Southern Folklore, Midwest Folklore, Mid-American Folklore, Journal of the Fantastic in the Arts, American Folklore: An Encyclopedia, Encyclopedia of Folklore and Literature,* and *Dream Garden: The Poetic Vision of Fred Chappell.*

JOHN LANG teaches American literature at Emory & Henry College, where he also edits the *Iron Mountain Review* and directs the Great Books

Program. He is the author of *Understanding Fred Chappell* and of numerous essays on southern writers.

TRACI LAZENBY is an independent scholar and bookseller who lives in Asheboro, North Carolina, with her husband and two sons. They are all students of both the mythic and the mundane.

PETER MAKUCK's short stories and essays, poems, and reviews have appeared in the *Hudson Review, Poetry,* the *Laurel Review,* and the *Sewanee Review.* Author of five volumes of poems, he has edited *Tar River Poetry* at East Carolina University for twenty-five years. His second collection of short fiction, *Costly Habits,* was published last year by the University of Missouri Press.

KAREN JANET MCKINNEY, a native of Mitchell County, North Carolina, teaches American literature at Mars Hill College, a small, liberal arts institution located in the North Carolina mountains. She has published articles on Native American authors in *Critique* and the *Asheville Poetry Review.* Her Ph.D. dissertation (University of New Mexico) on ethnological writings about and by white and Cherokee Appalachian peoples is nearing completion.

ROBERT MORGAN, a native of western North Carolina, has taught at Cornell University since 1971. He has published several books of fiction and poetry, most recently *Brave Enemies,* Algonquin Books of Chapel Hill, 2003, and *New and Selected Poems,* Louisiana State University Press, 2004. His novel *Gap Creek* won the Southern Book Award in 2000.

WARREN ROCHELLE is an assistant professor of English at Mary Washington College in Fredericksburg, Virginia. He has published articles on rhetoric and literature in *Emergency Librarian, Extrapolation, Presidential Studies Quarterly, Foundation, SFRA Review, Children's Literature Association Quarterly,* and the *North Carolina Literary Review.* His short fiction and poetry are published in *Aboriginal Science Fiction, Beyond the Third Planet, Forbidden Lines, Coraddi, Crucible,* the *Charlotte Poetry Review, GW Magazine,* the *Asheville Poetry Review,* the *North Carolina Literary Review,* and *Romance and Beyond.* A critical book on the fiction of Ursula Le Guin, *Communities of the Heart: The Rhetoric of Myth in the Fiction of Ursula K. Le Guin,* was published by Liverpool University Press in early 2001. Golden Gryphon Press published his first novel, *The Wild Boy,* in the fall of 2001 and his short story "The Golden Boy" in *The Silver Gryphon,* an anthology, in 2003.

REBECCA SMITH is professor of English and director of the Sam and Marjorie Ragan Writing Center at Barton College. Publications and conference presentations include work on the fiction of Lee Smith, Robert Morgan, Jill McCorkle, Kaye Gibbons, Doris Betts, Eudora Welty, and Ernest Gaines.

SHELBY STEPHENSON is professor of English at the University of North Carolina at Pembroke, where he is also editor of *Pembroke Magazine.* He has published several collections of poetry, including most recently *Fiddle-deedee.*

{ INDEX }